Gustavo Gutiérrez

THE GOD OF LIFE

Translated from the Spanish by
Matthew J. O'Connell

ORBIS BOOKS

Maryknoll, New York 10545

Originally published as *El Dios de la Vida*, copyright © 1989 by the Instituto Bartolomé de las Casas-Rimac, Ricardo Bentín 763, Apartado 3090, Lima 25, Peru and the Centro de Estudios y Publicaciones (CEP), Lampa 808, Of. 601, Apartado 6118, Lima, Peru. This text was a greatly expanded version of the book, published in 1982 under the same title, by CEP.

Unless otherwise indicated, all scripture quotes are from the *New American Bible*.

Library of Congress Cataloging-in-Publication Data

Gutiérrez, Gustavo, 1928-
  [Dios de la vida. English]
  The God of life / Gustavo Gutiérrez : translated from the Spanish
by Matthew J. O'Connell.
    p. cm.
  Translation of: El Dios de la vida.
  Includes bibliographical references and index.
  ISBN 0-88344-760-6
  1. God—Biblical teaching. 2. Kingdom of God. 3. Poor—Religious
aspects—Christianity. I. Title
BS544.G87 1991
231—dc20   91-15278
                                                     CIP

To Bishop Oscar A. Romero,
to sisters Maria Agostino and Irene McCormack,
assassinated in Peru,
and in their persons, to all those in Latin America
who have by their death borne witness (martyrdom)
to the God of life

Then David blessed the Lord in the presence of the whole assembly, praying in these words:

Blessed may you be, O Lord,
    God of Israel our father,
    from eternity to eternity.
Yours, O Lord, are grandeur and power,
    majesty, splendor, and glory.
For all in heaven and on earth is yours;
    yours, O Lord, is the sovereignty;
    you are exalted as head over all.
In your hand are power and might;
    it is yours to give grandeur and strength to all.
Therefore, our God, we give you thanks
    and we praise the majesty of your name.

But who am I, and who are my people that we should have the means to contribute so freely? For everything is from you, and we only give you what we have received from you. For we stand before you as aliens: we are only your guests, like all our fathers. Our life on earth is like a shadow that does not abide. O Lord our God, all this wealth that we have brought together to build you a house in honor of your holy name comes from you and is entirely yours. I know, O my God, that you put hearts to the test and that you take pleasure in uprightness. With a sincere heart I have willingly given all these things, and now with joy I have seen your people here present also giving to you generously. O Lord, God of our fathers Abraham, Isaac, and Israel, keep such thoughts in the hearts and minds of your people forever, and direct their hearts toward you.

(1 Chr 29:10–18)

CONTENTS

INTRODUCTION

In a vast open space, before about two million people who put the seal of their applause on each sentence spoken, two members of a community belonging to the Christian Workers' Movement are proclaiming the faith of the poor in the God of life. They are addressing an illustrious visitor who listens to them eagerly and attentively. Speaking from the experience of the marginalized folk of our country, these two individuals tell how they think of and perceive the God of biblical revelation; in their address, every word counts.

WE BELIEVE IN THE GOD OF LIFE

Victor and Irene Chero have been given a friendly introduction by Bishop Germán Schmitz, pastor of this area. Speaking in the name of the settlers in Villa El Salvador and of the shantytowns of Lima, they begin their greeting to John Paul II by saying: "Holy Father, we are hungry." The simplicity and frightfulness of these opening words set the tone for all that follows. "We suffer affliction, we lack work, we are sick. Our hearts are crushed by suffering as we see our tubercular wives giving birth, our children dying, our sons and daughters growing up weak and without a future." The reality of unjust and premature death is described in utterly unadorned language. Out of it comes, with renewed force, a profession of faith: "But, despite all this, *we believe in the God of life.*" The lack of the necessities for living a human life is contrary to the will of the God whom Jesus reveals to us. A profession of faith in that God implies a rejection of this inhuman situation; conversely, this situation gives content and urgency to the proclamation of the God of life.[1]

The conclusion is unavoidable: "We struggle for this life in the face of death." This is the fundamental choice, and it is made over a period of time. "Necessity has compelled us to leave our distant villages, bringing with us a deep faith in God, and inspired by the longing for a more human life." Theirs is the faith of emigrants; they are driven by their understanding of God and their desire for a different kind of life. That is why they undertake their journey. God "is known through one's feet," as Carlos Mesters beautifully says, referring to the great biblical image of the journey or the way as a search for the God whom Jesus, the itinerant preacher of Galilee, reveals to us. That is what these settlers, too, are experiencing.

In the course of this journey they become a people: "In the recently formed communities, shared need has united and organized us; it has created among us a solidarity in the struggle for life and the defense of our rights." The determination to be in solidarity characterizes the life of the poor. At the same time, they declare that they are followers of Christ: "From the outset we have journeyed with the church and in the church, and the church has journeyed in us and with us." That is what the church is, a journeying amid a people: a people that becomes a Christian congregation, and a church that becomes a people on its way to God. These are two processes that support each other and retain their full vitality in Latin America, even if they stir uneasiness and even anxiety in some.

The Christian communities that are on the increase "among our believing and poor people" are seeking to carry on the mission that Jesus announced (see Lk 4:16–20): to proclaim the good news to the poor, with all that this good news implies. The two settlers speak their final words: "Holy Father, may your visit once again make the words of Jesus effective among us: 'Today, the prophecy you have just heard is fulfilled.' Then," say the two speakers emphatically, "our *hunger for God* and our *hunger for bread* will both be heeded." These two needs characterize the life of this people that is Christian and, at the same time, poor and oppressed. The voices of the poor repeat the message of Jesus at Nazareth; thus they bring the good news and evangelize all who hear them.

The waves of applause that ripple across the sea of human beings here present attest to the identification the hearers feel with the words of Victor and Irene. The man to whom they are speaking, John Paul II, is visibly moved as he listens. He answers: "I have listened very attentively to the words of your representatives — this family, this husband and wife — I have listened very attentively," he repeats, and then uses the language of Victor and Irene, "and have heard that there is a hunger for God, a hunger for God. This hunger is truly a treasure of the poor, a treasure that must not be lost." A fruitful, and not very common, pastoral dialogue has begun. The pope continues: "There is here a hunger for bread, there is here a hunger for bread." To this repetition the crowd answers "Yes, yes!"

This situation gives rise to a demand, and the pope continues, speaking forcefully: "Everything must be done to see to it that this daily bread is not lacking, for such bread is a right, a right expressed when we pray in the Our Father: 'Give us this day our daily bread.' " Prayer and commitment are inseparably connected. In hesitant Spanish as he looks for the right words and leaves brief silences, which only give greater power to what he says and to the solidarity he voices, John Paul II declares: "I want this hunger for God to remain, but I want the hunger for bread to be satisfied; I want means to be found to supply this bread. I want there to be none who go hungry for daily bread: people should be hungry for God but not starved for their daily bread." The doubly hungry multitude welcomes the assertion of these two rights with loud applause.

Hungry for God, yes; starved for bread, no.[2] Faith in God must lead to elimination of the lack of bread. The exchange I have just reported expresses this incompatibility with unparalleled vigor: faith and starvation cannot be combined, because the God of Jesus is the God of life, of all life. Because of their experience the believing poor grasp the point clearly, for their experience is the insider's experience of a situation of conflict, abuses, and injustice, which the Christian conscience must reject.[3] Otherwise, we take the name of the Lord "in vain," for that is what happens when we appeal to God in order to justify and induce forgetfulness of the mistreatment of the poor, or in order to evade the scandal of this mistreatment. The passages I have been citing help us avoid this danger and set us on the right road to the true God, the God of the kingdom, whom Jesus Christ proclaims to us. The faith experience of the poor and oppressed that bursts into our lives and our theology is the vital context, the historical and social setting, for the following pages, which are intended as a reflection on the God of biblical revelation.

THINKING THE GOD OF THE BIBLE

In a well-known passage Blaise Pascal contrasts the "God of Abraham, Isaac, and Jacob," the "God of Jesus Christ," with the "God of the philosophers." The words occur in the "Memorial," which Pascal always carried on his person and which gives expression to a profound mystical experience. In other words, the God of the Bible is not the God of philosophy. This is an authentically Christian insight that has legitimately inspired many lived experiences and reflections. It is impossible not to agree with it.

As a matter of fact, philosophy—or at least a certain type of philosophy—has a great deal of trouble thinking the God of biblical revelation. To give an example: for thinking that is based on Aristotle, it is difficult to say that God is love. If one accepts the categories of Greek thought, love is a *pathos* or something undergone; it implies a need and therefore a dependence on something or someone. For this reason, love cannot be attributed to the perfect being. Now, all this is not a matter simply of conceptual stumbling blocks; at issue is the way in which human beings approach God.

According to the Bible, God is a mystery; that is to say, God is love that embraces all things. God is someone who self-manifests within history and, at the same time, is present in the heart of each individual. This mystery must be communicated and not kept for oneself; it is not the possession of any individual or group. In Christ, says St. Paul, there has been revealed "the mystery kept secret for long ages but now manifested through the prophetic writings and, according to the command of the eternal God, made known to all nations to bring about the obedience of faith"; to this God, "to the only wise God, through Jesus Christ be glory forever and ever. Amen" (Rom 16:25–26).

The act of believing is a vital and communal experience. The mystery of
God must be accepted in prayer and commitment; this is the phase of
silence and practice. Within this combined contemplation and practice
there arise the categories and language needed for communicating God to
others; this is the phase of speaking about God.[4] The communication must
be made with the profound respect felt by those who know their place
before God. In a passage that is steeped in the Old Testament faith, Paul
again shows us the way: "Oh the depth of the riches and wisdom and
knowledge of God! How inscrutable are his judgments and how unsearchable his ways! 'For who has known the mind of the Lord or who has been
his counselor?' 'Or who has given him anything that he may be repaid?'
For from him and through him and for him are all things. To him be glory
forever. Amen" (Rom 11:33–35; see Is 40:13).

The profound insight of Pascal does not, however, do away with the
necessity of thinking the God of biblical revelation; rather it warns us not
to follow the wrong way of doing it. My intention in these pages is to reflect
on the God of Abraham, Isaac, Jacob, and Jesus Christ. Jesus himself has
told us how to do this: "Whoever has seen me has seen the Father" (Jn
14:9). Augustine of Hippo tells us that Christ is the key to the Scriptures.
He makes known to us who God is, because "no one knows the Father
except the Son" (Mt 11:27). It is well known that in the Bible "knowledge"
is a very rich concept that is not limited to the intellectual realm but also
connotes taste, fellow feeling, and love. Knowledge here is a direct and
profound kind of knowledge that embraces all dimensions of the person
who is known and loved.[5]

Consequently, it is in the Son and in his light and through him that we
love the Father. This love puts its stamp on our knowledge of God. Because
we are God's children and because God loves us, the Lord makes known
to us "everything I have heard from my Father" (Jn 15:15). It is as friends
of Jesus that we shall seek to reflect on our common Father. This revelation
is the area in which I shall be making this present effort at understanding
the biblical faith. We read the Bible in the community of the followers of
Christ, the church.

Biblical revelation receives its unity from Christ: according to Vatican
II, which cites St. Augustine, God so ordered the two testaments "that the
New should be hidden in the Old, and that the Old should be made manifest in the New" (*Dei Verbum* 16).[6] For this reason, I shall seek to include
the entire Bible in these reflections. The underlying continuity of the Bible
does not mean forgetting the novelty to be found in "the words and works
. . . [the] death and glorious resurrection" of Jesus Christ (*DV* 4). The break
entailed in this witness and proclamation is an important guideline in the
pages that follow. It explains why under one and the same section heading
I deal separately with the texts of each testament.

The Lord tells us, moreover: "Do not think that I have come to abolish
the law or the prophets. I have come not to abolish but to fulfill" (Mt 5:17).

The demands that this "fulfillment" makes on the understanding of Scripture provide the basic criterion I shall be following in my presentation of the theme of God in the Bible. "The most intimate truth which this [divine] revelation gives us about God and the salvation of man shines forth in Christ, who is himself both the mediator and the sum total of Revelation" (*DV* 2).

I Feel God Differently

Human beings believe in God in the context of a particular historical situation; after all, believers have their place in a cultural and social fabric. For a long time, for example, the consciousness of their own limitations and their realization of their dependence on the external world, both natural and social, led human beings to emphasize the divine power and omnipotence. The consciousness of their finiteness sensitized them to the infinity of the supreme being. In our age, the assertion of the human person as subject of its own history, as well as its increasing ability to transform nature, have gradually led to a different approach to God. In the context of the phenomenon we call "secularization" (there is no need here of introducing nuances and distinctions) there is a growing sensitiveness to a God who is revealed in humility and suffering. Confronted with human beings who are conscious of their strength, theologians speak of a God who is "weak."[7]

Given their experience of death, the poor proclaim a God who liberates and gives life. The lived experiences of God and the reflection on God that originate in the impoverished and marginalized sectors of the human race emphasize this perspective. "I feel God differently," says a character in a book of J. M. Arguedas; she perceives him in the light of her experience as a woman,[8] a human being who is disregarded and looked upon as inferior. The same claim can be made by the unimportant people of this world, those who suffer abuse in body and dignity from the mighty. As in the case of the two settlers whose words I cited earlier, the experience of death ("we are hungry") leads to the affirmation of the God of life.

The mystery of God cannot be captured by any one of the approaches I have summarily described. Each of them represents certain values and reveals to us aspects of a reality that is ineffable; the framework they supply enables us to grasp the complexity of the mystery we are approaching. But precisely because the Bible is to a great extent the expression of the faith and hope of the poor, and above all because it reveals to us a God who has a preferential love for those whom the world passes over, the last approach just described has a broad and fruitful foundation in the Scriptures. I am undertaking to make this explicit while taking into account the challenges posed to us by our Latin American situation and by the lived experience of Christian communities there. These communities also look at the Bible differently and enter into a fruitful and complex dialogue with it. The avenues followed in this exchange have left their mark on the reflections offered in this book.

I approach the Scriptures in an attitude of faith. The intention of the books of the Bible is to speak to us of God and to communicate the faith of their authors and of persons, groups, and an entire people. The intention is pursued in various ways in these works. A passage from the Gospel of John sums up the approach: "Now Jesus did many other signs in the presence of his disciples that are not written in this book. But these are written so that you may [come to] believe that Jesus is the Messiah, the Son of God, and that through this belief you may have life in his name" (Jn 20:30–31). The intention, then, is to rouse faith in the Lord, to call the reader to life. Not everything that happened is recounted; the author proposes only to offer a selection of events (see the final verse of the same Gospel, 21:25). To read the Bible is to begin a dialogue *between faith and faith*, between the believers of the past and the believers of today: a dialogue that is taking place today within the ecclesial community as it pursues its pilgrimage through history.

The books of the Bible tell us stories, sometimes about an entire people, sometimes about a community; or they tell of personal journeys. These books in turn have their own history; they took form through a process of reading and rereading. The stories, whether they be based on real situations or are literary fictions, give voice to an authentic faith experience. The stories told are not inspired by any urge for scientific accuracy; they do not constitute a history written according to the principles of modern historical writing. They are testimonies. Their aim is to show the saving action of God. This is the important thing, and it manifests itself in historical events; the latter are the accounts and expression of that action.[9] I approach the Scriptures in terms of my own history, in terms of the situation of a people that suffers abuse and injustice but is organizing to defend its right to life and in keeping its hope in God strong. There is thus a dialogue *between history and history*. The biblical stories shed light on our present history, both collective and personal, and help us to see in it the intervention of the God who liberates.

The Latin American people, whose knowledge and use of the Bible has grown and deepened so much in recent years, perceive the word of God as very close to them. They hear it speaking directly to their everyday lives. When a passage is read, it is not unusual for someone to say, for example: "That is what happened to me a short time ago." Among the people there is a quick and extensive identification with the biblical texts. This experience of nearness is undoubtedly very valuable. The Bible is not a book like any other; it is the word of the Lord who, according to Deuteronomy, always speaks to us "today." At the same time, however, we cannot forget that we are dealing with writings that took shape millennia ago, in languages and cultural settings that are not our own. We must therefore make the effort to distance ourselves from them and to acquire knowledge of the cultural, social, and religious context of the texts. At the present time, there are countless serious works on history, social setting, and literary form that enable us nowadays to familiarize ourselves with the background. These studies are a basic tool to be used in drawing near to writings that we must at the same time admit are distant from us. The dialogue with the Scriptures will be more fruitful if we are aware that our relationship to the texts of the Bible is one of both *nearness* and *distance*. On the one hand, we will then avoid a facile closeness and even a possible manipulation of the Bible, but at the same time we will be prevented from succumbing to a literalism that pays no heed to human and social circumstances and turns every word into a timeless absolute.[10]

Contact with the Bible takes the form of reading it. It is a text. We go to it with the questions, worries, and hopes that derive from reality as we experience it. Such has been the church's practice throughout its history. These questions are the pre-text with which we approach the Bible and continually read and reread it. John Paul II spoke of this in Brazil: "The Church has meditated on these texts and messages from the beginning, but it is aware that it has still not penetrated their meaning as it would like (will it perhaps be able to do so some day?). In different concrete situations it *rereads these texts* and studies this message with the desire of finding a *new application* of it."[11] But when believers read Scripture, they know that the Scriptures also challenge them. The Bible is not a kind of depository of answers to our concerns; rather it reformulates our questions and sets us on unexpected paths. We can truly say that we read the Bible. But it in turn reads us, "penetrating even between soul and spirit, joints and marrow, and able to discern reflections and thoughts of the heart" (Heb 4:12). The dialogue must therefore also be one of *reading* with *reading*. When the reading of the Bible is done as a community, as a church, it is always an unexpected experience.

In summary: our starting point is our faith: we *believe* in the God of life. We aim to *think* this faith by going ever deeper into the content of biblical revelation. And we do this while taking into account the way in which the poor *perceive* God. Faith and reflection on God feed each other.

OUTLINE OF THE BOOK

The questions traditionally asked of God can be organized with the aid of "commonplaces," or general themes, from classic rhetoric.[12] On that basis it may be said that the fundamental questions are these:

An sit?	Does God exist?
Quid sit?	What is God?
Ubi sit?	Where is God?
Quo modo sit?	How are we to speak of God?
Cur sit?	Why God?

This sequence of questions can provide us with a helpful guiding thread.

I shall develop what I have to say in terms of the three basic questions (the second, third, and fourth). These will enable me to reply in a concrete way to the substance of the other two questions (the first and the last). After all, it would not be very profitable to discourse on the existence of God unless I first determined what God we are talking about.[13] The fifth question is essential and will therefore be very much in mind as I deal with the three main questions, since it cannot be separated from them.

My presentation, then, will have three main parts:

What is God? A God who is Love (Father and Mother).

Where is God? In the kingdom that Jesus proclaims.

How are we to speak of God? According to the prompting of the Spirit.

My hope is that the following pages will make the Scriptures accessible to a wide readership. I want the texts to speak for themselves (that is why the citations are so extensive). They will be accompanied by short commentaries that situate them, bring out certain key points, and show some relationships. For the same reason, I have tried to avoid technical language and to limit the number of notes and bibliographical references.[14]

My desire is that this book may help readers to know more fully the God of biblical revelation and, as a result, to proclaim God as the God of life.

PART ONE

GOD IS LOVE

"God is love" (1 Jn 4:8). This statement of John sums up the biblical revelation about God. Love gives life; therefore in the Bible God is frequently called Father. God is the origin of all that exists:

> Is the Lord to be thus repaid by you,
> O stupid and foolish people?
> Is he not your father who created you?
> Has he not made you and established you?
> Think back on the days of old, reflect on the years of age
>   upon age.
> Ask your father and he will inform you, ask your elders
>   and they will tell you.
>   [Dt 32:6-7; see Sir 34:20; Is 53:2]

The canticle of Mary, which is filled with Old Testament echoes, will likewise speak of God accepting Israel as his child (see Lk 1:54). The very name "Father" evokes a profound everyday human experience and underscores the truth that God is the fount of life. The same idea may be richly conveyed, in other cultural contexts, by calling God "Mother." In fact, the Bible itself refers to the maternal aspect of God's love.[1]

God causes all that exists to be because God is the source of all things; God gives life because God is life; God loves and gives the power to love because, in the words of Paul that John Paul II has repeated, God is "rich in mercy" (Eph 2:4). God the Father overflows with love and affection. It is significant that Jesus, and he alone, uses the Aramaic word *Abba* to address and refer to his Father; the best translation is our affectionate,

1

colloquial "papa" or "daddy."[2] The Father, communicator of life, is the God who is love. The Holy Spirit is the bond of love between Father and Son, between God and us, and between human beings. The presence of the Spirit in our hearts enables us, like Jesus, to call God *Abba* (see Gal 4:6). The mystery of the Trinity shows the fullness of life that is in God.

The God of life is present in human history; this presence reaches its supreme and unsurpassed expression in the incarnation of the Son. As James Cone rightly says, "to ask 'Who is God?' is to focus on what he is doing," on God's liberating action in history.[3] But it is important not to go astray here. God is not a liberator because God liberates; rather God liberates because God is a liberator. God is not just because God establishes justice, or faithful because God enters into a covenant, but the other way around. I am not playing with words here, but trying to bring out the primacy and transcendence of God and to remind ourselves that God's being gives meaning to God's action. According to the Bible, God's interventions in the life of God's people do not imply any kind of immanentism or any dissolution of God into history; rather they emphasize that God is the absolute and transcendent source of being.

God is simultaneously near and distant. We know God through God's action in history; knowing who God is, we know what we ought to do if we believe in God. We find repeatedly in the Bible a pattern that is summed up concisely in a passage of Deuteronomy: "Remember, you were once slaves in Egypt, and the Lord, your God, ransomed you from there; that is why I command you to observe this rule" (Dt 24:18).

Jesus makes his own this rhythm governing the life of believers when he commands: "Love one another as I love you" (Jn 15:12). The same teaching is to be seen in the parable of the wicked servant to whom the king says: "Should you not have had pity on your fellow servant, as I had pity on you?" (Mt 18:33).

The God of life manifests love by forming a family of equals through an act of liberation in which God does, and demands, justice amid the people and enters into an irrevocable covenant with them in history.[4] Liberation, justice, and covenant imply one another; each is necessary for the full meaning of the others. These actions reveal to us a living, holy, faithful God who leads believers to certain kinds of behavior. Such are the three points to be made in each of the chapters that follow.

The Bible also shows us the opposite of acknowledgment of the God of life: the idolatry that is a danger threatening every believer, because it supposes an option in favor of death.

CHAPTER I

GOD LIBERATES:
GOD IS LIFE

Oppression in any of its forms means death. This was the experience of the Jewish people in Egypt, a country that became a symbol of deprivation and exploitation as well as of sin, which is the ultimate cause of injustice. Set over against this experience was the experience of the exodus: liberation brings life. God liberates because God is the God of life. The messianic proclamation of Jesus Christ is likewise focused on liberation. The theme thus runs through the entire Bible and reveals to us a God who loves life; life is God's will for all beings. To believe in Yahweh, the God who liberates, and to maintain that Jesus, "the author of life" (Acts 3:15), is the Son of God, is to be a friend of life.

1. WITH OUTSTRETCHED ARM

God acts in history to set the people free. Consequently, the experience and perspective of liberation are a central element in the Scriptures.

The Exodus: The Foundational Deed

God is revealed in the works of God. We are all aware that the exodus is the event on which the faith of the Jewish people is based. This faith springs from historical experience of the action of Yahweh in the deliverance from Egyptian slavery and the journey toward the collective takeover of the promised land.[1]

The Lord said, "I have witnessed the affliction of my people in Egypt and have heard their cry of complaint against their slave drivers, so I know well what they are suffering. Therefore I have come down to rescue them from the hands of the Egyptians and lead them out of that land into a good and spacious land, a land flowing with milk and honey, the country of the Canaanites, Hittites, Amorites, Perizzites, Hivites and Jebusites. So indeed the cry of the Israelites has reached me, and I have truly noted that the Egyptians are oppressing them.

3

Come, now! I will send you to Pharaoh to lead my people, the Israelites, out of Egypt." [Ex 3:7–10]

This is the deed on which the faith of Israel is founded.[2] It involves the
experience of a people. In this deed God is shown to be a liberator by
means of an action that accompanies and gives meaning to the entire journey that leads the people to encounter with God. Liberation and worship
of the Lord are therefore closely connected. Yahweh says repeatedly to
Moses: "Go to Pharaoh and tell him: Thus says the Lord, the God of the
Hebrews: 'Let my people go to worship me'" (Ex 9:1; same idea in Ex
16:16 and 17:13). True worship is given to God only in a setting of freedom;
conversely, liberation reaches its full form in prayer to Yahweh, the God
of life. This connection is the nerve center of every experience of faith.

Faith therefore expresses itself in what have been called the "historical
credos"; I am referring to professions of faith in Yahweh, the God of the
covenant, which narrate and specify the meaning of a concrete historical
process.[3] I shall mention one of these historical credos, this one uttered
when "remembering" the taking over and cultivation of the promised land
and the subsequent offering to God of a basket containing the firstfruits of
the soil. It is important to note, therefore, that this credo is uttered in a
context of worship:

> The priest shall then receive the basket from you and shall set it in
> front of the altar of the Lord, your God. Then you shall declare before
> the Lord, your God. "My father was a wandering Aramean who went
> down to Egypt with a small household and lived there as an alien.
> But there he became a nation great, strong and numerous. When the
> Egyptians maltreated and oppressed us, imposing hard labor upon us,
> we cried out to the Lord, the God of our fathers, and he heard our
> cry and saw our affliction, our toil and our oppression. He brought
> us out of Egypt with his strong hand and outstretched arm, with
> terrifying power, with signs and wonders; and bringing us into this
> country, he gave us this land flowing with milk and honey." [Dt 26:4–
> 9]

Here is a simple yet profound remembrance of a historical event pregnant with consequences. The text recalls in a poetic manner the poor and
insignificant beginning ("a wandering Aramean") of the Israelite people,
who, though grown into "a nation great, strong and numerous," live in a
state of subjection and impoverishment in Egypt. They cry out to the Lord,
who is also called "the God of our fathers," who hears them and delivers
them from misery and oppression.[4] This is not the place for a detailed
commentary on the passage. We need note only that in expressing its *faith*
the Jewish people narrate the intervention of God in *history*: concretely in
the history of their deliverance from the yoke of the pharaoh, but with the

clear intention of thereby shedding light on their entire history as a people.[5]

There are many passages of the Bible that resemble the one just cited. Here are two of them: "It was I who brought you up from the land of Egypt, and who led you through the desert for forty years, to occupy the land of the Amorites" (Am 2:10). "Thus says the Lord: As the shepherd snatches from the mouth of the lion a pair of legs or the tip of an ear of his sheep, so the Israelites who dwell in Samaria shall escape with the corner of a couch or a piece of a cot" (Am 3:12).

Memory is the place where faith resides; consequently, memory is related to the present. For this reason, Deuteronomy offers us a searching meditation of the liberating events recounted in the Book of Exodus, with the evident intention of showing the demands these events make upon the Jewish people in the here and now.

Another passage representative of the "historical credos" brings out this point clearly:

> Later on, when your son asks you what these ordinances, statutes and decrees mean which the Lord, our God, has enjoined on you, you shall say to your son, "We were once slaves of Pharaoh in Egypt, but the Lord brought us out of Egypt with his strong hand and wrought before our eyes signs and wonders, great and dire, against Egypt and against Pharaoh and his whole house. He brought us from there to lead us into the land he promised on oath to our fathers, and to give it to us. Therefore, the Lord commanded us to observe all these statutes in fear of the Lord, our God, that we may always have as prosperous and happy a life as we have today; and our justice before the Lord, our God, is to consist in carefully observing all these commandments he has enjoined on us." [Dt 6:20–25]

God's action requires that the people put God's commandments into practice; it requires a certain behavior in the *today* of their lives. The requirement of actualizing the covenant is a characteristic element in the theology of Deuteronomy:

> Be careful not to forget the Lord, your God, by neglecting his commandments and decrees and statutes which I enjoin on you *today*. . . . Remember, then, it is the Lord, your God, who gives you the power to acquire wealth, by fulfilling, as he has now [or: *today*] done, the covenant which he swore to your fathers. But if you forget the Lord, your God, and follow other gods, serving and worshiping them, I forewarn you *this day* that you will perish utterly. [Dt 8:11, 18–19]

In this context Deuteronomy reminds us of the importance of our personal decision. God does not force a covenant on us; it is a gift, and therefore requires a choice on our part. A choice of life. This requirement has

a place of prominence in a central text: the "testament" that Moses leaves
to his people when he is prevented from entering the promised land. This
is a solemn moment, and the leaders of the tribes, the advisers and officials,
the women and children and all the inhabitants of Israel are in the presence
of Yahweh. As the people are thus gathered, shortly before they cross the
Jordan and take possession of the land "flowing with milk and honey,"
Yahweh speaks to them through the mouth of Israel's liberator and offers
them a definitive choice:

> Here, then, I have *today* set before you life and prosperity, death and
> doom. . . . I call heaven and earth *today* to witness against you: I have
> set before you life and death, the blessing and the curse. Choose life,
> then, that you and your descendants may live, by loving the Lord, your
> God, heeding his voice, and holding fast to him. For that will mean
> life for you, a long life for you to live on the land which the Lord
> swore he would give to your fathers Abraham, Isaac and Jacob. [Dt
> 30:15, 19–20]

The passage clearly confronts us with the alternatives, *life* or *death*; these
are two paths that open before us *today* and call for a decision. It also
reminds us of God's warning that we should choose life by "holding fast to
God" — a phrase filled with a sense of tenderness. To choose life means to
choose God, to hold fast to God as a child does to its parents, who are the
source and protectors of its life. The path of love is the path of blessing
and life.[6] Moses' final words to his people confirm this perspective. "Take
to heart all the warning which I have now given you and which you must
impress on your children, that you may carry out carefully every word of
this law. For this is no trivial matter for you; rather, it means your very life,
since it is by this means that you are to enjoy a long life on the land which
you will cross the Jordan to occupy" (Dt 32:46–47).

The law or Torah must be put into practice; it is life because it is a way
to God.

The Program of the Messiah

The Old Testament says that God gives life. Jesus Christ says the same
in his preaching. In his gospel John emphasizes the point that "God so
loved the world that he gave his only Son, so that everyone who believes
in him may not perish but may have eternal life" (3:16). Going even further,
Jesus reveals himself as "the way and the truth and the life" (Jn 14:6). The
theme of life is fundamental in the story told by John and by the New
Testament as a whole. Jesus makes it the focus of his proclamation.

In a section of the Gospel of Luke that is very familiar to us (4:16–20)
Jesus uses passages from the prophet Isaiah (61:1–2 and 58:6) to make a
public statement of his program.[7] The text in question plays a role in the

Gospel of Luke similar to that played by the exodus in the Old Testament.[8]
Both express God's will to set human beings free.

The Messiah states his mission as follows:

> The Spirit of the Lord is upon me,
>> because he has anointed me
>> to bring glad tidings to the poor.
>
> He has sent me to proclaim liberty to captives
>> and recovery of sight to the blind,
>
> To let the oppressed go free,
>> and to proclaim a year acceptable to the Lord.
>>> [Lk 4:18–19]

In this passage of his Gospel Luke is describing the beginning of the
ministry of Jesus. In like manner, he tells of the pentecostal event and
records Peter's first sermon as a way of showing that the work of the church
is beginning (see Acts 2). In his two books, then, Luke emphasizes the role
of the Spirit in the first phase of the journeys of Jesus and of the church
alike, both of them being anointed preachers of the good news.

In passages that can be looked upon as parallels to the one I am commenting on, Mark (1:14–15) and Matthew (4:12–17) speak of the beginning
of the preaching about the kingdom and its demands, but these two writers
do not tell us the content of this preaching as Luke does.[9] It is the reference
to Isaiah that allows Luke to proceed as he does:

> The spirit of the Lord God is upon me,
>> because the Lord has anointed me;
>
> He has sent me to bring glad tidings to the lowly [LXX:
>> the poor],
>> to heal the brokenhearted,
>
> To proclaim liberty to the captives,
>> and release to the prisoners;
>
> To announce a year of favor from the Lord
>> and a day of vindication by our God,
>> to comfort all who mourn. [Is 61:1–2][10]

Luke takes advantage of the scene during the visit to Nazareth, which
Matthew (13:53–58) and Mark (6:1–6) also report, to tell us in what the
messianic work will consist; he also takes great care to show its universal
scope. This work is not for the benefit solely of one nation among others;
the covenant is now to be with all the nations of the earth. This is undoubtedly the reason why Luke omits from his citation of Isaiah 61 the second
part of verse 2: "and a day of vindication by our God," with its connotation
of punishment for the pagans.[11] The same universalist outlook appears a

few verses later in the reference to Elijah and Elisha being sent to individuals who are gentiles (see Lk 4:25–27).

The various human situations mentioned (poverty, captivity, blindness, oppression) are manifestations of death. The preaching of Jesus, who has been anointed Messiah by the power of the Spirit, will cause death to withdraw, by introducing a source of life that is meant to bring history to its fulfillment. This programatic passage, therefore, confronts us again with the dilemma: death or life, which is central to biblical revelation and calls upon us, as we saw above, to make a radical choice.

We may ask ourselves, however, whether all the situations are located on the same level. The answer would seem to be that they are not. In fact, as is suggested by the penetrating analysis that J. Dupont makes of a passage related to one on which I am commenting, namely, Matthew 11:2–6 (see Lk 7:18–22), it is possible to maintain that in Luke 4:18–19, too, the most important thing is the proclamation of the good news to the poor.[12] In addition, the emphasis in the text itself seems to be that this is the primary purpose of the Messiah's mission. The poor (Greek: *ptochoi*; the same word is used in Is 61:1 LXX) in Luke are clearly those who lack the necessities of life (see Lk 6:20; 7:22; 14:13–21; 16:10, 22; 18:22; 19:8; 21:3). It is to these that deliverance is proclaimed. In accordance with the method of synonymous parallelism,[13] the good news preached to them is given concrete form in the three statements that follow: release for captives, sight for the blind, and freedom for the oppressed. In all these instances we find one and the same proclamation, the dominant idea being *freedom*.

Even Luke's expression "sight to the blind" is a reference to freedom, for the literal meaning of the Hebrew text of Isaiah 61:1 is: "and to those in chains the opening of the eyes." The image the prophet uses for the emergence from the darkness of a prison clearly signifies a liberation (this is why the text of Isaiah is rightly translated: "and release to the prisoners"). But the Greek translation of the Old Testament (the Septuagint), which Luke is following, gives a figurative version; the metaphor in the Hebrew original, "opening of the eyes," is replaced by "recovery of sight," and "to those in chains" by "to the blind." The Greek translation thus drops the reference to freedom for those in prison, which is clearly to be seen in the Hebrew text. If we go back to the latter, we recover the original meaning of the passage; "recovery of sight to the blind" must therefore likewise be understood in the perspective of liberation.

In addition, Luke replaces Isaiah's words "to heal the brokenhearted" with "to let the oppressed go free," which is an expression taken from Isaiah 58:6. By including this promise, which in its Isaian context is accompanied by others of the same kind, Luke emphasizes the liberation aspect of the Messiah's programatic statement.

> This, rather, is the fasting that I wish:
> releasing those bound unjustly,

untying the thongs of the yoke;
Setting free the oppressed,
   breaking every yoke. [Is 58:6]

"Oppressed" translates a word derived from the Hebrew verb *rss*, which indeed means to oppress, but with the connotations of to crush, to grind down, to smash physically. The good news the Messiah proclaims to the poor is focused on liberation. This perspective is further underscored by the phrase "a year of favor from the Lord" or, in Luke, "a year acceptable to the Lord," which is also to be proclaimed. The reference is to the jubilee year, meant to be celebrated every fifty years; during this year "every one of you shall return to his own property" (Lv 25:13), because in the final analysis Yahweh alone owns the land (Lv 25:23).

This jubilee clearly had to do with liberation: "This fiftieth year you shall make sacred by proclaiming liberty in the land for all its inhabitants" (Lv 25:10). By doing away with all unjust inequality, the year of the Lord's favor was meant to contribute to the permanent establishment of a fellowship among the members of the Jewish people and, in the final analysis, of communion with God.[14] The list of the actions to be taken by the Messiah is thus clearly concerned with life and liberation.

The reign of God, which is a reign of life, is the ultimate meaning of human history, but its presence begins even now as a result of the concern of Jesus for the least regarded participants in this human history. The passage in Luke attests to this: "Today this Scripture passage is fulfilled in your hearing" (4:21). The word "today" is a key term in Lucan theology (see 2:11; 3:22; 5:26), as it is in Deuteronomy; in Luke 4:21 the meaning is that the prophecy of Isaiah (the prophet most often cited in the Gospels) is fulfilled. This is the moment of integral liberation in Christ; therefore, in the person of Jesus the kingdom has become present in our midst (see Lk 17:21). But the life that he brings us is rejected by many.

Luke tells us that those who heard his sermon on this occasion wanted to throw him down from the top of the hill (see 4:28–30). The proclamation of the gospel of liberation to the poor is not an easy task. The giving of life may bring death at the hands of those who have chosen death against life. The experience of many parts of the Latin American church in recent years bears eloquent testimony of this.

2. THE LORD, FRIEND OF LIFE

The Bible is the book of life, of all life. This life has its origin in the love of God; believers in God must therefore be friends of life.

The Living God

The expression "living God" occurs very frequently in the Old Testament. "David now said to the men standing by, 'What will be done for the man who kills this Philistine and frees Israel of the disgrace? Who is this uncircumcised Philistine in any case, that he should insult the armies of the living God?' " (1 Sm 17:26). "Incline your ear, O Lord, and listen! Open your eyes, O Lord, and see! Hear the words of Sennacherib, which he sent to taunt the living God" (2 Kgs 19:16).

When the Jews recall the actions of Yahweh in behalf of the people, they say that the God in whom they believe is a living God: a God who sees and hears, who knows and feels. For this reason they mock the gods of foreigners:

> Their idols are silver and gold,
>   the handiwork of men.
> They have mouths but speak not;
>   they have eyes but see not;
> They have ears but hear not;
>   they have noses but smell not;
> They have hands but feel not;
>   they have feet but walk not;
>   they utter no sound from their throat.
> Their makers shall be like them,
>   everyone that trusts in them. [Ps 115:4–8]

Israel places its trust in Yahweh, a God who speaks and acts, who is not the product of human labor. The God of Israel is a living God. For this reason, the Bible often says that God does not grow weary, but is always ready to act in behalf of the people:

> Do you not know
>   or have you not heard?
> The Lord is the eternal God,
>   creator of the ends of the earth.
> He does not faint or grow weary,
>   and his knowledge is beyond scrutiny. [Is 40:28]

The prophets bear witness to the living God. According to the Puebla Document, a priest "can be a prophet only insofar as he has had experience of the living God" (no. 693). Yahweh is therefore looked upon as the permanent defender of life, especially the life of the poor, whom Yahweh delivers from oppression:

> For he shall rescue the poor man when he cries out,
>   and the afflicted when he has no one to help him.
> He shall have pity for the lowly and the poor;
>   the lives of the poor he shall save. [Ps 72:12–13]

This idea of God is based on the event that founds the faith of Israel: the liberation from oppression in Egypt. It expresses the will to life of a God who continually liberates and blesses the people.[15]

This approach to God shows in the names given to God. The Old Testament has various names for God, but the most important, and the one characteristic of the religion of Israel, is undoubtedly the well-known tetragram, which is revealed to Moses, YHWH:[16]

"But," said Moses to God, "when I go to the Israelites and say to them, 'The God of your fathers has sent me to you,' if they ask me, 'What is his name?' what am I to tell them?" God replied, "I am who am." Then he added, "This is what you shall tell the Israelites: I AM sent me to you." God spoke further to Moses, "Thus shall you say to the Israelites: The Lord [Yahweh], the God of your fathers, the God of Abraham, the God of Isaac, the God of Jacob, has sent me to you. This is my name forever; this is my title for all generations." [Ex 3:13–15]

The passage is from the Yahwist tradition. It is well known, and it will be enough, therefore, to remind the reader that it is part of the scene in which Moses receives and accepts the task of liberating the Jewish people from oppression in Egypt. The immediate context, therefore, of this revelation of God in the Book of Exodus is the commissioning of a human being for a historic mission of liberation.[17] Moses' approach to the question of God's name is determined by the context—namely, God's call and mission, as well as his own response to the task laid upon him.

The priestly tradition observes that what is revealed by the name Yahweh is something new, something different from what is said in other names for God. "God also said to Moses, 'I am the Lord [Yahweh]. As God the Almighty [El Shaddai] I appeared to Abraham, Isaac, and Jacob, but my name, Lord [Yahweh], I did not make known to them'" (Ex 6:2–3).

Verses 6, 7, and 8 of chapter 6 repeat the formula "I am Yahweh," always in the context of the task of liberation given to Moses.

This brings me to the meaning of God's name. According to the Jewish mind, a name is not something accidental; it not only points to the person but captures the meaning of the person. In the prayer we know as the Our Father, the words "hallowed be your name" mean "hallowed be you, Father." In like manner, when Genesis tells us that God authorized Adam to name all the animals and other things on earth, the implication is that God was giving him dominion over them. Far from proposing that Adam engage in a simple exercise of the imagination, the biblical message is that in giving him the assignment of naming creatures, God grants him dominion and recognizes him as lord of all creation. If, then, the name is the person, the question "What is your name?" is the same as asking "Who are you?" When Moses echoes this question, he shows his concern to transmit the answer to the people whose liberation the Lord is entrusting to him.

The translation of "Yahweh" is a headache for the exegetes; its inter-pretation has given rise to many philological and philosophical speculations. The most common translation is "I am who I am," but others are possible: "I am he who is," and even "I am who I will be," "I will be who I will be," or "I will be who I am." These are interesting nuances, but I shall certainly not linger on them here.[18] The important thing is that a new presence of the God of the Israelites is revealed here. The formula "Yahweh Elohim" (see Ex 9:1) uses the plural (in the abstract meaning of "divinity") of the ancient name El for God; the point is perhaps to attribute to Yahweh, the God of the covenant, the fullness of meaning hitherto given to the word "God."

Let me emphasize, however, one possible meaning of this new presence of God that is of special interest for the theme I am now developing. As understood in the Bible, "to live" always means "to live with," "to live for," "to be present to others"; in other words, life implies communion. Death is utter isolation. That is why, for example, in the time of Jesus, lepers, who are cut off from the community, are regarded as dead; a healing restores them to life not only because it cures them of an illness, but also because it reincorporates them into the human community, the body social. This is the reason for Jesus' command when he cures lepers: "Go, show yourself to the priest, and offer for your cleansing what Moses prescribed; that will be proof for them" (Mk 1:44). It is very probable that the much discussed name Yahweh is to be interpreted along these lines and that it means: "I am he who is with you; I am life." The divine presence is at once creative and liberating.[19]

"I am life" ("I am who I am"): such is Yahweh. We are faced here once again with the idea of the origin or source of life. But the text adds: "I AM sent me to you" (Ex 3:14). The fact that God is an absolute principle does not mean that God is unconcerned about history. On the contrary, by revealing God's name (which is not a concept), Yahweh makes known the decision to intervene in history. The divine being is linked to the course of history. The eternal becomes present in time, the absolute in history. More-over, God is not only a presence but a communication, a gift. The two passages that tell us of the manifestation of God's name also tell us of God's will to liberate and give life: "I have decided to lead you up out of the misery of Egypt into . . . a land flowing with milk and honey" (Ex 3:17). "I am the Lord. I will free you from the forced labor of the Egyptians and will deliver you from their slavery. I will rescue you by my outstretched arm and with mighty acts of judgment" (Ex 6:6). In the beginning is this love, this gift of life. "He rescued me, because he loves me" (Ps 18:20).

But there is more. God is also revealed as "Yahweh, the God of your ancestors." God's name "forever," which the Israelites are ordered to use "for all generations" in invoking God, inseparably unites "I am who I am" and "the Lord, the God of your ancestors." There is thus both newness and continuity. The God who is transcendent but also present in history is at the same time the God of tradition. These two aspects find expression in Moses' mission or, concretely, in the deliverance of the Jewish people from the pharaoh who is oppressing them. In this liberation, God is revealed, an action that implies a clear and very precise reference to the historical vicissitudes of the peoples. "I am" (Yahweh), the absolute and active principle, the origin of all things, is also the God of the past, the God of the patriarchs or ancestors of the people to whom Moses is now being sent.

It is possible, therefore, to say that while "I am" lacks a past insofar as God is absolute, faith in God does have antecedents. Faith in God is always historical, because it is accepted and professed by persons who live in time, to whom God becomes present. "I am" is the origin of everything; God is a Father; faith in God has a history. In light of the mission it is possible to understand who God is. Jesus will adopt this approach, but, as always, he will do so with complete freedom and creativity.

I Am the Life

When Jesus is called "Lord" in the New Testament, the word carries all the implications I have pointed out. If "Lord" is a translation of what the word "Yahweh" means,[20] then to confess that Jesus is the Lord is to affirm that he is God. He himself will say to us, "I am the life" (see Jn 14:6), using an expression that has its roots in the Old Testament and has many resonances. Another major Johannine theme, that of light, also signifies life when applied to Jesus: "Jesus spoke to them again, saying, 'I am the light of the world. Whoever follows me will not walk in darkness, but will have the light of life' " (Jn 8:12).

This passage has for its setting the feast of booths, which celebrated the deliverance from Egypt.[21] The connection between light, liberation, and life is also found in Isaiah:

> I, the Lord, have called you for the victory of justice,
> I have grasped you by the hand;
> I formed you, and set you
> as a covenant for the people,
> a light for the nations,
> To open the eyes of the blind,
> to bring prisoners out from confinement,
> and from the dungeon, those who live in darkness.
> [Is 42:6-7]

We have already met these synonyms: darkness and prison, on the one hand, and light and liberation, on the other.

Jesus manifests this will to life by means of his miracles. These are never accomplished in order to astonish their beneficiaries or any bystanders;

neither are they means of exerting a personal power. The miracles of Jesus take the form of restoring physical health and, as a consequence, social health as well. Connected with this restoration is liberation from sin, from everything that prevents us from fully accepting the gift of divine love, along with its demands. The miracles point to and manifest the kingdom that the Lord is proclaiming. That is why the Gospel of Mark establishes a revealing equivalency between kingdom and life:

> If your hand causes you to sin, cut it off. It is better for you to enter *into life* maimed than with two hands to go into Gehenna, into the unquenchable fire. And if your foot causes you to sin, cut it off. It is better for you to enter *into life* crippled than with two feet to be thrown into Gehenna. And if your eye causes you to sin, pluck it out. Better for you to enter *into the kingdom* of God with one eye than with two eyes to be thrown into Gehenna. [Mk 9:43-47]

To enter the kingdom is to enter into life. The resurrection of Jesus is the Father's confirmation of the gift of life made in the Son. It signifies, if I may so put it, the death of death; since the Lord is alive, we must not seek him among the dead (see Lk 24:5; also Acts 1:3). In the eyes of Paul, who makes the resurrection of Jesus (and therefore our resurrection) the cornerstone of his message and his thought, to deny the resurrection is to be ignorant of God (see 1 Cor 15:14).

Christians must bear witness to the resurrection. Yet at first that witness was in doubt, as Luke and John tell us. The women among the disciples of Jesus went to the tomb and found it empty. The Lord's body was not there (Lk 24:4). Their first reaction was bewilderment: "We don't know where they put him" (Jn 20:2), then sadness: "Mary stayed outside the tomb weeping" (Jn 20:11). Once informed by the women, the other disciples did not believe them (people never believe those they regard as "inferior"), but they too returned home "amazed at what had happened" (Lk 24:12). And yet this emptiness, this absence, points to a fullness of presence. The body of Jesus is not in the tomb, because he is alive. The Lord's messengers ask: "Why do you seek the living one among the dead?" (Lk 24:5).

The God in whom we believe is the God of life. Belief in the resurrection entails defending the life of the weakest members of society. Looking for the Lord among the living leads to commitment to those who see their right to life being constantly violated. To assert the resurrection of the Lord is to assert life in the face of death.

Now, for Christians the resurrection is a passover or passage. Passover in the Bible is the passage from oppression in Egypt to the promised land. The celebration of Passover meant remembering the gift of deliverance. It is in this context that Jesus located his own work, which was a passage from sin, oppression, and death to grace, freedom, and life. There is no affirmation of life that does not entail passing through death, confronting death.

This is the witness that so many in Latin America have given to us in our time. The message of the resurrection of Jesus and of our resurrection in union with his is clear: life, not death, has the final word in history.

For this reason, the resurrection is the heart of the first Christian preaching. The disciples come forward as witnesses to this foundational event. As Peter says in the house of Cornelius, the disciples "ate and drank with him after he rose from the dead" (Acts 10:41). The source of the testimony the disciples give is an experience they had often shared before with the master but now takes on a very special meaning. Then, too, food is connected with life, and their experience of the risen Lord takes the form of sharing a meal with him ("we ate and drank"), something that is peculiar to beings who are alive.

In his second sermon, Peter refers to Jesus as "the author of life" (Acts 3:15) who was handed over to death while a "murderer" was set free (see Lk 23:13–19). The Greek word *archegos*, which is here translated as "author," can mean "leader, guide." The word is used twice again in Acts (5:31; 7:35); in these instances it describes Moses as the one who liberated and gave life to his people by rescuing them from unjust death in Egypt and leading them to the promised land.[22]

In Christ's name Peter gives life and health to the crippled man who asks him for alms at the gate of the temple. "I have neither silver nor gold," he tells him, "but what I do have I give you: in the name of Jesus Christ the Nazorean, [rise and] walk" (Acts 3:6). Money, no; life, yes. A little earlier, in his first sermon, he applies Psalm 16 to Jesus and tells his listeners that Jesus has "made known" to us "the paths of life" (Acts 2:28). That is, the paths along which we are to be led by the author of life who calls us to make decisive choices. The bishops of Chile have written:

> Consideration of the past and the challenges of the present have led us to meditate and to pray to the Lord of our faith. We have repeatedly asked ourselves in our reflection what fundamental attitude God our Father is asking us to adopt during the pastoral year now beginning. And we have not the least doubt *that the Lord is calling us to a profound, even radical, option for him as the God of life*.

A little further on, the bishops draw conclusions for the life of the church: the church "needs to show itself to the world, and especially to our country, as a great sacrament of life. ... When the Church puts itself at the service of life, it is simply making its own the attitude of Jesus."[23]

God Did Not Make Death

Some reflections on the Book of Wisdom are in place here. This is a late pre-Christian book that seems to have been written at Alexandria toward the middle of the first century before Christ (some scholars regard it as almost contemporaneous with him). In any case, we are dealing with the last book of what we call the Old Testament. The Jews living in Egypt had been persecuted shortly before by Ptolemy II; moreover, at this time the period of Roman domination was beginning. The purpose of the author of Wisdom, in these days of difficulty and crisis, is to confirm believers in their hope; to this end, he rereads (in the Greek version known as the Septuagint) the great books that are part of the Bible, with the aim of bringing out the fundamentals of their message. In this re-reading he will establish a solid connection between *God* and *life*.

The clouds visible on the horizon should not dismay believers. They should be able to think correctly of God, and it is the declared intention of this writing to ensure that they do. At the very beginning the author says: "Love justice, you who judge the earth, think of the Lord in goodness [or: in the right way] and seek him in integrity of heart" (Wis 1:1). If we keep the God of the Bible before us, we necessarily desire righteousness: this is the most authentic prophetic tradition. For "God is just and loves justice" (Wis 11:7). Love of God inevitably leads us to want what God loves; consequently, the practice of justice is not something added from outside to our friendship with God, but is an intrinsic element in our relationship with God. God must be sought "in integrity of heart." In the words of an old popular Chilean song, God could say to us: "Divided hearts I do not want." This is a matter of personal integrity. It is not possible to "serve God and mammon," Jesus tells us in the Gospel of Matthew (6:24). No one can love God and practice injustice, because the exploitation and despoilment of the poor, like the resultant rejection of God, is a choice of death.

In this context the Book of Wisdom has a statement that may at first sight be surprising: God is not the author of death. "Court not death by your erring way of life, nor draw to yourselves destruction by the works of your hands; because God did not make death, nor does he rejoice in the destruction of the living" (Wis 1:12–13). The author reminds his readers that the persecution and death they may be facing do not come from God; this means that this situation should not be thought of as finding support in God's will or as something inevitable. It is up to us to transform the time in which we live; it is our responsibility to change the course of events. There is no room, then, for an easy resignation that seeks reasons, including religious reasons, to hide our cowardice.

God "fashioned all things that they might have being; and the creatures of the world are wholesome, and there is not a destructive drug among them nor any domain of the nether world on earth" (1:14). The Lord wills life. The created world does not contain a poisonous seed of death that must someday inexorably grow. Creatures have been made to live in health; the earth exists to feed and receive the living. When our rural brothers and sisters in Latin America claim the land to which they have a (human and historical) right, they are not seeking to have their names entered in the public record books of the country; they are asking only to exercise their

right to life. The domain of Hades, the world of darkness, does not control
and ought not control the earth and the life it sustains. For the same reason
and in the same way, the Bible rejects the shedding of blood, and not only
of innocent blood; the latter case is doubtless the one that calls most loudly
for attention, but the rejection extends to every attack on human life.

The full importance of life emerges in the theme of the promised land.
The promised land is not simply a place where human beings find daily
food. It is also the space wherein they enjoy personal freedom and dignity.
These too are elements in the life that has God for its author. In a land in
which men and women cease to be aliens and wanderers and instead
become owners who are able fully to exercise their rights, they will be able
to offer God a worship "in spirit and in truth."

After this reaffirmation of life, the Book of Wisdom brings out the
oblique but nonetheless strong links between the wicked—that is, those
who do not practice righteousness—and death: "For justice is undying. It
is the wicked who with hands and words invited death, considered it a
friend, and pined for it, and made a covenant with it, because they deserve
to be in its possession" (Wis 1:15-16). To say that justice is undying is to
maintain that it is an element of life and comes from God; only by practicing
it can one think correctly of God. This is an important idea for the author;
that is why we find repeated that "justice is undying" (v. 15). The wicked,
on the other hand, are friends of death; they invite it; they gesture to it to
show their affection for it; they die for it, so to speak. They sow it everywhere by violating the rights of others.

Chapter 2 tells us in what precisely the wickedness of these friends of
death consists. The author is referring to those who exploit and mistreat
the poor and do not love justice. He puts on their lips a description of their
own conduct:

> Let us oppress the needy just man;
>> let us neither spare the widow
>> nor revere the old man for his hair grown white with
>>> time.
> But let strength be our norm of justice;
>> for weakness proves itself useless. [2:11–12]

The author is not speaking simply of occasional misdeeds; the matter is
far more serious: those who "knew not the hidden counsels of God" (2:22)
make a pact with death, a kind of countercovenant. The covenant with
Yahweh, the God of life, turns its signatories into defenders of life within
history. Those, on the contrary, who enter into an agreement with death
form a party of assassins and try to give death the last word in human
history. As in so many other books of the Bible, life and death are here
opposed. Deuteronomy told us we must choose between the two (see Deut
30:15). We cannot avoid hearing the question: To which party do we

belong? To those who actively or by omission participate in the violence that is presently crushing and grinding others, especially the poor? Or to those who endeavor, likewise "with hands and words" and against wind and tide, to bear witness to life, at times at the cost of their own lives?

From this point of view, chapter 11 of the Book of Wisdom is especially important. The immediate context is a reflection on Exodus 7:25–8:11, where the sacred writer speaks of the liberating action of Yahweh who rescues the people from the situation of oppression and death that was theirs in Egypt. The Book of Wisdom reflects on God's life-giving purpose: "With you great strength abides always; who can resist the might of your arm? Indeed, before you the whole universe is as a grain from a balance, or a drop of morning dew come down upon the earth" (11:21–22). The author is meditating here on the will to deliver and the liberating power of Yahweh, who removed the people from slavery in order to make them free and bring them to the land "flowing with milk and honey." Every relationship with God begins with an acknowledgment of God's greatness.

"But you have mercy on all, because you can do all things; and you overlook the sins of men that they may repent" (Wis 11:23). God's omnipotence does not cause believers to be frightened or insecure; quite the contrary, because God's omnipotence motivates the divine compassion. Conversely, God's nearness to creatures helps them better understand the meaning of God's power. God wants all human beings to be converted; God wants all of them to set out on the way of life, even the wicked, the friends of death, of whom I spoke above. It is for this reason that God overlooks our sins and that God's plan of love knows no limits. Yahweh is compassionate power and compassion that has power at its service.

Everything begins with God's love. "You love all things that are and loathe nothing that you have made; for what you hated, you would not have fashioned. And how could a thing remain, unless you willed it; or be preserved, if it had not been called forth by you?" (Wis 11:24–25). Creation itself is an expression—the first expression—of God's love. God's love is a free and unmerited love, which the Lord makes the root of all being. When we approach the subject of creation as philosophers, we sometimes think of creation as an action done once for all and now over with; as something like a push given by a first mover that sets in motion a chain of movers with whom God then ceases to have anything to do. In the Bible, however, God's creative action is presented as something that abides. God creates all the days, as it were, because God loves all the days. God rejects nothing that has been made, but keeps created reality in existence. God's love enfolds everything.

To sin against God is to turn, at least for a time, into a partisan of death; it is to demand death. Such a position alienates us from God. But even here God's mercy is always open-armed and ready to have us return to the way that leads to the kingdom. "You spare all things, because they are yours, O Lord and lover of souls [or: friend of life]" (v. 26). God's love is universal and nothing is excluded from God's forgiveness, for to forgive is to give life. "Lord and lover of the living" is a beautiful and profound way of describing God that sums up the message of the Book of Wisdom, just as it sums up the demand with which the book confronts all believers. To believe in God is to be, like God, a lover of life, in contrast to the companions on the way of death. As the Book of Proverbs says: "The fear of the Lord is a fountain of life, that a man may avoid the snares of death" (Prov 14:27).

A few last words to end this section. Liberation embodies a will to life. The action of liberation is directed against oppression, servitude, and death; against a situation that has at its root the breaking of friendship with God and others—that is, sin. Hence the essential importance of the liberation from sin that brings us into a new communion with the Lord and others. Liberation expresses a will to life; consequently, by liberating us God is shown to be a liberating God, a living God, and the friend of life.

To be a Christian is to be a friend of the author of life, Jesus the Christ.

CHAPTER II

GOD DOES JUSTICE:
GOD IS HOLY

The God of Israel makes justice and judgment the foundations of the divine reign:

> Justice and judgment [or: righteousness] are the
> foundations of your throne;
> kindness and truth go before you. [Ps 89:15]

For this reason, ever since God made the promise to Abraham (see Gn 18:18–19), God has required the practice of justice and righteousness. In addition, Yahweh has become an intimate friend of each member of the Jewish people and asserts their rights, especially the right of the poor and the helpless to life. This entrance into the rough places of human existence, far from imperiling God's holiness, throws it into greater relief. The difference between God and creation does not mean a divine indifference to human history. On the contrary, God's followers must reflect God's holiness in themselves if they are to be in true solidarity with others.

1. THE *GO'EL* OF ISRAEL

Go'el is an important name of God in the Bible. It arises from the familial and the historical experience of the Hebrew people.

God Defends the Poor

Ga'al means "to liberate"; a *go'el* is one who liberates, one who ransoms; a redeemer, a protector, an avenger of blood. We find its original meaning in the history of Israel. The closest relative of those who are victims and deprived has the obligation to avenge and to buy back the possessions and persons of these individuals who have fallen into alien or foreign hands. Such a person is a *go'el*. The Book of Leviticus says:

> When one of your countrymen is reduced to such poverty that he sells
> himself to a wealthy alien who has a permanent or a temporary res-

20

idence among you, or to one of the descendants of an immigrant family, even after he has thus sold his services he still has the right of redemption; he may be redeemed by one of his own brothers, or by his uncle or cousin, or by some other relative or fellow clansman; or, if he acquires the means, he may redeem himself. [Lv 25:47–49]

The act of ransom or redemption may go further and turn into vengeance if there is question of an injustice done to relatives defending themselves: "If a man strikes another with a death-dealing club in his hand and causes his death, he is a murderer and shall be put to death. The avenger of blood may execute the murderer, putting him to death on sight" (Nm 35:18–19).

The institution of the *go'el* is thus rooted in the solidarity created by blood, in the family clan. A *go'el* is the official protector of relatives. By an extension and deepening of this original meaning, Yahweh comes to be called the *go'el* of Israel. Yahweh is seen as the nearest relative, the protector and avenger of the people, and especially the poor of the Jewish nation. The people with whom Yahweh establishes the covenant thereby become Yahweh's family; consequently, when they are wronged, Yahweh comes to their defense. Many passages in the Scriptures express this thought.[1]

God is revealed as the one who does justice in behalf of the people. Many passages of the Bible recall this kind of intervention in the history of Israel. Yahweh, under the title of "Lord of hosts," intervenes again and again to deliver the Israelite people from foreign oppression, as, for example, when Yahweh rescues them from the Babylonian captivity. "Thus says the Lord, your redeemer, the Holy One of Israel: for your sakes I send to Babylon; I will lower all the bars, and the Chaldeans shall cry out in lamentation" (Is 43:14).

Yahweh, the only God, is revealed as creator and redeemer and is acknowledged as such by the people:

> Thus says the Lord, Israel's King
>   and redeemer, the Lord of hosts:
> I am the first and I am the last;
>   there is no God but me. . . .
> Thus says the Lord, your redeemer,
>   who formed you from the womb:
> I am the Lord, who made all things,
>   who alone stretched out the heavens;
>   when I spread out the earth, who was with me?
> [Is 44:6, 24]

God is revealed as the relative and the national protector of Israel; in addition, and above all, God is revealed as the defender, the *go'el,* of the poor within the Jewish nation.[2] I need cite only one passage:

> The father of orphans and the defender of widows
>   is God in his holy dwelling.
> God gives a home to the forsaken;
>   he leads forth prisoners to prosperity. [Ps 68:6–7]

Affirmation of Nationhood and Defense of the Poor

When we speak of God as redeemer of the people and defender of the poor, we are not talking of two juxtaposed activities. Rather, the second (*"go'el* of the poor") gives meaning to the first. Yahweh is protector of the Israelite people *to the extent* that Yahweh is defender of the poor, for the defense of the poor is the ineradicable seal that permanently marks the covenant.

To put it another way: Israel's identity, or what it means to belong to the Hebrew people, consists in doing justice to the poor and restoring their trampled rights. Consequently, when the Jewish people do not do justice to the poor, they are traitors to themselves. This means that not only do they act in evil ways, but that violations of the covenant are directly contrary to what identifies them and originally gave rise to them as a people: namely, the liberating event of the exodus and the historical experience of having come forth from Egypt thanks to God's intervention.

The failure to do justice to the poor means turning one's back on the true identity of Israel as a nation. It so happens that the defense of the poor is the very meaning of the Jewish people's claim to nationhood. For this is a nation that, ever since the promise was given to Abraham, has been called upon to enthrone justice and right:

> The Lord reflected: "Shall I hide from Abraham what I am about to do, now that he is to become a great and populous nation, and all the nations of the earth are to find blessing in him? Indeed, I have singled him out that he may direct his sons and posterity to keep the way of the Lord by doing what is right and just, so that the Lord may carry into effect for Abraham the promises he made about him." [Gn 18:18–19]

"To do what is right and just": this command completes the one given to Abraham when God told him to leave his own country and travel to an unknown land where he would make him father of a great people (see Gn 12:1–2), a people that would be characterized precisely by the doing of what is right and just in order to create a society of equals. What else is meant by the preference for the poor that runs through the Bible than that those we insist on marginalizing should be brought instead to the level of equality? That is what is meant by "keeping the way of the Lord"; it is therefore also the condition that must be met if God is to carry out the promise.[3]

The identity of Israel is rooted in the relation between the poor and the nation; the chosen people lose their dignity if they do not establish justice in their midst. For this reason, in many passages I need not list here, the prophets, speaking in the name of God, describe the powerful in their own Jewish nation as "foreigners." They are, in effect, foreigners to their native land because they do not do what is right and do not establish justice as prescribed in the covenant that justifies the existence of the Hebrew people. Those who domineer may belong to the collectivity but they are foreign as regards that which is the very wellspring of the nation's existence. So too, an affirmation of nationhood that leaves aside the effort to make justice reign in the land is a lie and a form of manipulation.

We see this same manipulation of God's will today in many people who claim to be Christian. I have no room here to digress on the present-day implications of this aspect of biblical revelation, but I do want to stress the importance of it for the church — that is, for the people of God, the family of God, the sacrament of salvation in history. The building of the Christian community acquires its full meaning to the extent that this community defends and protects the poor, who are the privileged members of the kingdom; otherwise, there is a contradiction of the very essence of the ecclesial community. In other words, as I shall say more particularly further on, the community goes against the very meaning of the witness it gives to the Lord's resurrection.

Yahweh is the *go'el* or defender of Israel because Yahweh asserts the rights of the poor. More than this, God rejects the chosen nation when it does not practice justice. This is a recurring theme in the prophetic books — for example, in chapters 21 and 22 of Jeremiah, from which I shall cite a few verses:

> Hear the word of the Lord, O house of David!
>   Thus says the Lord:
> Each morning dispense justice,
>   rescue the oppressed from the hand of the oppressor,
> Lest my fury break out like fire
>   which burns without being quenched,
>   because of the evil of your deeds. . . .

Thus says the Lord: Do what is right and just. Rescue the victim from the hand of his oppressor. Do not wrong or oppress the resident alien, the orphan, or the widow, and do not shed innocent blood in this place. If you carry out these commands, kings who succeed to the throne of David will continue to enter the gates of this palace, riding in chariots or mounted on horses, with their ministers, and their people. But if you do not obey these commands, I swear by myself, says the Lord: this palace shall become rubble. . . .

Many people will pass by this city and ask one another: "Why has the Lord done this to so great a city?" And the answer will be given:

"Because they have deserted their covenant with the Lord, their God,
by worshiping and serving strange gods." [Jer 21:11–12; 22:3–5, 8–9]

It is made clear again and again throughout the Bible that the connection
between the poor and the nation is solidly involved in the covenant; that
in it is to be seen the true meaning of Israel's claim to nationhood. The
prophets constantly remind their hearers of it; that is why they are called
traitors and are imprisoned and threatened with death by the leaders of
the people who have forgotten the requirements of the covenant. The
prophets are regarded as disloyal because even at times of serious national
crisis they insist that it is meaningless for Israel to claim to go forward as
a nation if the poor in its midst are oppressed.

Such, for example, was the lot of Jeremiah. The prophet comes into
conflict with the notables of his people because he calls for the fulfillment
of the covenant and threatens punishment in the form of a Babylonian
military victory over Israel. A response in the form of an accusation comes
quickly: " 'This man ought to be put to death,' the princes said to the king;
'he demoralizes the soldiers who are left in the city, and all the people, by
speaking such things to them; he is not interested in the welfare of our
people, but in their ruin' " (Jer 38:4).

Jeremiah has put his finger on the sore. The prophets remain faithful to
their obligation of reminding others of the meaning of the covenant,
because they know that the assertion of nationhood is meaningless if it
glosses over the destruction of the poor, the oppression of laborers, and
the deprivation of the marginalized. There is a kind of nationalism that is
simply "dust thrown in the eyes," because it covers over radical problems
within the nation. In fact, what goal can a nation have except to build itself
up in terms of justice and the common good? Any alleged national value
that forgets what is fundamental is a swindle.

Yahweh is, therefore, the *go'el* of the people because Yahweh is the *go'el*
of the poor among the people. This truth causes the prophets constantly
and unyieldingly to reject the oppression that the powerful practice, often
in sophisticated ways:

> Hark! the Lord cries to the city.
>   Hear, O tribe and city council,
> You whose rich men are full of violence,
>   whose inhabitants speak falsehood
>   with deceitful tongues in their heads!
> Am I to bear any longer criminal hoarding
>   and the meager ephah that is accursed?
> Shall I acquit criminal balances,
>   bags of false weights? [Mi 6:9–12]

Furthermore, Israel gradually comes to understand that Yahweh is the
go'el of the poor in all the peoples of the earth. The great Old Testament

theologian of God's universal love is Second Isaiah. When Yahweh presents his servant, Yahweh says: "Upon him I have put my spirit; he shall bring forth justice to the nations" (42:1). The servant's task of establishing justice and righteousness expresses God's will to life:

> I, the Lord, have called you for the victory of justice,
>   I have grasped you by the hand;
> I formed you, and set you
>   as a covenant of the people,
>   a light for the nations,
> To open the eyes of the blind,
>   to bring prisoners out from confinement,
>   and from the dungeon, those who live in darkness.
>   [Is 42:6–7]

Jesus was given a response like that which Jeremiah had experienced. John reports the harsh and revealing words that Caiaphas, the high priest, spoke shortly before the Lord went up to Jerusalem for the last time; the words bring to light the meaning of his condemnation to death. The powerful men among his people are alarmed by the success of Jesus' preaching; they see it challenging their interests, which they have grown accustomed (we know of similar cases today!) to identifying with the interests of the people as a whole. They are dismayed by the implications of a message that they reject, and they ask each other: "What are we going to do? This man is performing many signs. If we leave him alone, all will believe in him, and the Romans will come and take away both our land and our nation" (Jn 11:48–49). To permit Jesus to go on preaching is a dangerous course for them, and they acknowledge it without beating about the bush. Caiaphas, who has a clear grasp of what is at issue, coldly draws the necessary conclusions and replies to them in oracular fashion: "You know nothing, nor do you consider that it is better for you that one man should die instead of the people, so that the whole nation may not perish" (Jn 11:49–50). The death of the disturbing preacher from Galilee will permit the situation to continue as before; the powerful will again be able to breathe easy.

Jesus' proclamation of the kingdom of life places him in the main prophetic line. He was fully aware of this. In a harsh controversy with the Pharisees and scribes that Luke reports for us, he accuses them of complicity with those who in the past had put to death the messengers God had sent to remind the people of the requirements of the covenant. Jesus addresses them ironically: "Woe to you! You build the memorial of the prophets whom your ancestors killed. Consequently, you bear witness and give consent to the deeds of your ancestors, for they killed them and you do the building" (Lk 11:48).

In addition, Jesus in his mission takes up and underscores the universalism of the prophets. The Gospel of Matthew in particular will emphasize the universalist aspect of his preaching of the kingdom of love and life, a preaching in which he declares blessed all the poor of the earth.[4]

2. I Am Not a Human Being

God commits himself to the people; therefore God intervenes in history as their *go'el*, liberator and avenger, in order to establish justice and righteousness. But the God of the Bible also says repeatedly that God is holy — that is, different.

The Wholly Other

In Karl Barth's well-known phrase, God is the "Wholly Other" — that is, the one who is completely different, which is what "holy" means. The Lord says as much in response to the people's tendency to interpret God's action in history in purely human categories:

> I will not give vent to my blazing anger,
>   I will not destroy Ephraim again;
> For I am God and not man,
>   the Holy One present among you;
> I will not let the flames consume you. [Hos 11:9]

God, and not a human being: this is a reassertion of the essence of biblical revelation about God. To say that God is "holy" is to assert that God is unique. God alone is God. One of God's fundamental demands is to be recognized as such. There are indeed stages in the Jewish people's understanding of the truth, but the demand is there from the beginning:

> I, the Lord, am your God, who brought you out of the land of Egypt, that place of slavery. You shall not have other gods besides me. You shall not carve idols for yourselves in the shape of anything in the sky above or on the earth below or in the waters beneath the earth; you shall not bow down before them or worship them. For I, the Lord, your God, am a jealous God. [Dt 5:6–9]

This, then, is a God who is jealous of holiness and defends it against any distortion, because it means the safeguarding of the freedom and fruitfulness of God's relationship with the people. "You shall not worship any other god, for the Lord is 'the Jealous One'; a jealous God is he" (Ex 34:14):

> "Holy, holy, holy is the Lord of hosts!" they cried one to the other. "All the earth is filled with his glory." [Is 6:3]

This, of course, is the text of the Sanctus in the eucharistic liturgy. The holiness of God is in fact a central theme in the preaching of Isaiah:

You are my witnesses, says the Lord,
　my servants whom I have chosen
To know and believe in me
　and understand that it is I.
Before me no god was formed,
　and after me there shall be none.
It is I, I the Lord;
　there is no savior but me. [Is 43:10–11]

The Bible brings home the holiness of God through great and terrifying images provided by certain theophanies (manifestations of God), as well as through images of God's love, mercy, and forgiveness. The essential point is that the life of God immeasurably surpasses any human measure or anticipation. This is also the experience of every believer; J. Cone puts it well: "God is always more than our experience of him."[5] It is this God of whom Paul is thinking in his hymn:

Oh, the depth of the riches and wisdom and knowledge of God! How inscrutable are his judgments and how unsearchable his ways!
　"For who has known the mind of the Lord
　　or who has been his counselor?"
　"Or who has given him anything
　　that he may be repaid?"
　For from him and through him and for him are all things. To him be glory forever. Amen. [Rom 11:33–35]

The Scriptures teach us that the God of the Bible irrupts into history, but at the same time they show us that God is not as it were watered down by the historical process. On the contrary, as Paul says at the Areopagus, in God "we live and move and have our being" (Acts 17:28).[6] We may therefore say that the holy God is a God who makes a covenant with the people and that the God of the covenant is the "Wholly Other," the Holy One. These are two distinct aspects of God but each implies the other.

The fact is that we may not simply juxtapose the several approaches to God that I have been taking. I said earlier that the Lord's self-revelation begins with the mission of liberation. The people whom God has gathered together and with whom God enters into a covenant is a sacrament, or efficacious sign, of life and liberation within history. The living God sets free; the liberating God is holy. A text in Isaiah brings these two dimensions together in a short formula: our redeemer's "name is the Lord of hosts, the Holy One of Israel" (Is 47:4).

God makes the people a sign of liberation and holiness within history. A passage is Leviticus is relevant here:

Be careful to observe the commandments which I, the Lord, give you, and do not profane my holy name; in the midst of the Israelites I, the

Lord, must be held as sacred. It is I who made you sacred and led you out of the land of Egypt, that I, the Lord, might be your God. [Lv 22:31–33]

Yahweh sanctifies the people and brings them into the holy camp, by freeing them from oppression. In turn, this free nation, made up of persons whose right to life and justice is respected, must bring others into the sphere of the Holy One. To this end, they must observe the commandments given them by the Lord. The holiness of Yahweh is manifested in the holiness of believers in Yahweh. If they are to give this kind of witness, they must undergo an interior change and begin to follow a different path:

I will prove the holiness of my great name, profaned among the nations, in whose midst you have profaned it. Thus the nations shall know that I am the Lord, says the Lord God, when in their sight I prove my holiness through you. For I will take you away from all the foreign lands, and bring you back to your own land. I will sprinkle clean water upon you to cleanse you from all your impurities, and from all your idols I will cleanse you. I will give you a new heart and place a new spirit within you, taking from your bodies your stony hearts and giving you natural hearts. I will put my spirit within you and make you live by my statutes, careful to observe my decrees. [Ez 36:23–27]

The restoration of life causes the nation to bear witness within history to the God who liberates; it does this to the extent that it practices justice. To establish justice and righteousness is to prolong the liberating action of God; such actions embody fidelity to the covenant made between God and God's people; in other words, it is a step toward the fullness of life. The word "justice" thus acquires such weighty and rich connotations in the Bible that it becomes equivalent to "salvation." St. Paul, for example, will speak of salvation as justification. The justice of God thus marks God's saving action in history.[7]

With Radiant Face

The norm set for the behavior of the people whom the God of life brings into existence is precisely that they should give life. This means acting in such a way that life is asserted against every power that seeks to destroy it; against death and therefore against oppression, hunger, selfishness, sickness, injustice, and, in the final analysis, against sin, which is the characteristic stamp of death.

In fact, liberation from sin goes to the root of evil; it means that in the Bible the process of transformation leading to a just society and a new kind of human being is an experience and way of holiness. It is not surprising, therefore, that the word "just" becomes synonymous with "holy." Both are used in the New Testament to describe the disciples of Jesus:

> As he who called you is holy, be holy yourselves in every aspect of your conduct, for it is written, "Be holy because I [am] holy." Now if you invoke as Father him who judges impartially according to each one's works, conduct yourselves with reverence during the time of your sojourning. [1 Pt 1:15–17]

The holiness of God is the source and model of our holiness; our holiness is to find expression in deeds, and it is by these that we shall be judged. At the end of a forceful summons to the justice proper to the new covenant, Matthew places an unexpected demand of the Lord: "Be perfect, just as your heavenly Father is perfect" (Mt 5:48). The command calls all Christians to holiness, but the requirement is meant to be a source of deep joy. As Clotilde, the "poor woman" of Leon Bloy's novel of that name, says at the end of the book: for a Christian "there is but one sadness: not to be a saint" *(La femme pauvre)*.

The practice of justice, with all that it implies, takes us into the realm of holiness, into the sphere of God. Deeds are the way to holiness. Pedro Casaldáliga writes with beauty and power of the holiness of God and of his closeness to us in Jesus:

> Into the plantation of our short-lived clay
> the nameless sea of his light does not fall.
> No tongue ventures to speak his truth.
> No one has seen God. No one knows him. . . .
> His hands and his dust-covered feet,
> his face of flesh, son of the Hidden One:
> translation of God into human littleness![8]

To proclaim the gospel is to transmit the holiness of God. Paul of Tarsus had a keen sense of this.

A beautiful but mysterious passage of Exodus tells us that after conversing with Yahweh on Mount Sinai, Moses came down "with radiant face," thereby inspiring a reverential awe in Aaron and the leaders of the community, who did not dare approach him in these circumstances. But Moses summoned them to enjoin on them "all that the Lord had told him on Mount Sinai." After that, he put "a veil over his face." The same sequence was repeated each time that Moses contemplated the holiness of God (see Ex 34:29–35). The interpretation Paul gives of the famous "veil of Moses" is a key for understanding his own mission.

The event that took place on the road to Damascus was Paul's investiture as an apostle; his own references to it are nonetheless discreet, especially by comparison with Luke's account of it (Acts 9:1–30). He tells the Galatians: "You heard of my former way of life in Judaism. . . . But . . . [God], who from my mother's womb had set me apart and called me through his grace, was pleased to reveal his Son to me, so that I might proclaim him to the gentiles" (1:13–16). This last is the main point for Paul: his special mission, his task in the church, is to proclaim the gospel to the gentiles. "I did not immediately consult flesh and blood, nor did I go up to Jerusalem to those who were apostles before me; rather, I went into Arabia and then returned to Damascus" (Gal 1:17).

Paul thus claims to be an apostle, someone who has received a direct revelation and therefore has no need of asking anything of anyone. He would eventually visit Peter, but without haste: only three years later. The same for James (see Gal 1:16–19). He thereby emphasizes that he is in touch with the tradition. Once these visits had been made, he went into the regions of Syria and Cilicia. "I was unknown personally to the churches of Judea that are in Christ; they only kept hearing that 'the one who once was persecuting us is now preaching the faith he once tried to destroy.' So they glorified God because of me" (Gal 1:22–24). These last words are very important because they give the meaning of the entire story he has been telling — namely, that it is God's work. Therefore Paul, too, gives thanks to God. In other words, his claim of apostolic responsibility is not an unbased self-assertion; it is not the result of pride; it does not reflect a desire to put himself in the foreground. Rather it is an honest statement about himself and the task that God has entrusted to him. To glorify God is to acknowledge and proclaim God's holiness.

The event on the road to Damascus has been described as a moment of conversion. Strictly speaking, however, "conversion" is the wrong word, if one means by it the transition from unbelief to belief. Paul was a religious man, a devout Jew, a Pharisee filled with zeal for God. His encounter with Christ will be in a sense the fulfillment of the faith that he already has and will continue to have. What the event brings, then, is a light that illumines his own Jewish faith from within, but that at the same time launches him on new paths.

The Damascus event brings to light the relation that exists between, on the one hand, the continuity of the Christian faith with Old Testament revelation and, on the other, the break that the Christ event supposes and the tremendous newness it brings. And, in fact, one of the key points in the Lord's message is precisely the prolongation of the message of the patriarchs and prophets, but at the same time a break with it. Paul, a good Jew, had to face the difficulties met in every attempt to explain the continuity and at the same time to account for the break. He tackled the problem with the energy and boldness that characterize his entire work.

He gets into the subject by attempting an interpretation of the text of Exodus that I cited above (Ex 34:29–35). The important thing here is not the correctness of his exegesis but the self-understanding that it expresses:

Their thoughts were rendered dull, for to this present day the same veil remains unlifted when they [Jews] read the old covenant, because through Christ it is taken away. To this day, in fact, whenever Moses is read, a veil lies over their hearts, but whenever a person turns to the Lord the veil is removed. Now the Lord is the Spirit, and where the Spirit of the Lord is, there is freedom. [2 Cor 3:14–17]

Only in Christ, through encounter with the Lord, was the veil drawn back for him, enabling him truly to understand the revelation to which he had previously assented and, consequently, to give an account both of the continuity and of the newness and the division or break that the newness entails. The Lord is the Spirit, and where the Spirit of the Lord is, there is freedom. Seeing the Lord is a source of freedom. Freedom is the outlook proper to the believer, an outlook born of Christ who by drawing aside the veil enables us to understand the word of God in a new light.

The Damascus event is therefore a call rather than a conversion. "God called me to be an apostle to the gentiles" (see Gal 1:15–16); of this Paul is deeply convinced. Moreover, the task is inseparable from the call. This link does not exclude a development in time whereby we mature and understand better the task to which we are invited.

In the same Letter to the Galatians Paul gives the basis of his call to be an apostle to the gentiles. "The one who worked in Peter for an apostolate to the circumcised worked also in me for the gentiles" (Gal 2:8). Paul is speaking of one and the same universal proclamation, in which nonetheless there are different paths to follow. There is a real division of labor. Consequently, no circumcision and no submission to the law is required of the pagans who convert to Christianity, though some outsiders are trying to impose these on the church of Galatia. To discover Christ is to become free; to go back to the law is to submit anew to slavery. This is a major point in Paul's thought. The difficulties arising in the Galatian community give Paul an opportunity to write a letter on Christian freedom. This letter draws its inspiration from the newness brought by the witness of Jesus, the free man.

Furthermore, Galatians 2:8, cited a moment ago, makes it clear that due to the graciousness and holiness of God all are called to salvation. The call of Paul to evangelize the gentiles brings out the universality of the proclamation of Jesus Christ. If limitations are placed on this universalism, the message is distorted and mutilated, and an attempt is made to set up barriers to the inspiration of the Spirit. Contemplation of the holiness of God makes our faces radiant, as it did the face of Moses, with a radiance that is a reflection of God's action in us. Under no circumstances is the veil appropriate; Christ has removed it once and for all. For, "all of us, gazing with unveiled face on the glory of the Lord, are being transformed into the same image from glory to glory, as from the Lord who is the Spirit" (2 Cor 3:18).

The love of God must be proclaimed at every moment with radiant face, for this radiance is a sign of God's holiness present in history and in us. Justice must be done not with bitterness and dejection but with joy and hope (see Is 64:4).

CHAPTER III

GOD MAKES A COVENANT: GOD IS FAITHFUL

The Bible reveals a God who is near to us and faithful. God's nearness finds expression in the covenant made with the people, a commitment that closely binds the two parties together and lives on in the memory of God and in believers who put the requirements of the covenant into practice. The old and new covenants alike reveal to us the divine fidelity that is always ready to forgive but at the same time is always demanding.

1. I WILL BE YOUR GOD AND YOU SHALL BE MY PEOPLE

The covenant that God makes with the people is a central theme of the Bible; some have therefore looked upon it as the nucleus around which an entire biblical theology can be developed.[1]

A Mutual Belonging

The promise given to Abraham includes a covenant between God and the people to be born of Abraham: "I will give to you and to your descendants after you the land ... and I will be their God" (Gn 17:8). This covenant is to be "an everlasting pact" (Gn 17:7, 19), which is all the more reason for requiring Abraham and his descendants to observe the requirements of the covenant.

The basic formula that expresses the meaning and content of the covenant is this: "I will take you as my own people, and you shall have me as your God" (Ex 6:7; see also Jer 7:23); it is a statement that runs throughout the Bible. Covenant means mutual belonging and possession. That is why the conjugal relationship becomes one of the most widely used and deeply meaningful images in the Scriptures for the bond between Yahweh and Yahweh's people. It is a daring image, which the prophets use to bring out the full meaning of the love involved. Husband and wife belong to each other. Yahweh says to the people:

> I will espouse you to me forever:
> I will espouse you in right and in justice,

in love and in mercy.
I will espouse you in fidelity,
  and you shall know the Lord.
On that day I will respond, says the Lord;
  I will respond to the heavens,
  and they shall respond to the earth. [Hos 2:21–23]

Heaven and earth shall hear each other. The love God offers is a faithful love, but it requires in return a fidelity to the covenant that will seek to put the establishment of justice and right on a solid footing. Love is the foundation of this mutual possession. St. Paul uses the same image for the relation between Christ and the church (see Eph 5:21–33).

The covenant formula, which is repeated with almost obsessive frequency, represents a key element in the national identity of the Jewish people. This point needs to be stressed. Faith in Yahweh makes it possible for Israel not only to know its religious status but also to assert itself as a people, as one nation among the others of history. Israel is a human group that has its own God and belongs to this God; it is a people that has entered into an agreement with the Lord and has received the gift of the covenant.

This approach to God leaves an ineradicable mark on biblical faith, which will always have the form of an agreement entered into with God who takes the initiative: "Here, then, is the covenant I will make" (Ex 34:10). To be more specific: the covenant is made with a people, with a human group, not an individual person. Since faith is something that lives within a community, the individual's life of faith is put right, regulated, and judged by the entire people called to the covenant with the Lord.

This is one reason why in the perspective of the Bible it is impossible for believers to manipulate God; they are not God's masters. Yahweh comes to meet a people who accept God and acknowledge in response that they belong to God: such is the context for the faith of the individual. Over against this twofold belonging, which is the very meaning of the biblical covenant, there is the abiding temptation to understand faith as something purely individual, and to claim, consequently, to be independent of the views of others and of any community judgment and control of the life of faith. This is a tendency that ultimately leads to persons turning in on themselves and shutting out anything new.

Once, however, we accept that belief in God is something communal, we are constantly open to the new, the unlimited, the unpredictable. Others will realize, and experience, new demands made by faith in God — demands that would have not occurred to us as isolated individuals. The community, which possesses a variety of charisms and functions, will regulate the faith of its individuals and will, in its turn, be enriched by the varied experiences of the persons making it up. It is the people as a whole that belongs to Yahweh. There is no question of a thou and an I, but of a thou and a we.

The bond uniting God to the people implies fidelity on both sides. The

Lord does his part: "Though the mountains leave their place and the hills be shaken, my love shall never leave you, nor my covenant of peace be shaken, says the Lord, who has mercy on you" (Is 54:10). The ultimate source of this fidelity is love: "With enduring love I take pity on you, says the Lord, your redeemer" (Is 54:8). The God of the Bible is thus a God who makes a covenant and who, as the Scriptures repeatedly tell us, always has in mind the motive that led to this covenant: "Since the Lord, your God, is a merciful God, he will not abandon and destroy you, nor forget the covenant which under oath he made with your fathers" (Dt 4:31).

"God will not forget the covenant": fidelity is, first of all, a remembering. To be faithful is to remember, not to forget our promises, to retain a sense of tradition. Fidelity to the covenant supposes remembrance of the origin and demands of the agreement. This is a point we have already seen when I spoke of the historical credos. The God of the Bible is a God who is mindful of the covenant and asks in turn that the people likewise keep God before them. The Lord remembers all and each of the members of the people with whom he has made his covenant; the Lord is especially mindful of the most helpless and poor among them.

True fidelity, however, requires more than that; it also requires—and this is less clear at first sight—a projection into the future. To remember does not mean being fixed in the past. It is important to remember yesterday, but this is because it helps us to risk the morrow, to move ahead, to travel by unknown ways. Fidelity does not mean simply remembering well-trodden paths, without taking any initiative of our own; it means rather that we constantly renew our ways. Fidelity leads us, or should lead us, to innovate, to change, to plan new undertakings. It is a manifestation of that trust in the other that the Bible attributes to God and that becomes therefore an obligation for believers.

When faced with the oppression and murder of the American Indians, Bartolomé de Las Casas was to express this aspect of biblical revelation about God in a fine statement: "God remembers in an ever fresh and vivid way the least and most forgotten."[2] A remembrance that is fresh and vivid, and therefore a permanent source of new gestures of love. God's remembrance both nourishes and challenges the memory of the church in which our life of faith goes on.

Fidelity implies a creative launching out into the future; consequently, the covenant always carries within it the possibility of a new covenant, of something new and different that is taking shape. And in fact, when the Bible proposes the new covenant, it presupposes the former covenant but also goes beyond it. The prophet speaks as follows in a classic passage:

> The days are coming, says the Lord, when I will make a new covenant with the house of Israel and the house of Judah. It will not be like the covenant I made with their fathers the day I took them by the hand to lead them forth from the land of Egypt; for they broke my

covenant and I had to show myself their master, says the Lord. But
this is the covenant which I will make with the house of Israel after
those days, says the Lord. I will place my law within them, and write
it upon their hearts; I will be their God, and they shall be my people.
[Jer 31:31–33]

Fidelity between two individuals means loyalty and attachment to the
sources of the love they have for one another, but it also supposes an ability
constantly to renew this love. There is no relationship between human
beings, nor between God and human beings, nor between God and the
people, that cannot be damaged by sin. In the context of the covenant, sin
is always an infidelity. In this situation, loyalty to the other does not consist
in climbing on a platform from which one is then satisfied simply to
denounce the infidelity of the other; no, it consists, above all, in the ability
to suggest ways in which the other one may start life again or, better, in
which together they may renew their lives. In other words, fidelity means
offering the possibility of a new covenant and promising such a covenant;
in everyday life we would speak of "giving someone another chance." The
partner who has remained faithful. forgives — that is, gives the other an
opportunity to recover and start anew — because the forgiving partner
believes in the other. This, after all, is what love is: forgiveness, stubbornness, persistence, trust in the future. This, too, is fidelity, an attitude that
acknowledges and constantly re-creates a mutual belonging.

The parable of the talents (Mt 25:14–30) provides a good illustration of
this outlook. The parable describes two attitudes: that of those who pass
on to others what they have received from God, and that of those who keep
for themselves what the Lord willed to bestow on them. Furthermore, the
emphasis in the parable is on the criticism of this second attitude. From
the outset, in the image of the absence of the "man who was going on a
journey," Christians are reminded of their responsibility in history. There,
in everyday life with its good and bad moments, its tensions and conflicts,
the disciples of Jesus must bear witness to life. We must therefore "stay
alert," St. Paul tells us (1 Thes 5:6). That is precisely what the first two of
the three servants do; moreover, their watchfulness is translated into service, and as a result of their labors the Lord's gifts bear fruit.

The attitude of the third servant in the parable is quite different (v. 25).
A small-minded and fearful person, he wants to stand in well with God
without leaving his own world. In his view, the life of faith is something
that goes on solely between himself and God. He has not grasped the
meaning of the gospel's demands, but has understood them rather to be
religious norms for exact and formal observance. Other people, all those
around him, play no role in his life. Relationships with them can even be
dangerous for him; perhaps they will draw him away from the path he has
set for himself and prevent him from carrying out his obligations as a
believer. He prefers, therefore, to take no risks but to give back to the Lord

what he has received from him. This way, he feels more secure; St. Paul will describe him as one who is asleep (1 Thes 5:6).

He will soon learn, and with him all of us, that his supposed "path" leads him not into the light but into darkness. In his small-mindedness he can imagine only a God who is limited to rewards and punishments. But the God of Jesus never wearies of loving freely and making constant demands. His gratuitous love overflows the dikes of our self-centeredness and false securities. Faith is not something to be kept in a strong cage for protection; it is a life that finds expression in love and self-giving to others. In the Gospels, fear means a lack of faith. How is it possible to love without taking risks? Without entering the world of the have-nots of our country who are struggling for their right to live? Solidarity with them will expose us to unforeseen dangers and conflicts, and perhaps to misunderstandings within our own universe of relatives, friends, and fellow Christians. But the parable of the talents teaches us that a Christian life focused not on formalities and self-protection but on self-giving and a feeling for others represents true fidelity to the Lord.

The Gourd Plant and the Worm

The God who remembers also knows how to forget. When the people are unfaithful, God calls them to conversion and, finally, promises them a new covenant; then God erases from mind all their former sins. The passage on the new covenant that I cited earlier from Jeremiah goes on to say: "No longer will they have need to teach their friends and kinsmen how to know the Lord. All, from least to greatest, shall know me, says the Lord, for I will forgive their evildoing and remember their sins no more" (Jer 31:34).

As we already understand, to "know" Yahweh means to love Yahweh. Forgiveness creates friendship, because it supposes forgetfulness of the sin of the other and is an expression of love that calls for reciprocity. To be able to forgive is part of being faithful. The announcement of the new covenant makes known the fidelity of God, for the new covenant is based on the forgiveness of faults and the forgetting of sins. By forgiving, God constantly gives rise to our freedom and trusts in our potentiality for renewal. In God's eyes, the actions of human beings are not predetermined; this conviction leads God to attack a deeply rooted idea of the Jewish people regarding the punishment of children for the sins of their parents:

> Thus the word of the Lord came to me: Son of man, what is the meaning of this proverb that you recite in the land of Israel:
> "Fathers have eaten green grapes,
>   thus their children's teeth are set on edge"?
> As I live, says the Lord God: I swear that there shall no longer be anyone among you who will repeat this proverb in Israel. [Ez 18:1–3]

Jesus also set himself against the idea that sickness, misfortune, and poverty result from the sins of those who suffer them (see Lk 13:1–6). Even today there are remnants of this mentality, so that the situation of the poor and the sick is further burdened by a painful sense of guilt. The contrast in mentalities is illustrated by the lengthy story of the man born blind in the Gospel of John (see chapter 9). By healing the man (giving him life), Jesus declares this idea of sin and punishment unacceptable, and restores the blind man to freedom and the ability to make personal choices. "Do you believe in the Son of Man?" The Lord asks. "He said, 'I do believe, Lord' " (vv. 35 and 38). Faith is always a free act. Thus the insignificant person who at the beginning of the story is described as a beggar passively sitting there (v. 8) grows, responds sarcastically to the Pharisees, and ends with a clear confession of faith.

Such is the result of forgiveness: it gives life and freedom. It marks a new beginning. This is the meaning of the new covenant, which continues and transcends the first covenant and brings it to fulfillment. The Lord is stubborn and moves beyond the Jewish people to reach every human being and have mercy on every repentant sinner.

An odd prophetic writing reminds us in a dramatic, and at the same time humorous, way that the biblical God's will to reconciliation is greater than God's severity toward those who have not done "what is right and just." It is also greater than the human ability to forgive. I am speaking of the book that tells the story of Jonah, though it does not supply information about his person or his social background. A third person tells the story, and in excellent prose; the majority of the commentators regard the book as a literary composition, a parable with didactic purposes.

Yahweh addresses the prophet and gives him a mission: "Set out for the great city of Nineveh, and preach against it; their wickedness has come up before me" (1:2). Without giving us Jonah's reason, the narrator tells us that Jonah tried to flee to Tarshish, a name which, it is thought, designates a city at the other end of the Mediterranean (in modern Spain). A terrible storm threatens the vessel in which the fleeing Jonah is traveling; he is thrown into the sea by the terrified crew, swallowed by a large fish, and then thrown up on to the land.

Yahweh persists and repeats his commission: "Set out for the great city of Nineveh, and announce to it the message that I will tell you" (3:2). This time, Jonah sees no alternative; he goes to Nineveh, the capital of the Assyrian empire, a bitter enemy and conqueror of the Jewish people. The inhabitants of the great city heed the message and are transformed: "The people of Nineveh believed God; they proclaimed a fast and all of them, great and small, put on sackcloth" (3:5). Every one of them is converted "from his evil way and from the violence he has in hand" (3:8). For this "violence" the author uses the Hebrew word *hamas*, which signifies the extensive and severe injustices that one people commits against another, as well as the oppression that the powerful practice against the weak.[3] This conversion causes God to change his mind: "When God saw by their actions how they turned from their evil way, he repented of the evil that he had threatened to do to them; he did not carry it out" (3:10).

The flight of Jonah is now explained. This was what he had feared from the outset: knowing God, he realized that God would not carry out the threats if the Ninevites repented; he knows that this God forgives and constantly calls human beings to life:

> But this was greatly displeasing to Jonah, and he became angry. "I beseech you, Lord," he prayed, "is this not what I said while I was still in my own country? This is why I fled at first to Tarshish. I knew that you are a gracious and merciful God, slow to anger, rich in clemency, loathe to punish." [4:1–2]

The prophet's displeasure is very great, because as a good Jew he hated the Assyrian oppressors who had destroyed his country. The fact that he behaves with restraint in the task God has given to him is an occasion for the Ninevites to cease their evil behavior and ask for mercy. God will hear them because, as is said in language classical in the prophets, God is "a gracious and merciful God, slow to anger, rich in clemency, loathe to punish" (see Jl 2:13 and Ex 34:6). Jonah prefers punishment and death for those who have committed so many crimes against his country. The prophet's suffering and displeasure are very great: this time God's mercy has gone too far. It is therefore not worth being a prophet or even living on. In his distress he cries: "Lord, please take my life from me; for it is better for me to die than to live" (4:3). What Jonah finds unforgivable, if I may so put it, is the universal and unrestricted forgiveness of God. If this were a God who stayed on the level of justice, God's actions could be foreseen; but the God of the Bible, as the Book of Job says with unequaled power, is a God who loves gratuitously, a God who refuses to be contained by our categories and to submit to a standard of conduct based on a quid pro quo. God is an unpredictable God.

Yahweh now proceeds to reeducate his messenger. "Have you reason to be angry?" he asks affectionately and in high spirits (4:4). Jonah, half-resentful, half-resigned, does not answer and once again chooses to leave the city. The story now shifts into the language of symbolism. The prophet builds himself a hut and sits down under it to see what will happen. In a friendly spirit, God causes a gourd plant to grow up there as shade for the prophet. Jonah's joy at the relief this plant affords does not last long, for God sends a worm that kills the plant. God then repeats the question that had gone unanswered: "Have you reason to be angry?" But this time God adds: "over the plant?" Jonah's vexation has only intensified; his reply is terse and dry, drier even than the condition in which the worm had left the plant: "Angry enough to die" (4:9). Then, in language full of deep feeling, Yahweh voices concern for the Ninevites, whom Jonah had hated so much, and not without reason:

Then the Lord said: "You are concerned over the plant which cost
you no labor and which you did not raise; it came up in one night
and in one night it perished. And should I not be concerned over
Nineveh, the great city, in which there are more than one hundred
and twenty thousand persons who cannot distinguish their right hand
from their left, to say nothing of so many cattle?" [4:10–11]

These people, too, are the work of God's hands; they are also human
beings endowed with freedom and therefore with the possibility of changing
their ways. Moreover, are all of them equally guilty of what their nation
has done to the Jewish people? The passage ends with a final consideration
that may surprise the reader: the life of the animals ("many cattle") is also
important to Yahweh. That is why after the flood the Lord is careful to
repeat that the covenant is with every living thing in the world that God
made and continually makes anew. God promises Noah and his sons: "I
will recall the covenant I have made between me and you and all living
things" (Gn 9:15). The Lord endeavors devotedly and affectionately to
make them understand that belief in God entails an understanding of God's
will to life for all living things. While Jonah was sorry about the gourd plant,
which he had neither sown nor cultivated, Yahweh has compassion on those
God created and wants them, be they Jews or non-Jews, to change their
ways and live.

Life and not death is what God desires for all, even evildoers, provided
they abandon their evil ways and do "what is right and just." Everyone (the
Book of Jonah emphasizes this universality) can and must do this; all are
called to life. God makes this clear through the prophet Ezekiel:

If the wicked man turns away from all the sins he has committed, if
he keeps all my statutes and does what is right and just, he shall surely
live, he shall not die. None of the crimes he committed shall be
remembered against him; he shall live because of the virtue he has
practiced. Do I indeed derive any pleasure from the death of the
wicked? says the Lord God. Do I not rather rejoice when he turns
from his evil way that he may live? [Ez 18:21–23; see also 33:11]

God's mercy is a gift, but it is not something arbitrary; it requires a
behavior, a practice that gives life to others. This is what is implied in the
establishment of right and justice, in the recognition of the legitimate claims
to life that all, especially the weakest members of society (the poor and the
oppressed), have as God's gift. To forgive is to give life.

A Death That Brings Life

The covenant with God is located historically within a dialectic of death
and life. After proclaiming the new covenant in a passage that is a parallel
to that of Jeremiah, which I cited earlier, Ezekiel says:

Thus says the Lord God: When I purify you from your crimes, I will repeople the cities, and the ruins shall be rebuilt; the desolate land shall be tilled, which was formerly a wasteland exposed to the gaze of every passer-by. "This desolate land has been made into a garden of Eden," they shall say. "The cities that were in ruins, laid waste, and destroyed are now repeopled and fortified." Thus the neighboring nations that remain shall know that I, the Lord, have rebuilt what was destroyed, and replanted what was desolate. I, the Lord, have promised, and I will do it. [Ez 36:33–36]

Destruction and ruin are followed by rebuilding and life. This is God's will; therefore the gift and demands of the covenant represent an option for life (see Dt 30). Paradoxically, it is for this reason that the covenant is sealed with blood. Deliverance from oppression in Egypt and journey to the promised land mark the celebration of the first Passover according to the account in Exodus. It is on this same feast that the Lord celebrates his final meal with his friends.

Then he took the bread, said the blessing, broke it, and gave it to them, saying, "This is my body, which will be given for you; do this in memory of me." And likewise the cup after they had eaten, saying, "This cup is the new covenant in my blood, which will be shed for you." [Lk 22:19–20]

It is the event that we commemorate in every eucharistic celebration, in every consecration of bread and wine, which are the basic foods needed to sustain human life. This is why in the context of the liturgy the consecrated bread and wine signify life that is sacrificed, death that is overcome, food for a new life. Body and blood of Christ: these are present in every communal remembrance of Christ's action and in the text about the institution of the eucharist that I just cited. The blood that is shed is, then, connected with the covenant; it is part of the covenant of faith, hope, and love that God establishes with the people. This covenant implies communion and mutual service. That is the point that John is emphasizing when he replaces the account of the eucharist with an account of the prophetic gesture of Jesus as he fraternally and humbly washes the feet of his disciples (see Jn 13:1–15).[4]

The fact that death, one kind of death, can give life is something we see in the experience of Jesus. His martyrdom, his passover, his passage through death helps us understand the meaning of the resurrection—that is, that he really overcomes death and enters the fullness of life. As César Vallejo said in one of his *Poemas humanos*: "In short, I cannot express my life but only my death."

In the "Christmas cycle" of the Christian liturgy there is a commemoration that risks being passed over or misinterpreted: the feast of the holy

Innocents. Although it has been turned into an occasion for jokes in good or bad taste, the celebration is nonetheless pregnant with meaning. The birth of a child on the outskirts of a small town disturbs Herod. The scent of the manger reaches the palace of this villainous man. The fear that the recent birth inspires in him will lead to the assassination of many innocent children. A premature and unjust death cruelly dogs the life that has just come into being. Tragedy keeps watch at the joy of birth. The event presages the blood that will be shed on the cross by those who oppose the divine proclamation of life by that child who is now an adult.

Is this not also the experience of a great part of the Latin American people today? This is true especially of some places in the continent where this oppressed Christian people have no other way of manifesting their life than by their own death, by surrendering that life. Theirs is a life that in a sense is denied or taken from them in many ways by a social order in which things are more important than persons. Their passage through death is their passover, the final step to the revelation of an authentic life. The covenant is a covenant of life.

2. A FAITHFUL GOD

Yahweh's initiative in establishing a covenant with the people implies a fidelity to them. A key text in Exodus recalls this truth, while at the same time naming other attributes of the God of the covenant. On Mount Sinai, a privileged place of God's self-manifestation, Yahweh passes before Moses and declares himself to be "the Lord, the Lord, a gracious and merciful God, slow to anger and rich in kindness and fidelity" (Ex 34:6).

Fidelity heightens the other attributes of God. Yahweh is stubbornly compassionate and merciful. Yahweh's love does not appear and disappear like a flash of lightning but rather has the persistence of river waters that penetrate the rocks and stubbornly, patiently, scour the bed they have made for themselves. Those who draw nourishment from the river can always rely on the constancy of its course.

Tender Love and Demands

This is a faithful God who seeks to keep alive the twofold relationship of belonging implied in the covenant. God therefore repudiates the continuing resentment that springs more from self-love than from concern for the other:

> Then the Lord said to me: Rebel Israel is inwardly more just than traitorous Judah. Go, proclaim these words toward the north, and say:
> Return, rebel Israel, says the Lord,
>   I will not remain angry with you;
> For I am merciful, says the Lord,
>   I will not continue my wrath forever. [Jer 3:11–12]

The faithful God does not relax into a petrified attitude of stern rejection. On the other hand, mercy does not exclude divine claims on human beings but rather supposes them:

> Only know your guilt:
>   how you rebelled against the Lord, your God,
> How you ran hither and yon to strangers
>   [under every green tree]
>   and would not listen to my voice, says the Lord.
>   [Jer 3:13]

Yahweh's fidelity is nourished by tender love; Yahweh loves the people as parents love their little child:

> When Israel was a child I loved him,
>   out of Egypt I called my son. [Hos 11:1]

Yahweh is father of all the people but especially of the poor. "The father of orphans and the defender of widows is God in his holy dwelling" (Ps 68:6). Those who believe in God must act in the same way; Sirach 4:10 therefore says, "to the fatherless be as a father." It is in this perspective that Job adduces as proof of his innocence that "I was a father to the needy" (29:16).

The Bible interprets this love that God has as the love of a father, but it also compares it to the love of a mother:

> Can a mother forget her infant,
>   be without tenderness for the child of her womb?
> Even should she forget,
>   I will never forget you. [Is 49:15]

The Hebrew word for "womb" (*rahamim*) refers to the maternal womb, the place where a woman receives life and gives it. The word is then used for the "heart" of God:

> Is Ephraim not my favored son,
>   the child in whom I delight?
> Often as I threaten him,
>   I still remember him with favor;
> My heart stirs for him,
>   I must show him mercy, says the Lord. [Jer 31:20]

The compassion of God thus has a profoundly tender maternal dimension.[5] God's love is also compared with a uniquely female experience that is filled with meaning:

> I have looked away, and kept silence,
> > I have said nothing, holding myself in;
> But now, I cry out as a woman in labor,
> > gasping and panting. [Is 42:14]

In the passages I have shown Yahweh as a tender God; a Lord who is both father and mother, and holds the people of Israel on his knees the way a parent holds a child. The Lord is a God who, like human beings, but with greater reason, gives children what they ask for. The relationship of God with children, the people, is seen to be filled with sensitivity and affection.

When Yahweh has momentarily lost patience with the people because of their sins, he is able to reverse himself and faithfully restore the attachment that has been broken:

> For a brief moment I abandoned you,
> > but with great tenderness I will take you back.
> In an outburst of wrath, for a moment
> > I hid my face from you;
> But with enduring love I take pity on you,
> > says the Lord, your redeemer. [Is 54:7–8]

At the same time, however, biblical revelation speaks to us of a God who makes demands, who requires concrete kinds of behavior, who lays commandments on the people, and who even threatens to punish the failure to carry out these commandments:

I, the Lord, am your God, who brought you out of the land of Egypt, that place of slavery. You shall not have other gods besides me. You shall not carve idols for yourselves in the shape of anything in the sky above or on the earth below or in the waters beneath the earth; you shall not bow down before them or worship them. For I, the Lord, your God, am a jealous God. [Ex 20:2–5]

He is a God who is jealous when it comes to observance of the covenant made with the people. Possible rejection and the threat of punishment by Yahweh is only the reverse side of Yahweh's love. Yahweh's is a faithful love that demands fidelity in return. It calls for an enduring recognition of the God who delivered the people from the oppression and want that they experienced in Egypt, and an ongoing establishment of justice and right in the new land in which they now live. It calls, too, for "love and mercy" on the part of the covenanted people.

The same outlook is to be seen in the New Testament. Jesus compares God's love with the love of a father for his family:

Everyone who asks, receives; and the one who seeks, finds; and to the one who knocks, the door will be opened. Which one of you would hand his son a stone when he asks for a loaf of bread, or a snake when he asks for a fish? If you then, who are wicked, know how to give good gifts to your children, how much more will your heavenly Father give good things to those who ask him? [Mt 7:8–11]

This passage is part of the Sermon on the Mount, which sets forth the main lines of the ethics of the kingdom. It deals not simply with norms but with attitudes, with a sensitivity to the needs of others.

Worship and Justice

One expression of the jealousy of this God who is once faithful, demanding, and tenderly loving is the necessary connection between worship and the practice of justice, between sacrifice and fellowship among human beings, between religious offering and the work of liberation. Biblical passages calling for the practice of authentic worship are many and well-known. Let us look at one of them:

> This, rather, is the fasting that I wish:
>   releasing those bound unjustly,
>   untying the thongs of the yoke;
> Setting free the oppressed,
>   breaking every yoke;
> Sharing your bread with the hungry,
>   sheltering the oppressed and the homeless;
> Clothing the naked when you see them,
>   and not turning your back on your own. [Is 58:6–7]

The passage lists in detail liberating actions and commitments that believers in Yahweh must make their own, those believers who themselves have just been released from the Babylonian yoke. At the same time, the passage summons them to an ongoing attitude of human fellowship and calls upon them not to turn their backs on their own flesh. All this is implied in the idea of "fasting" and in the prayer that is so necessary. The prophets constantly and resolutely reject the oppression that the powerful practice, at least in sophisticated ways:

> Hark! the Lord cries to the city. . . .
>   Hear, O tribe and city council,
> You whose rich men are full of violence,
>   whose inhabitants speak falsehood
>   with deceitful tongues in their heads!
> Am I to bear any longer criminal hoarding
>   and the meager ephah that is accursed?

> Shall I acquit criminal balances,
>   bags of false weights? [Mi 6:9–12]

These and many similar passages will be clearly echoed in the Gospels. For in the latter we find the same prophetic outlook. Here is a classic and trenchant passage of the Gospels:

> If you bring your gift to the altar, and there recall that your brother has anything against you, leave your gift there at the altar, go first and be reconciled with your brother, and then come and offer your gift. [Mt 5:23–24]

Due to his extensive experience of church life, Matthew was well aware that the divorce between prayer and justice, which Jesus denounces and which runs through his controversy regarding authentic worship with the Pharisees, was, and still is, a danger for the Christian community.

The danger has, unfortunately, become a painful reality in many cases and it leads to harsh reactions such as Alejandro Romualdo, a Peruvian poet, voices in a forceful poem:

> Pray, Christian, pray. But let your God
> not starve my comrade to death.
> But let your God
> restore the land to those who work it.
> But let your God
> not bury forever in hell
> those whose hearts are full of hatred
> because they love.
> Pray, Christian, pray.
> O, if only the fire of your hell might warm
> the dreams of the poor!
>
> And if you see my comrade
> dead of rage against the earth,
> and if you see him, night and day,
> dead of cold under the sky,
> and if you know that on the morrow
> he will be persecuted
> and kicked
> and put against a wall and shot
> at dawn,
> do not pray, Christian, do not pray,
> for words accomplish nothing.[6]

But the poet's noble-hearted call only reminds us of the prophetic and evangelical teaching on prayer. God wants not sacrifice but repentant hearts (see Ps 51:19); God wants us to rend our hearts and not our garments (see Jl 2:13); God does not want offerings and prayers that are unconcerned about the injustices and sufferings that human beings experience in this world. Prayer to the God of the Bible is not a discreet way of escaping history, but rather an occasion for uttering words that are enfleshed. Prayer is a space available for gratuitousness and freedom in the life of the believer, or, better, a special moment of gratuitousness that ought to fill up all the corners of our life, even during our most concrete tasks.

Prayer is a privileged way of being in communion with the Lord and, like his mother, keeping "all these things in her heart" (Lk 2:51). To pray is to be with the Lord during the moments when he went aside to speak to the Father (see Mk 1:35). Contemplation plays a central role in the life of Jesus. During one of the most painful hours of his life, he reproaches his disciples for having been unable to be with him during his final prayer, which had turned into a fierce struggle with approaching death. "He was in such agony" as he struggled for his life, says Luke, that his sweat became "like drops of blood" (Lk 22:45). Our communion with the prayer of Jesus should reach this extreme of "agony"—that is, of struggle, because that is what "agony" means. This is something that in fact is readily grasped by those who risk their own lives in their commitment to the lot of the deprived peoples of Latin America.

Thus, prayer to the God who liberates and does justice does not remove us from the historical process, but rather compels us to immerse ourselves in it so that we may responsibly exercise our solidarity with the poor and the oppressed. Christians can pray only from the tent that the word has pitched in our midst, in a world that wavers between acceptance and rejection of his message of life (see Jn 1:1–18).

The worship God desires is inseparable from the practice of justice. The union of these two—worship and justice—brings out a fundamental aspect of faith in the God of the covenant. Authentic fasting consists in liberating the oppressed and breaking the yokes that hold them captive. Worship of God demands justice toward others; gratitude for the gift of being God's children implies the establishment of brotherhood and sisterhood. Then, as the Bible repeatedly says, worship "in spirit and in truth" will be possible. We are faced here, once again, with the two fundamental dimensions of Christian life: contemplation and commitment, gratuitousness and justice.[7]

These two should nourish each other, so that we will "rejoice to do what is right" (Is 64:4 NRSV). Solidarity with the poor and the oppressed should be a source of joy, not of strain, just as gratitude to God will be pregnant with effective commitment here and now.

CHAPTER IV

IDOLATRY AND DEATH

The struggle against idolatry occupies an important place in the Bible. It helps us, in a negative way, to determine exactly the content of faith in the true God.

The rejection of God is described in the Scriptures not as atheism but as idolatry—that is, as the acceptance of a false God. We of the twentieth century may think the word "idolatry" refers to an ancient or even primitive problem, one peculiar to "uncivilized" people. We think of idolatry as a stage we have gotten beyond, and we feel safe against any danger of it.

The Bible, however, sees idolatry as a danger lying in wait for every religious person; more than that, as a permanent temptation. Idolatry means that believers place their ultimate trust in something or someone who is not God or that they play fast and loose with the ambiguous position of turning to God while at the same time seeking other kinds of ultimate support.[1] The position of the Bible with regard to idolatry is therefore clear and incisive. "How long will you straddle the issue? If the Lord is God, follow him; if Baal, follow him" (1 Kgs 18:21).

The alternatives are clear; one choice excludes the other. There is no middle ground. The theme is repeated in a forceful and original way in the New Testament, where it is again expressed in terms of a choice: God or mammon (see Mt 6:24).

This view of idolatry has special validity in Latin America. A tragic characteristic of this continent—the only continent in which the majority are at the same time Christian and poor—is the danger of claiming to be able to straddle the issue: to declare oneself in words for the God of Jesus Christ while in practice serving mammon by mistreating and murdering God's favorites, the poor (the same situation occurs, of course, in other parts of the world as well). This attempt, rather than the pure and simple denial of God's existence, is the great challenge to the proclamation of the gospel on our continent.[2] The true disciples of Jesus must turn the whole of their lives into a language in which yes means yes and no means no (see Mt 5:37).

48

1. CHOOSING DEATH

The theme of idolatry originates in the setting of worship. Yahweh claims the right to be the sole God of Israel, a people living in the midst of nations that worship a variety of gods. The prophets remove the subject from this limited framework and show that the question of idolatry touches many other aspects of the life of believers. Unless we attend to the social and economic context, some of the important meanings of idolatry will elude us.

Idolatry is first and foremost a behavior, a practice. The key question, therefore, is this: Whom, in practice, do you serve? The God of life or an idol of death? Even while denouncing idolatrous behavior, the Old Testament describes it for us. Three characteristics seem to emerge from its handling of the subject.

Trust and Submission

As I said above, idolatry consists in putting one's trust in something or someone who is not God. This is what happens with money or power. The just will say of one who takes this route:

> This is the man who made not
> > God the source of his strength,
> But put his trust in his great wealth,
> > and his strength in harmful plots. [Ps 52:9]

The subjection of one's life to the dictates of wealth contrasts with the attitude of one who puts trust in the Lord:

> Only in God be at rest, my soul,
> > for from him comes my hope.
> He only is my rock and my salvation,
> > my stronghold; I shall not be disturbed....
> Trust in him at all times, O my people!
> > Pour out your hearts before him;
> > God is our refuge! ...
> Trust not in extortion; in plunder take no empty pride;
> > though wealth abound, set not your heart upon it.
> > > [Ps 62:6–7, 9, 11]

There is an important passage on this subject in the Book of Job. Eliphaz, one of Job's friends, urges him to abandon a way of life that in his estimation is sinful. In his fervor, he calls upon Job very eloquently to renounce behavior that is based on an idolatrous trust in wealth and to recognize that true joy is in God.

> If you return to the Almighty, you will be restored;
>   if you put iniquity far from your tent,
> And treat raw gold like dust,
>   and the fine gold of Ophir as pebbles from the brook,
> Then the Almighty himself shall be your gold
>   and your sparkling silver.
> For then you shall delight in the Almighty
>   and you shall lift up your face toward God.
> You shall entreat him and he will hear you,
>   and your vows you shall fulfill. [Jb 22:23–27]

Job is moved by the reproach contained in this exhortation, but he believes that he has never adopted such an attitude. He replies without mincing words:

> Have I put my faith in gold,
>   saying to fine gold, "Ah, my security"?
> Have I ever gloated over my great wealth,
>   or the riches that my hands have won?
>   [Jb 31:24–25 NJB]

At work here is an outlook inspired by the prophets. In his oracle of doom Zephaniah announces the coming of a day of wrath (the well-known *dies irae*) on which the Lord will destroy those who act unjustly and rely on wealth to sustain and give meaning to their lives. At that time:

> Neither their silver nor their gold
>   shall be able to save them
>   on the day of the Lord's wrath,
> When in the fire of his jealousy
>   all the earth shall be consumed.
> For he shall make an end, yes, a sudden end,
>   of all who live on the earth. [Zep 1:18]

Echoes of this same vision are to be found in other prophetic texts:

> Thus says the Lord:
> Let not the wise man glory in his wisdom,
>   nor the strong man glory in his strength,
>   nor the rich man glory in his riches;
> But rather, let him who glories, glory in this,
>   that in his prudence he knows me,

Knows that I, the Lord, bring about kindness,
  justice and uprightness on the earth;
For with such am I pleased, says the Lord. [Jer 9:22–23]

To "glory" (or "boast") is to find one's security and pride in these possible idols: knowledge, courage in battle, and wealth. In contrast, the prophet says that only knowledge (that is, love) of Yahweh can be a reason for confidence. This confidence will, moreover, find expression in loyalty and in doing what is just and right, because such is the will of the God of life.

Work of Our Hands

Idols are things that human beings make with their hands and then turn into fetishes; as a result, they entrust their lives to them. The Bible is clear about the origin of idols. In language that shows a certain appreciation of the undertaking, Second Isaiah describes the craftsmen at work:

The smith fashions an iron image, works it over the coals, shapes it with hammers, and forges it with his strong arm. He is hungry and weak, drinks no water and becomes exhausted.
  The carpenter stretches a line and marks with a stylus the outline of an idol. He shapes it with a plane and measures it off with a compass, making it like a man in appearance and dignity, to occupy a shrine. [Is 44:12–13]

To this description the prophet then adds some sarcastic reflections on the material of which idols are made:

He cuts down cedars, takes a holm or an oak, and lays hold of other trees of the forest, which the Lord had planted and the rain made grow to serve man for fuel. With a part of their wood he warms himself, or makes a fire for baking bread; but with another part he makes a god which he adores. Half of it he burns in the fire, and on its embers he roasts his meat, and then warms himself and says, "Ah! I am warm, I feel the fire." Of what remains he makes a god, his idol, and prostrate in worship before it, he implores it, "Rescue me, for you are my god." [Is 44:14–17]

With biting irony, Isaiah shows how the wood that enables human beings to warm and feed themselves is also the material for the making of an idol. In addition, he suggests that trees are more useful as firewood than as material for idols. The prophet is trying to bring out the absurdity of veneration paid to a work of our own hands. In a comparable passage, Jeremiah takes the satire further. Idols are:

wood cut from the forest,
Wrought by craftsmen with the adze,
    adorned with silver and gold.
With nails and hammers they are fastened,
    that they may not totter.
Like a scarecrow in a cucumber field are they,
    they cannot speak;
They must be carried about,
    for they cannot walk.
Fear them not, they can do no harm,
    neither is it in their power to do good. [Jer 10:3b–5]

The Jews, then, have no reason to fear idols that are incapable of walking. They are harmless and can do no evil, but neither are they capable of doing good; they are simply wood. Over against them stands Yahweh, who "is true God, he is the living God, the eternal King" (Jer 10:10).

A passage from Ezekiel (another that echoes the text of Zephaniah cited above) reminds us that silver and gold can be shackles on the journey toward the God of the poor. On the day of Yahweh's judgment, which will come at a time when "lawlessness is in full bloom, insolence flourishes, violence has risen to support wickedness" (Ez 7:10), the wicked:

Shall fling their silver into the streets, and their gold shall be considered refuse. Their silver and gold cannot save them on the day of the Lord's wrath. They shall not be allowed to satisfy their craving or fill their bellies, for this has been the occasion of their sin. In the beauty of their ornaments they put their pride: they made of them their abominable images [their idols]. For this reason I make them refuse. [Ez 7:19–20]

On that day, the unjust will see how absurd it was for them to have put their trust in wealth. The text clearly links this reliance—which not only does not save them but condemns them before the wrath of Yahweh—with the making of idols. All these are fetishes that, like gold, are nothing but refuse.

Wealth, too, is the product of a human activity. Human beings fall into idolatry when they rank gold and silver above those who have made them, thus allowing themselves to be seduced by the success of their own handiwork. Money thus becomes a god that enslaves its maker. To make a fetish of money is to fall into idolatry, to worship an antigod.[3]

It is clear to the prophets that the trust placed in idols can seem sound for a time, but in the end will disappoint. Trust placed not in God but in a work of our own hands that gives us strength and power over others is a source of alienation and death. In the passage from Isaiah 44 cited above, the prophet goes on to speak of the utter confusion that comes upon idolaters:

> The idols have neither knowledge nor reason; their eyes are coated so that they cannot see, and their hearts so that they cannot understand. Yet he [the idolater] does not reflect, nor have the intelligence and sense to say, "Half of the wood I burned in the fire, and on its embers I baked bread and roasted meat which I ate. Shall I then make an abomination out of the rest, or worship a block of wood?" [Is 44:18–19]

The prophet rebukes the idolater: "He is chasing ashes — a thing that cannot save itself when the flame consumes it; yet he does not say, 'Is not this thing in my right hand a fraud?' " (v. 20). At this point, a chaos of blood and crime, of theft and fraud, prevails everywhere. This brings me to the third and last characteristic that I want to emphasize.

Demand for Human Victims

The god of idolatry is a murderous god. A great deal of blood is shed because of the desire for money. Many passages of the Bible speak of this; I shall cite a few of them.

In a harsh warning to King Jehoiakim, Jeremiah contrasts his behavior with that of his father, who "dispensed justice to the weak and poor" (Jer 22:16). Jehoiakim acts differently and has other goals:

> But your eyes and heart are set on nothing
>   except your own gain,
> On shedding innocent blood,
>   on practicing oppression and extortion. [Jer 22:17]

The yearning for money and power stops at nothing; it tramples underfoot the rights of others and disregards the commandments of the God who calls for the protection of the poor and oppressed. This self-seeking causes the powerful among the Jewish people to shed innocent blood and turn Israel into a "bloody city" (Ez 22:2), on which the Lord will pass judgment:

> Her nobles within her are like wolves that tear prey, shedding blood and destroying lives to get unjust gain. . . . The people of the land practice extortion and robbery; they afflict the poor and the needy, and oppress the resident alien without justice. [Ez 22:27, 29]

Oppression of the poor is here called by its true name: murder. God turned into an idol requires the shedding of blood. The author of the Book of Sirach says as much in unforgettable language:

Tainted his gifts who offers in sacrifice ill-gotten goods!
  Mock presents from the lawless win not God's favor.
The Most High approves not the gifts of the godless,
  nor for their many sacrifices does he forgive their sins.
Like the man who slays a son in his father's presence
  is he who offers sacrifice from the possessions of the
  poor.
The bread of charity is life itself for the needy;
  he who withholds it is a man of blood.
He slays his neighbor who deprives him of his living;
  he sheds blood who denies the laborer his wages.
                                         [Sir 34:18–22]

This passage is also interesting because it uses cultic language when it speaks of sacrifices offered in the desire for wealth and domination; this language only makes the denunciation more biting. The sacrifices here are macabre: the lives of the poor offered on the altar of the idol under pretence of worshiping God. What we are really faced with is murder committed from a desire of gain and power. The religious justification offered only makes the fact more scandalous. This is a "sacrifice" that is in fact sacrilegious, being offered to the true God who loves all, especially the poor, as a father.[4]

One of the parables in Matthew is that of the murderous vine growers. The name is an accurate one and, as we shall see, not only because it speaks of the murder of the son of the vineyard's owner. The focus of the parable is on the fact that the vineyard has not yielded any fruit. The workers responsible for it are unwilling to render any account and, in addition, respond with violence to the owner's emissaries when they come to obtain the results of the laborers' work:

Hear another parable. There was a landowner who planted a vineyard, put a hedge around it, dug a wine press in it, and built a tower. Then he leased it to tenants and went on a journey. When vintage time drew near, he sent his servants to the tenants to obtain his produce. But the tenants seized the servants and one they beat, another they killed, and a third they stoned. Again he sent other servants, more numerous than the first ones, but they treated them in the same way. Finally, he sent his son to them, thinking, "They will respect my son." But when the tenants saw the son, they said to one another, "This is the heir. Come, let us kill him and acquire his inheritance." They seized him, threw him out of the vineyard, and killed him. What will the owner of the vineyard do to those tenants when he comes? They answered him, "He will put those wretched men to death and lease his vineyard to other tenants who will give him the produce at the proper times." Jesus said to them, "Did you never read in the Scriptures:

The stone that the builders rejected
   has become the cornerstone;
by the Lord has this been,
   and it is wonderful in our eyes?
Therefore, I say to you, the kingdom of God will be taken away from
you and given to a people that will produce its fruit." [Mt 21:33–43]

What is this "fruit"? This question is the key to the meaning of the
passage. The allusion (sometimes a word-for-word citation) to a passage in
Isaiah (5:1–7) will help us in finding the right answer (the liturgy in Cycle
C joins the passage from Isaiah with this passage from the Gospel). In his
"vineyard song" Isaiah tells us that when the Lord planted this vineyard
(namely, Israel), "he looked for judgment, but see, bloodshed! for justice,
but hark, the outcry!" (5:7). The establishment of what is right and just is
one of the great demands made by God in the Old Testament. It is mainly
in the meeting of this demand that fidelity to covenant between God and
his people is to be found. The God of life and love wants justice to reign
among his people, and he wants the rights of all, especially those of the
poorest, to be respected. Such is the fruit that the vineyard was to yield,
which the Lord had planted and cared for.

Such is also the essence of the parable on which I am commenting: the
tenants have not done what is right, they have not established justice. Worse
still: among them, murders are committed, and complaints are heard about
the ill treatment and extortion in which they indulge. The Bible often speaks
of the oppression of the poor as a form of murder. It is not surprising,
therefore, that the tenants react to the Lord's messengers with the same
contempt for life that they show in their everyday behavior. The vine growers are thus murderers not only because they kill these messengers and
even the son, but also because they rob the poor and violate their rights.
The people who hear the parable of Jesus are aware of this background.
They too are murderers as soon as they fail to produce the fruits of justice
for which the Lord asks. Therefore the kingdom of God will be given into
other hands: the hands of those "not invited" to the banquet, as they are
described in the parable of the wedding feast, which immediately follows
on that of the tenants in the Gospel of Matthew. These "uninvited" are
the least members of society. Matthew's parable of the tenants leads us to
ask ourselves whether in our own daily lives we are guilty of any complicity
with the murderous vine growers.

When we see the victims of the various fetishes we understand more
clearly the meaning of idolatry and the reason why God rejects it in such
a radical fashion. Idolatry brings the death of the poor; money victimizes
the have-nots. As Leon Bloy says, "money is the blood of the poor." If (as
we shall see in the pages that follow) Jesus Christ ranks money as an antigod
and sets before us the inescapable choice of following the one or the other,

it is, in the final analysis, because the worship of mammon entails shedding the blood of the poor.

This is precisely what has happened in the various concrete forms of exploitation and oppression of the poor in the course of human history. When the poor are oppressed and their rights trampled underfoot, their blood is shed; this is against God's will. The idolatry of money, of this fetish produced by the work of human hands, is indissolubly and causally connected with the death of the poor. If we thus go to the root of the matter, idolatry reveals its full meaning: it works against the God of the Bible, who is a God of life. Idolatry is death; God is life.

2. GOD OR MAMMON

The problem of idolatry as a danger for every believer in God and therefore as an abiding possibility on the journey of a believing people is, as we have just seen, a classic and recurring theme in the Old Testament. Its meanings are extensive and numerous. Therefore, contrary to interpretations based on readings of the Bible from the standpoint primarily of religious philosophy, idolatry cannot be reduced to a kind of process of intellectual and religious cleansing on the way to monotheism, a process that supposedly went on throughout the history of the Jewish mind. Without abandoning the realm of the cultic, the prophets forcefully point out that the idolatry of the people also takes the form of placing their trust in power and wealth, which they turn into real idols. Their behavior means that they follow principles that differ from, and are opposed to, those that spring from the covenant they have made with Yahweh, the only God and the Lord of Israel. The outlook of the prophets will be even more strongly present in the New Testament.

No One Can Serve Two Masters

Jesus makes his own the strong prophetic criticism of idolatry and presents it anew in an original and unusual way: "No one can serve two masters. He will either hate one and love the other, or be devoted to one and despise the other. You cannot serve God and mammon" (Mt 6:24).

In a parallel text (16:9–15), Luke presents the same radical choice and again speaks of wealth as "mammon," a word that seems to derive from the Aramaic root *'mm*, which means "that on which one relies." The name "mammon" gives money a pejorative nuance[5]; Luke therefore speaks of "dishonest wealth" (vv. 9, 11). These two passages are the only ones in the New Testament to use *mamōnas* for wealth (once in Matthew; three times in the parallel passage in Luke).[6]

In these passages Jesus sets up an opposition between God and mammon; the latter thus becomes a power, an idol. The Lord therefore calls upon his disciples to make an uncompromising choice; the words "love" and "hate" underscore the impossibility of compromise and refer to a decision that must be made (see Gn 29:31; Dt 21:15–17). Furthermore, the verse on which I am commenting has for its context in Matthew a series of alternatives, all of which call for a choice. The decision is made in the realm of practice. The critique of idolatry begins a little earlier in the same chapter:

> Do not store up for yourselves treasures on earth, where moth and decay destroy, and thieves break in and steal. But store up treasures in heaven, where neither moth nor decay destroys, nor thieves break in and steal. For where your treasure is, there also will your heart be. [Mt 6:19–21]

In Matthew's vision, "heaven" and "earth" do not stand for an opposition between the present and the future life; rather, they are symbols that lend intensity to the choice that must be made between wealth and God. We have seen passages of the Old Testament in which this same position is foreshadowed; the message of Jesus is characterized by the fact that it puts the concrete contrast between God and wealth in new and forceful terms.

Jesus uses a word that is pregnant with consequences: to "serve" (Greek: *doulein*). The word has a cultic flavor: one serves God. The passage in Matthew speaks, therefore, of the possibility of serving wealth or mammon as though it were God. This attitude is the key to idolatrous behavior; it implies a complete and daily self-surrender to what is regarded as the absolute in our lives. To serve mammon means concretely to turn it into an alternative to the Lord.

After stating the choice, Luke notes the resistance of the Pharisees to what Jesus has said. "The Pharisees, who loved money, heard all these things and sneered at him" (Lk 16:14). These "friends of money" (Greek: *philargyroi*)—that is, servants of mammon—feel, and rightly so, that the words of Jesus apply to them, and they respond by snubbing him. Luke here points to the deepest root of the opposition between Jesus and the Pharisees: their love of money makes them idolaters, men who, despite appearances, do not believe in the true God. Jesus answers their mockery with one of his harshest parables: that of the unnamed rich man and the poor man Lazarus (Lk 16:19–31). It is especially meaningful.

Rarely do the parables give names to the personages in them. Furthermore, the one named here is a poor man, one of those who are usually anonymous in human history; in contrast, the rich and important man (who must have had a prestigious family name) has no name here. We would be mistaken if we thought this point unimportant; proof of the surprise it elicits is the curious custom of supplying the rich man, too, with a name: Dives (in Spanish versions: Epulon, "the banqueter"). The name is certainly not in the text. When the story of the two men is read in the perspective of the kingdom a reversal takes place. The man who was the more important when judged by the standards of power and prestige is anonymous in God's sight; and the man who was regarded as worthless and nameless is the one who is important to the God of the kingdom.

The friends of wealth despise the poor and therefore are distant from God. They want to "justify themselves in the sight of others," but God knows what shoes they wear; God "knows your hearts" and is not deceived: their behavior may win "human esteem" but it is "an abomination in the sight of God (Lk 16:15). The parable, which is found only in Luke, calls upon us to change our way of looking at things. The Gospel tells us in many ways that the last are first. They should also be first in our commitment, in our endeavor to build the church and establish a new society: a society and a church made up of the Lazaruses who today are despised by those who are the really anonymous folk of human history.

When the rich man asks that someone go to warn his relatives about the consequences of their love of money and their disdain for the poor, Father Abraham replies, without mincing his words, that the Scriptures are sufficient to teach them how to live as believers. They have no need of miracles, which in any case would be useless for people who are not responsive to the words of the prophets. "If they will not listen to Moses and the prophets, neither will they be persuaded if someone should rise from the dead" (Lk 16:31). Even today, despite the clarity of the gospel message, we look for excuses and we ask for startling interventions so that we may evade its demands.

These passages (amounting to an entire chapter in Luke) on the necessity of choosing to serve either God or wealth show the importance of this subject in the teaching of Jesus.[7] Ezekiel came close to this idea. Yahweh speaks to him and says:

> As for you, son of man, your countrymen are talking about you along the walls and in the doorways of houses. They say to one another, "Come and hear the latest word that comes from the Lord." My people come to you as people always do; they sit down before you and hear your words, but they will not obey them, for lies are on their lips and their desires are fixed on dishonest gain [or: their soul goes after wealth]. . . . They listen to your words, but they will not obey them. [Ez 33:30–32]

Idolatry consists in not walking toward God but following a fetish.[8] The theme is classic in the Bible, where it is said, for example, that the Israelites, "abandoning the Lord . . . followed the other gods . . . and by their worship of these gods provoked the Lord" (Jgs 2:12). In the passage cited from Ezekiel, those who hear the prophet's words but do not put them into practice follow not Baal or any other god of a neighboring nation but wealth.[9] The contrast between hearing and practicing is meant to highlight the concrete way in which the idolatry of money works; it is marked by a subtlety and a risk-taking that are not found in other forms of idolatry.

Matthew 6:24 speaks clearly of this real, concrete service, even if not in so many words. The alternatives are two forms of service. It is by specific behavior and not by words that idolatry is judged. Matthew signals this perspective in a fine passage on abandonment to divine providence, using as a springboard the image of the birds of the air and the lilies of the field (Mt 6:25–34).

This is not a glorification of frivolity but a call to freedom. Trust in God means that we place our lives in the hands of God's providential love and remain free to serve God and the poor. There is, therefore, no question of evading our responsibilities or of scorning human works and the means needed to achieve them. Furthermore, the passage ends with the exhortation: "Seek first the kingdom [of God] and his righteousness" (Mt 6:33); but seeking means putting into practice. The gospel is calling upon us not to mix up our priorities; it is calling upon us especially to accept the radical demand made by the gratuitousness of God's love. It would be simplistic and mistaken, therefore, to see in this passage any opposition between abandonment to providence and commitments within history. What is at issue is rather the freedom that enables us to accept these commitments.

Another passage in Matthew refers to this same freedom in regard to money:

> Then the Pharisees went off and plotted how they might entrap him in speech. They sent their disciples to him, with the Herodians, saying, "Teacher, we know that you are a truthful man and that you teach the way of God in accordance with the truth. And you are not concerned with anyone's opinion, for you do not regard a person's status. Tell us, then, what is your opinion: Is it lawful to pay the census tax to Caesar or not?" Knowing their malice, Jesus said, "Why are you testing me, you hypocrites? Show me the coin that pays the census tax." Then they handed him the Roman coin. He said to them, "Whose image is this and whose inscription?" They replied, "Caesar's." At that he said to them, "Then repay to Caesar what belongs to Caesar and to God what belongs to God." When they heard this they were amazed, and leaving him they went away. [Mt 22:15–22]

The passage is often interpreted as referring to the distinction between two powers: the religious and the political. But such an interpretation reads into this passage of the Gospel a later, though legitimate, concern of the Christian community. As it stands in Matthew, the passage points to something deeper. As usual, Jesus does not agree to remain within the limits of the question asked him, a question formulated in such a way as to create problems for him either with the authorities occupying his country or with his own followers. Once again, as often before, he answers by asking a question: "Whose image is this and whose inscription?"

On the basis of the answer given, Jesus develops his own position. The Pharisees had spoken of "paying" Caesar. The Lord uses the same verb (in Greek: *didomi* = give), but he adds a prefix (Greek *apo-didomi*), which shifts the emphasis and gives the meaning "repay." Paying and repaying are not the same thing. The coin bears the image of its owner; the money belongs to the Roman oppressor and must be given back. The matter is important, because if the Pharisees' question suggests the possibility of not paying the tribute, it also suggests the possibility of keeping the money. Their vaunted nationalism did not go so far as to make them give up the money. Jesus goes to the root of the matter: all dependence on money must be rooted out. It is not enough to throw off foreign political domination; one must also break away from the oppression that arises from attachment to money and the possibilities it creates of exploiting others. Return the money to Caesar, Jesus is telling them, and you yourselves will be free of the power exercised by wealth, by mammon; then you will be able to worship the true God and give God what belongs to God.

When human beings place all their hopes on money, they leave no room for others. It is against this background that Luke issues his curse: "Woe to you who are rich, for you have received your consolation" (Lk 6:24). The rich are thus excluded from the beatitudes, since their source of security and joy is money and not God. In money they find their ease and their reward; they shall not enter the kingdom because they are, in the final analysis, idolaters.

The idolatry of money, then, is an abiding, always real, temptation for the people of God; it is the opposite of the service—that is, the true worship—of God. For this reason, in his parable of the sower Matthew does not hesitate to place this explanation on the Lord's lips: "Worldly anxiety and the lure of riches choke the word and it bears no fruit" (Mt 13:22). Greed is a rival of God's word and is able to suffocate it in the hearts of some people. When they allow money to seduce them, they render God's word sterile and prevent its bearing fruit.

The well-defined position taken by Jesus leads Paul to describe the greedy explicitly as idolaters: "and the greed that is idolatry" (Col 3:5); "Be sure of this, that no immoral or impure or greedy person, that is, an idolater, has any inheritance in the kingdom of Christ and of God" (Eph 5:5).

In the final analysis, to succumb to greed (Greek *pleonexia*, "a desire to have more") is to be an idolater, that is (in the language of Jesus), to serve riches as though they were God. The texts just cited are part of the lengthy lists that contrast the "old self," which is characterized by sin, and the "new self," with which the Christian community must clothe itself, for to this it is called. In another list, the idolater comes immediately after the greedy person. Here Paul urges his readers not to associate "with anyone named a brother, if he is immoral, greedy, an idolater, a slanderer, a drunkard, or a robber" (1 Cor 5:11). Note that according to the apostle such people can claim to be brothers. The texts thus remind us that the danger of falling into idolatry always lies in wait for those who regard themselves as Christians.

Greed divinizes money and turns it into an absolute. The First Letter to Timothy says: "The love of money is the root of all evils, and some people in their desire for it have strayed from the faith" (1 Tm 6:10). The attraction of riches (mammon) estranges us from the service of the God of Jesus Christ. The Gospels therefore speak carefully and emphatically of the impossibility of "serving two masters" and not simply of "believing in two masters." "To serve" means to act in accordance with the will of the one accepted as master.[10]

The first evangelizers of this continent found that the idolatry of Christians was the greatest obstacle to their work. They had come to proclaim the gospel to pagan peoples, whom many regarded as idolaters, but they felt in their own flesh the truth of Paul's statement that greed is a form of idolatry. Bartolomé de Las Casas testified to this traumatic experience. When the Dominican saw how the American Indians were being oppressed and dispossessed, he realized that those who come to the Indies "have deliberately subjected themselves and made themselves the servants and captives of greed, as is clear from the deeds they have done there."[11] Deeds speak. These men do not admit their true belief, but their deeds prove that those who stop at nothing in pursuit of gold have made wealth their master. Las Casas goes a step further and gets to the root of the meaning of greed; in the Indies, he says, "there is less veneration and worship of God than of money."[12] Fray Bartolomé cites a sentence from Ecclesiastes: "A covetous man shall not be satisfied with money" (5:9 Vg). Gold is the real god of those who mistreat the Indians.[13]

Las Casas was particularly scandalized by the fact that this real idolatry is disguised as though it were a service of the true God. Regarding the regimen imposed on the Indians, he says that:

> In order to gild a very cruel and harsh tyranny that destroys so many villages and people, solely for the sake of satisfying the greed of men and giving them gold, the latter, who themselves do not know the faith, use the pretext of teaching it to others and thereby deliver up the innocent in order to extract from their blood *the wealth which these men regard as their god*.[14]

A supposed proclamation of the true God serves to disguise the idolatrous behavior of those who themselves are completely ignorant of the faith.

In this Dominican friar's judgment, the worst idolatry is that of Christians and not that of the Indians. The primary distinguishing mark of idolatry in the Bible is that one trusts in an idol and not in God. Las Casas rediscovers this truth through his experience in the Indies. It is useless, in his view, to claim belief in the God of the Bible if one subsists "on the blood of the

Indians."[15] Idolatry is death; God is life. Henceforth, the defense of the life and temporal well-being of the Indians will be, for Las Casas, a way of preaching the living God of whom Jesus Christ tells us.

Friends of Life

In the passage from the Book of Wisdom on which I commented earlier (in chapter I), the Lord is called "friend of life" (11:26). He is one who wants life for all. This is the ultimate motive of his forceful call to conversion and "the doing of what is right and just." The prophet Ezekiel gives us a beautiful and profound statement of this will to life. Yahweh bids the prophet keep watch over the people, alert them to the perils threatening them, and remind those who act unjustly of the danger they are running. But Yahweh also commands him to tell them that Yahweh desires their conversion: "As I live, says the Lord God, I swear I take no pleasure in the death of the wicked man, but rather in the wicked man's conversion, that he may live" (Ez 33:11).

This is a very revealing key text. What Yahweh wants is life, not death. If life is to be attained, sinners must change their ways: "If he does what is right and just, turning back pledges, restoring stolen goods, living by the statutes that bring life, and doing no wrong, he shall surely live, he shall not die. None of the sins he has committed shall be held against him; he has done what is right and just, he shall surely live" (Ez 33:14–16).

The statutes in question are those who command the giving of life; their fulfillment will therefore win life for one who shortly before was threatened with punishment and death. Yahweh's will to life inspires and energizes the entire process.

In his first sermon after Pentecost, as the Christian community begins its proclamation of the gospel, Peter speaks of the death of Jesus at the hands of the leaders of the Jewish people. But he also emphasizes the fact that God raised Jesus up and that he, Peter, is proclaiming this new life. He rebukes his hearers for having pardoned a murderer and condemned "the author of life" (Acts 3:14–15). He is speaking of Jesus the Messiah; the Messiah's followers must bear witness to him in the historical circumstances in which it is given them to live.

This is certainly true for us today. In my own country, life nowadays is marked by a hellish cycle of different kinds of violence, each giving rise to the next with increasing rapidity. Each kind of violence has its own characteristics; therefore, in addition to bearing in mind the three aspects of the situation, it is important to take note of the peculiarities of each. The most murderous kind of violence, the one that kills most children, is the one that Medellín (and Puebla) calls "institutionalized," because it is even accepted as the "legal order." To this can be added the unjustifiable violence inflicted by terrorists of varying tendencies, which continues to fill us with horror and revulsion. On the one hand, the repressive violence that violates human rights and is applied with the excuse of battling terrorism is unacceptable and particularly scandalous since it claims to be defending the human values of our society. We cannot resign ourselves to this state of affairs. Nor is there room for lack of interest in the matter on the grounds that we are not directly affected by it. On the other hand, the quest of vengeance, whether personally or through others, will simply heap wood on the fire that now threatens to reduce the country to ashes.

The question we must ask ourselves in this context is: How are we to be friends of life in present-day Peru? One of the great tasks of Christians and of the entire church is to defend the human rights that the three types of violence mentioned trample down every day. In our day we have learned that in Peru and in Latin America generally this defense means confronting powerful interests, especially when the defense is mounted by the weakest members of society, the poor and the oppressed. But the command laid upon us as a Christian community, a church, is not to survive but to serve. In Latin America today the church is bringing into play the sense of its own identity as the community of disciples of him who came that we might "have life and have it more abundantly" (Jn 10:10). The assertion of its identity depends on its witness.

The choice is clear. Either we detach ourselves from what is going on, under the pretext that it is not our direct responsibility; we restrict ourselves to poetic requests that all become one; we draw back in fear and claim to be above the oppositions found in Peruvian society today; but then we have summoned death and joined its party, as the Book of Wisdom says, at the very moment when we claim to be making no choice. Or we set aside disdainful neutrality and are usually present where the forces opposed to the reign of love and justice are every day aggressively violating the most elementary human rights; then we are beginning to act as friends of life.

The theme of life and death is crucial in the biblical revelation of God:

> If you hide your face, they are dismayed;
> if you take away their breath, they perish
> and return to their dust.
> When you send forth your spirit, they are created,
> and you renew the face of the earth. [Ps 104:29–30]

At the beginning of this first part of my book, I reminded the reader that the relation between death and life is very important in the revelation of God as love. I have tried to bring out something of this relationship in these first chapters. I shall end this section by citing a passage that is well known but that always seems new because of its power and beauty. I am referring to the unforgettable passage of Ezekiel on the dry bones:

> The hand of the Lord came upon me, and he led me out in the spirit of the Lord and set me in the center of the plain, which was now filled with bones. He made me walk among them in every direction

so that I saw how many they were on the surface of the plain. How dry they were! He asked me: Son of man, can these bones come to life? "Lord God," I answered, "you alone know that."

Then he said to me: Prophesy over these bones, and say to them: Dry bones, hear the word of the Lord! Thus says the Lord God to these bones: See, I will bring spirit into you, that you may come to life. I will put sinews upon you, make flesh grow over you, cover you with skin, and put spirit into you so that you may come to life and know that I am the Lord.

I prophesied as I had been told, and even as I was prophesying I heard a noise; it was a rattling as the bones came together, bone joining bone. I saw the sinews and flesh come upon them, and the skin cover them, but there was no spirit in them.

Then he said to me: Prophesy to the spirit, prophesy, son of man, and say to the spirit: Thus says the Lord God: From the four winds come, O spirit, and breathe into these slain that they may come to life.

I prophesied as he told me, and the spirit came into them; they came alive and stood upright, a vast army.

Then he said to me: Son of man, these bones are the whole house of Israel. They have been saying, "Our bones are dried up, our hope is lost, and we are cut off." Therefore, prophesy and say to them: Thus says the Lord God: O my people, I will open your graves and have you rise from them, and bring you back to the land of Israel. Then you shall know that I am the Lord, when I open your graves and have you rise from them, O my people! I will put my spirit in you that you may live, and I will settle you upon your land; thus you shall know that I am the Lord. I have promised, and I will do it, says the Lord. [Ez 37:1–14]

The love of God is mightier than death and keeps the hope of a people alive. God is life.

PART TWO

THE KINGDOM
IS AMONG YOU

To the question "What is God?" the Scriptures answer: God is love
(Father and Mother). Jon Sobrino says: "God showed himself to Jesus as
Father, but the Father showed himself as God."[1] We know the Lord from
his works; these make it clear to us, as we have now been reminded, that
God liberates because God is a liberator, and not conversely, as we tend
to think; that God does what is just because God is just; that God enters
into covenants because God is faithful. God sanctifies because God is holy,
and gives life because God is life, because God is what God is. These
various statements are certainly expressions of what God meant in the self-
description to Moses: "I am who I am" ("I am life"), on which I have
already commented.

Let me turn now to another question that likewise derives its traditional
formulation from the experience of believers and from reflection on this
experience: "Where is God?" This is the question the psalmist asks:

> My tears are my food day and night,
>   as they say to me day after day, "Where is your God?"
> Those times I recall,
>   now that I pour out my soul within me,
> When I went with the throng
>   and led them in procession to the house of God,
> Amid loud cries of joy and thanksgiving,
>   with the multitude keeping festival. . . .
> It crushes my bones that my foes mock me,

> as they say to me day after day, "Where is your God?"
> (Ps 42:4–5, 11)

Where is your God? As I pointed out earlier, in the Bible the revelation of God is given, and the most radical questions regarding it are asked, in a specific historical context. In this psalm they arise out of the experience of exile, suffering, and oppression that the Jewish people underwent in Babylon. It is in such circumstances that the just are forced to face up to the challenging question of their enemies: Where is your God? While reaffirming his faith, the psalmist asks himself anxiously why God is absent — that is, why the Lord seems to have forgotten him and his people. At difficult moments in our own lives we ask the same question: Where is God?

This was the question that a Peruvian Indian, Guaman Poma de Ayala, asked when he traveled the ancient land of the Incas and saw how the Indians were suffering from the injustices and tribulations they experienced at the hands of the conquistadors and landowners. "Where are you then, my God?" he exclaims; "will you not hear me and help your poor?"[2] The experience of faith, which also finds expression in the Scriptures, has a specific historical and social context.

But the question "Where is God?" does not arise solely out of suffering and distress. It is an utterance of faith; the failure to ask it is a kind of forgetfulness for which Yahweh rebukes the people:

> Listen to the word of the Lord, O house of Jacob!
>   All you clans of the house of Israel,
>   thus says the Lord:
> What fault did your fathers find in me
>   that they withdrew from me,
> Went after empty idols,
>   and became empty themselves?
> They did not ask, "Where is the Lord
>   who brought us up from the land of Egypt,
> Who led us through the desert,
>   through a land of waste and gullies,
> Through a land of drought and darkness,
>   through a land which no one crosses,
>   where no man dwells?"
> When I brought you into the garden land
>   to eat its goodly fruits,
> You entered and defiled my land,
>   you made my inheritance loathsome.
> The priests asked not,
>   "Where is the Lord?"
> Those who dealt with the law knew me not:

the shepherds rebelled against me.
The prophets prophesied by Baal,
and went after useless idols. [Jer 2:4–8]

When we ask "Where is the Lord?" we are seeking to be near him, to "cleave" to the God of our faith; we are desirous of making our own his plan for human history. God takes the initiative: "God so loved the world that he gave his only Son" (Jn 3:16) to tell us that he is the God of the kingdom and that this term means what the gospels call the will of God. We find God to the extent that we make our own God's plans for history and our lives. In the prayer that Jesus taught us, we call God Father and holy, and then ask that "your kingdom come" (Lk 11:2). To this petition Matthew's version of the Our Father adds: "Your will be done, on earth as it is in heaven" (Mt 6:10). In fact, both petitions mean basically the same thing, since the Father's will is precisely that the kingdom of life and liberty become a reality. Where the kingdom is established, there is God.

If we separate God from God's plan, we do not really believe in God, for the separation means the rejection of God's reign, God's will that life, love, and justice reign in history. Jacques Prévert, a French poet of the people, placed on unbelieving lips a prayer that many Christians perhaps pray in practice: "Our Father who art in heaven, stay there!" In other words, "Don't come and bother us with your demands; don't enter into our history; leave us alone to do our will there and not yours." The behavior of Jesus is quite different, for he says repeatedly, in the Gospel of John, for example, that he feeds on the Father's will—that is, that his food is the Father's intention to reign, his plan of life, his kingdom.

The God of the Bible is inseparable from God's plan, God's kingdom. Consequently, every effort to find and understand God while divorcing God from God's reign is, in the language of the Bible, an attempt to construct an idol, to make a god according to our own image and desires, to trust in someone who is not God, to fall into idolatry. And indeed a god without a kingdom is a fetish, a work of our hands, a denial of the Lord, because such a separation is contrary to God's will. The God of Jesus Christ is the God of the kingdom, the God who has a message and a purpose for human history.

But Jesus goes further. When asked about the moment when the kingdom will come, he replies: "The kingdom of God is among you" (Lk 17:21). This is the unqualifiedly new element in his message: Jesus the Messiah is the kingdom. He himself is the center of God's creative and redemptive work; "However many are the promises of God, their yes is in him [Jesus Christ]; therefore, the Amen from us also goes through him to God for glory" (2 Cor 1:20). To speak of the kingdom is to speak of Jesus, who makes the kingdom the center of his message. He is God, who comes into history and makes of this particular moment the favorable time for proclaiming the gift of the kingdom. To accept the gift is to commit oneself to meet its demands.

CHAPTER V

THE GOD WHO COMES

The God of the Bible is the God who comes to the people. Yahweh says: "I have come down to rescue them from the hands of the Egyptians" (Ex 3:8; see 18:20), and "I will come to you" (Ex 20:24). John the Evangelist says of the Word: "He came to his own house" (Jn 1:3, literal) and he "made his dwelling among us" (v. 14). The Apocalypse begins (Rv 1:4, 8) and ends (Rv 22:20) with the promise of the definitive coming of the Lord. God is present where God's life-giving plan takes flesh. This prompts me to reflect on a dialectic often found in the Bible: the tension between God's visibility and invisibility, between God's obviousness and hiddenness. This tension is renewed by the incarnation of the Son of God, where it is marked by both continuity and discontinuity. The tension provides us with new forms of God's presence and absence in history.

1. GOD HAS DEPARTED

When and where God's reign and demand that we "do what is right and just" are denied, God is not present. There is a philosophically inspired theology that has difficulty in handling the biblical assertion of God's absence. As children we learned that God is everywhere, and knows and sees everything. From a metaphysical viewpoint that is correct. But the Bible also and quite frequently speaks to us of God's absences, of spaces deprived of God's presence. If we restrict ourselves to the categories of traditional philosophy, we will see these biblical statements as absurdities: What kind of a God is it who *is not* in a particular place? If we take that approach, we will be guilty of confusing a particular philosophy with reflection on the God of the Bible.

The Scriptures offer us three important examples of God's absence that will help us think about the God of biblical revelation.

The Empty Temple

The temple is clearly a place where God must necessarily dwell. Yet the Bible says that God is not there, if those trying to find God do not put into practice the commandment of life and justice:

The following message came to Jeremiah from the Lord: Stand at the gate of the house of the Lord, and there proclaim this message: Hear the word of the Lord, all you of Judah who enter these gates to worship the Lord! Thus says the Lord of hosts, the God of Israel: Reform your ways and your deeds, so that I may remain with you in this place. Put not your trust in the deceitful words: "This is the temple of the Lord! The temple of the Lord! The temple of the Lord!" Only if you thoroughly reform your ways and your deeds; if each of you deals justly with his neighbor; if you no longer oppress the resident alien, the orphan, and the widow; if you no longer shed innocent blood in this place, or follow strange gods to your own harm, will I remain with you in this place, in the land which I gave your fathers long ago and forever. [Jer 1:1–7]

The prophet is calling for a radical conversion in those who wish to find God. He makes it fully clear that until there is a commitment to the rights of the poor, God will not dwell with them in the temple; God will be absent. Observe that Jeremiah is speaking here of a holy place—that is, a space that has classically been God's dwelling place. Even so, God orders the prophet to proclaim that God will not be found there if those who claim to be approaching God are exploiting the poor and shedding the blood of the innocent. Here God is absent from the temple because the people do not practice justice, especially toward the weakest among them.

The prophet therefore criticizes those who claim to be seeking help in the temple but who in fact profane it by their behavior: "And yet [they] come to stand before me in this house which bears my name, and say: 'We are safe; we can commit all these abominations again.' Has this house which bears my name become in your eyes a den of thieves? I too see what is being done, says the Lord" (Jer 7:10–11).

Jesus likewise forcefully rejects the hypocrisy that such an attitude represents. Using various passages from the Old Testament (Is 56:7; Zec 14:21; Ps 69:10), the Synoptic evangelists tell us of the expulsion of the tradesmen from the temple. It is significant that while the Synoptics place this incident toward the end of Jesus' ministry, John places it at the beginning. One of the passages to which Jesus alludes is the one just cited from Jeremiah, which helps us understand the meaning of the passage in the gospels:

They came to Jerusalem, and on entering the temple area he began to drive out those selling and buying there. He overturned the tables of the money changers and the seats of those who were selling doves. He did not permit anyone to carry anything through the temple area. Then he taught them, saying, Is it not written:
My house shall be called a house of prayer for all peoples?
But you have made it a den of thieves. [Mk 11:15–17]

Here we have Jesus confronting the leaders of the Jewish people (the first of his confrontations with them according to the parallel passage in John). The Lord is in Jerusalem (John says he is there to celebrate Passover, the feast of deliverance) and, when he enters the temple, he finds an especially scandalous kind of oppression of the people. Money has become a mediator between God and the faithful, with the result that the latter are faced by an oppressive tyrant and not by the Father who delivers them from slavery. The house of the God who loves the people and sets them free has been turned into a marketplace that exploits and degrades. The business transacted in the temple enriches the high priests; it is they who are behind the trade. The sellers of animals and the money changers who accept Roman money (which is pagan and cannot be offered in a holy place) and give in exchange money minted by the temple itself, are simply intermediaries.

The expulsion by Jesus is therefore an attack on powerful interests, the interests of those who, without denying God with their lips, have replaced God with greed, which, as we saw, Paul regards as idolatry. The substitution is adroit and disguised, and paradoxically, often justified by religious arguments. No one is free to engage in such a perversion of the faith. The special harshness with which Jesus treats the sellers of doves is worth noting (John also emphasizes it). The fact is that the dove, being the smallest and cheapest of animals, is for that reason used by the poorest in sacrifices of purification. The people engaged in selling doves are therefore using worship to exploit the poor. This is why such business is especially scandalous, and it is why Jesus is so resolute in his expulsion of the dove sellers. We may hide our desire for power and money behind arguments and even religious motives; but the Lord, who knows what is in human nature (as John says at the end of his account of the expulsion: 2:25), will not allow "his name to be taken in vain" (see Ex 20:7).

The service of money ends in oppression of the poor. Whether God dwells or does not dwell in a particular place depends on whether true worship is offered there, the worship that the Gospel of John describes as "worship in Spirit and truth" (Jn 4:24). If such worship is being offered, then God is there for all and especially for those looked down upon and regarded as unimportant. Citing a universalist text from Second Isaiah (56:7), Jesus says that the temple shall be called a house of prayer "for all peoples" (Mk 11:17). In the passage parallel to the one on which I am commenting, Matthew notes that "the blind and the lame approached him in the temple area, and he cured them" (Mt 21:14). The healing is a prophetic gesture that underscores his rejection of what was going on in the temple; his giving of life is the opposite of the exploitation of the poor and the substitution of money for God. It is not surprising, therefore, that the people hurt by the attitude of Jesus react aggressively. Immediately after the incident, Mark tells us, "The chief priests and the scribes came to hear of it and were seeking a way to put him to death, yet they feared him because the whole crowd was astonished at his teaching. When evening came, they went out of the city" (Mk 11:18–19).

The World of Bribery

Those in authority over the people are obligated to respect the law and to establish right and justice. They do not always do so in practice:

> Hear this, you leaders of the house of Jacob,
>   you rulers of the house of Israel!
> You who abhor what is just,
>   and pervert all that is right;
> Who build up Zion with bloodshed,
>   and Jerusalem with wickedness!
> Her leaders render judgment for a bribe,
>   her priests give decisions for a salary,
>   her prophets divine for money,
> While they rely on the Lord, saying,
>   "Is not the Lord in the midst of us?
>   No evil can come upon us!"
> Therefore, because of you,
>   Zion shall be plowed like a field,
>   and Jerusalem reduced to rubble,
> And the mount of the temple
>   to a forest ridge. [Mi 3:9–12]

The passage is an indictment. The mighty of the nation are betraying their responsibility and causing the death of the innocent. All of this is an assault on the will of the God of life.

When the prophet attacks those who "build up Zion with bloodshed," he is attacking greed, the idolatry of mammon—that is, the bribery, the pay, and the money that turn judicial and religious activities into a commodity. Yet "they rely on the Lord"! The prophet is infuriated; these idolaters even claim their actions are devout; they claim that God is with them and that God guarantees their security. Since the argument from God's presence is manipulated to justify unjust behavior, God maintains that God will abandon Zion and punish it for the sins of its leaders—that is, the very men whose responsibility it is to teach the people and lead them to faith in Yahweh. God is absent from these men because they are idolaters; in fact, we already know from St. Paul that the greedy, those who worship money, are idolaters.

In one of his harshest attacks on the religious leaders of his people, Jesus rebukes them to their faces: "Woe to you, blind guides, who say, 'If one swears by the temple, it means nothing, but if one swears by the gold of the temple, one is obligated.' Blind fools, which is greater, the gold, or the temple that made the gold sacred?" (Mt 23:16–17).

As the reader will know, a great deal of money was stored in the temple as a result of the offerings made by devout Jews. If this money had any meaning, it derived it from the place in which it was stored. But, to the scandal of having money thus accumulate, there was added the scandal created by the priorities that the beneficiaries had introduced into temple practice.

"Which is greater, the gold or the temple?" The question is a cutting indictment. Jesus is bringing to light a profound deviation in those who claim to represent the law of God, although in fact they "love places of honor at banquets, seats of honor in synagogues, greetings in marketplaces, and the salutation 'Rabbi' " (Mt 23:6). Honors and money give these religious leaders a power that makes them unable to put up with Jesus.

Theirs is an intolerance that does not fear even to commit murder when they see their privileges questioned and the dishonesty of their religion exposed. God is not with religious leaders who betray their task nor does God give them backing. The blood of Jesus can seal the new covenant, which he inaugurates because he dies as a just man at the hands of those who refuse to accept the God of life whom he preaches. But the covenant of love will abide; it will carry the indelible mark of the lamb of God, of the Lord's sacrifice but also of his resurrection.

Evil Deeds

We are familiar with the many passages in which the prophets denounce acts of worship that they regard as empty of content, because those performing them do not practice justice:

> I hate, I spurn your feats,
>> I take no pleasure in your solemnities;
> Your cereal-offerings I will not accept,
>> nor consider your stall-fed peace offerings.
> Away with your noisy songs!
>> I will not listen to the melodies of your harps.
> But if you would offer me holocausts,
>> then let justice surge like water,
>> and goodness like an unfailing stream. [Am 5:21–24]

As I said earlier, offerings to Yahweh, the God of the covenant, must be linked to the establishment of what is right and just. Otherwise they are not acceptable to God; they are hollow actions:

> Is this the manner of fasting I wish,
>> of keeping a day of penance:
> That a man bow his head like a reed,
>> and lie in sackcloth and ashes?
> Do you call this a fast,

a day acceptable to the Lord?
This, rather, is the fasting that I wish:
   releasing those bound unjustly,
   untying the thongs of the yoke;
Setting free the oppressed,
   breaking every yoke;
Sharing your bread with the hungry,
   sheltering the oppressed and the homeless;
Clothing the naked when you see them,
   and not turning your back on your own.
                                    [Is 58:5–7]

Sharing our bread with the poor, making of them our "bread-sharers" (this is the etymology of "companion"): that is the fast God wants. Only under these conditions will God be present:

Then your light shall break forth like the dawn,
   and your wound shall be quickly healed;
Your vindication shall go before you,
   and the glory of the Lord shall be your rear guard.
Then you shall call, and the Lord will answer,
   you shall cry for help, and he will say: Here I am!
                                    [Is 58:8–9]

A passage of the New Testament repeats these reasons for the absence of God from allegedly religious activities:

Not everyone who says to me, "Lord, Lord" will enter the kingdom of heaven, but only the one who does the will of my Father in heaven. Many will say to me on that day, "Lord, Lord, did we not prophesy in your name? Did we not drive out demons in your name? Did we not do mighty deeds in your name?" Then I will declare to them solemnly, "I never knew you. Depart from me, you evildoers." [Mt 7:21–23]

"I never knew you; depart from me" is a classical formula of the Bible for a complete and unconditional rejection. "On that day" those rejected will be termed "evildoers," because they did not feed the hungry or give drink to the thirsty (see Mt 25:31–45). The actions that such people claim as religious (prophesying, expelling demons, working miracles) were simply ritual gestures empty of concrete love for the poor brothers and sisters; therefore God was not in these actions. Moreover, the exercise of these charisms becomes the practice of evil (in Greek: *anomia*, lawlessness); that is, the very opposite of love (Greek: *agape*), which is God's law as explained in the Sermon on the Mount, of which the present passage is a part.[1]

"Evildoers" is a bold and harsh term that allows no loopholes. When one tries to justify the failure to love the poor and the oppressed by claiming that one is occupied in worshiping, one is in fact doing evil. God is not bound to accept our religious works; if they are not inspired by a will to life and justice, God is not present in them.

All these passages recall different ways in which God is absent: from the temple, from the leaders of the people, and from religious activities. But all these absences have a single theological meaning: God is not there because the reign of God is not accepted; because God's will is not carried out. As the elderly sacristan says in *Todas las sangres*: "God is here in Lahuaymarca. He has left San Pedro, and, I think, forever." God departs from places and persons that have committed so many injustices against the Indians. The philosophical argument offered by the priest—"God is everywhere, everywhere"—is irrelevant. The old sacristan ponders: "Was God in the hearts of those who broke the body of innocent Master Bellido?" Is he in the hearts of those who rob and kill? No, God has left them. Arguedas's poetic intuition matches the biblical outlook. When the grace of God's reign is not accepted, when God's demands are not met, the God of the kingdom is absent.

2. DWELLING OF GOD

The presence of God is one of the major themes of the Bible. There is an exact term that expresses God's dwelling within history: the *shekinah* of Yahweh.[2] The people of Israel are profoundly convinced of God's nearness, and this nearness motivates a constant sense of gratitude. "What great nation is there that has gods so close to it as the Lord, our God, is to us whenever we call upon him?" (Dt 4:7). God is present in the midst of the people, but not only there, for God is also present in the cosmos—that is, in everything that is the result of God's creative action. The coming of Christ hastens and deepens this presence in history and in the least of history's participants.

The Cosmos Speaks of God

The poetry found in many books of the Bible has for one of its favorite themes the traces of God in the natural world. In that world God is clothed in beauty:

> Bless the Lord, O my soul!
>   O Lord, my God, you are great indeed!
> You are clothed with majesty and glory,
>   robed in light as with a cloak.
> You have spread out the heavens like a tent-cloth;
>   you have constructed your palace upon the waters.
> You make the clouds your chariot;

you travel on the wings of the wind.
You make the winds your messengers,
    and flaming fire your ministers. [Ps 104:1-4]

God's presence is signaled by these beautiful garments; God is found in the "tent" from which his message reaches us. The natural world speaks of God:

The heavens declare the glory of God,
    and the firmament proclaims his handiwork.
Day pours out the word to day,
    and night to night imparts knowledge;
Not a word nor a discourse
    whose voice is not heard;
Through all the earth their voice resounds,
    and to the ends of the world their message.
                                    [Ps 19:2-5a]

In part, perhaps, because it springs from a rural world, the Bible likes to sing of this presence of God and to do so along with the rest of creation. A fine example of this approach is the beautiful hymn of the three young men, Hananiah, Azariah, and Mishael, in the Book of Daniel:

Sun and moon, bless the Lord;
    praise and exalt him above all forever.
Stars of heaven, bless the Lord;
    praise and exalt him above all forever.
Every shower and dew, bless the Lord;
    praise and exalt him above all forever.
All you winds, bless the Lord;
    praise and exalt him above all forever
Fire and heat, bless the Lord;
    praise and exalt him above all forever. [Dan 3:62-66]

It is important, however, to observe that the main reason for these exclamations of wondering praise is not the fact that heaven, earth, and the phenomena of nature raise questions that human beings have difficulty in answering, so that they fall back on mystery and try to find God in what is hidden and in interstellar space. The Bible does indeed refer to this experience, but its emphasis on the theme is due much more to the fact that it sees God revealed in the grandeur and harmony of the cosmos, in the majestic beauty of the natural world. Like Dante at the end of his *Divine Comedy*, the Bible speaks to us of "the love that moves the sun and the stars."

It is for this reason that Francis of Assisi with his insight into the gospel sees the creatures of the natural world as our brothers and sisters:

> All praise be yours, my Lord, through all that you have
> made,
> And first my lord Brother Sun,
> Who brings the day; and light you give to us through
> him.
> How beautiful he is, how radiant in all his splendour!
> Of you, Most High, he bears the likeness.
> All praise be yours, my Lord, through Sister Moon and
> Stars;
> In the heavens you have made them, bright
> And precious and fair. . . .
> All praise be yours, my Lord, through Sister Water,
> So useful, lowly, precious and pure.
> All praise be yours, my Lord, through Brother Fire,
> Through whom you brighten up the night.
> How beautiful he is, how gay! Full of power and
> strength.[3]

This vision of things is extremely important, and we need to recover it through contemplation and the celebration of the liturgy. It represents the phase of silence to which I referred in the introduction to this book. If we lose the dimension of beauty, we deny ourselves an approach to the God who loves us, as well as to understanding of liturgy. All the symbols used in the liturgy are realities of the natural world: fire, water, light, fruits. The presence of God undoubtedly spurs us to stress the ethical perspective, but no less certainly the finding of God in contemplation has an esthetic dimension. Do we not see this in the experience of the great mystics, such as St. John of the Cross ("Seeking my loves, I will go o'er yonder mountains and banks") in his relationship with nature? The sensitivity of the Bible to this aspect of reality causes it to assert the presence of God in the beauty of the universe. In the addresses of God in the Book of Job (chapters 38–41), for example, the beautiful description of the natural world serves as a revelation of the gratuitousness of God's love.

On the other hand, the effort to draw near to the mystery of God moves along lines that are apparently opposed among themselves. This is because we are engaged in a dialectical approach to the ineffable. God is revealed through events that cannot fail to be seen and even produce fear: the storm, for example, and devouring fire:

> On the morning of the third day there were peals of thunder and
> lightning, and a heavy cloud over the mountain, and a very loud trum-
> pet blast, so that all the people in the camp trembled. But Moses led

the people out of the camp to meet God, and they stationed themselves at the foot of the mountain. Mount Sinai was all wrapped in
smoke, for the Lord came down upon it in fire. The smoke rose from
it as though from a furnace, and the whole mountain trembled vio-
lently. [Ex 19:16–18]

But God is also present in situations that rise into consciousness only if
we are attentive to them, as, for example, the light breeze:

Then the Lord said, "Go outside and stand on the mountain before
the Lord; the Lord will be passing by." A strong and heavy wind was
rending the mountains and crushing rocks before the Lord—but the
Lord was not in the wind. After the wind there was an earthquake—
but the Lord was not in the earthquake. After the earthquake there
was fire—but the Lord was not in the fire. After the fire there was a
tiny whispering sound. When he heard this, Elijah hid his face in his
cloak and went and stood at the entrance of the cave. A voice said
to him, "Elijah, why are you here?" [1 Kgs 19:11–13]

God is manifested on the mountain and in the storm, and in fire amid
thunder and lightning. But, according to the beautiful passage just cited,
God is also manifested in the "tiny whispering sound" of a breeze,[4] in the
light caress that restores calm after the terrifying storm. In these different
ways that are based on events of nature the Bible seeks to approach the
limitless plenitude of God's presence.

It is to be noted, however, that in all cases it is the same God who is
revealed and makes identical claims. Thus the manifestation of God in the
form of a light breeze does not relieve Elijah of the necessity of covering
his face when Yahweh is near, nor does it soften the terms of the mission
he receives. On the other hand, the theophany in the storm on the mountain
does not keep Moses from speaking freely to Yahweh and experiencing
Yahweh's intimate presence.

I Shall Dwell in Your Midst

God is present in the cosmos, but God is also present in the midst of
history. The living God is present and active in the historical movement of
human society. God has decided that it should be so. God's being with us
is a central and profound idea, and one that is not reducible to simplistic
visions of reality. The prophets supply two correctives against errors of
interpretation that can occur in the effort to understand this presence more
fully and define it more closely.

The first is to remind their hearers that no space and no time can contain
God fully. God dwells in the cosmos and in concrete human history, but
these cannot enclose God or set limits to God's presence. The holy mountain cannot, nor can the ark or the temple or any reality or dimension of

society; neither can any experience or any historical event set limits to the divine action. This is one of the reasons why the Old Testament is so opposed to the making of images: God cannot be represented; God transcends any likeness.

For this reason, when the Jewish people, remembering the presence of God on Mount Sinai and their experience of God's company in the wilderness, build a temple for God—that is, a particular spot in which God's dwelling is fixed—the prophets immediately broaden the horizon and caution that the true dwelling place of God is in the heavens. Thus, in the presence of the imposing temple built of cedar of Lebanon to be a house for Yahweh, Solomon exclaims before the entire assembly: "Can it indeed be that God dwells among men on earth? If the heavens and the highest heavens cannot contain you, how much less this temple which I have built!" (1 Kgs 8:27).

Implicit in the conviction that no place and no historical event is capable of containing God is the great biblical idea that God cannot be manipulated. God is beyond the reach of every effort to limit the scope of God's freely adopted plans. Human beings must not delude themselves: Yahweh agrees to the building of a temple, but this is not the sole place in which God dwells, nor is God's dwelling there guaranteed.

For the same reason temporal limits cannot be imposed on God; that is, God cannot be enclosed in time. When the rulers of the city of Betulia decide that they will hand the city over to the enemy if Yahweh does not come to its aid within five days, Judith responds in the purest prophetic tradition:

Listen to me, you rulers of the people of Betulia. What you said to the people today is not proper. When you promised to hand over the city to our enemies at the end of five days unless within that time the Lord comes to our aid, you interposed between God and yourselves this oath which you took. Who are you, then, that you should put God to the test this day, setting yourselves in the place of God in human affairs? It is the Lord Almighty for whom you are laying down conditions; will you never understand anything? You cannot plumb the depths of the human heart nor grasp the workings of the human mind; how then can you fathom God, who made all these things, discern his mind, and understand his plan?

No, my brothers, do not anger the Lord our God. For if he does not wish to come to our aid within the five days, he has it equally within his power to protect us at such time as he pleases, or to destroy us in the face of our enemies. It is not for you to make the Lord our God give surety for his plans.

God is not man that he should be moved by threats, nor human, that he may be given an ultimatum. [Jdt 8:11–17]

This fine passage clearly asserts the transcendence of God and the utter freedom with which God loves. Those who demand guarantees of God do not understand God: you cannot give God ultimatums. God is beyond all space and all time. God will act, utterly freely, if it pleases God to do so.

The prophets constantly recall the majesty of Yahweh and thus counteract the tendency, often found in believers, to seek to domesticate faith in God. For this reason they frequently met with resistance and hostility among their own people. In our own day, even to speak of God and the poor is to go counter to a world that creates a religion for its own private use, one that sees no problems and raises no questions.

The second corrective of the prophets relates to a point to which I have already referred. Isaiah puts it this way: "Truly with you God is hidden, the God of Israel, the savior!" (Is 45:15). The Lord certainly dwells within history, but, as the prophet makes clear, God's presence is often hidden; God is present in what is insignificant and anonymous.[5] On many occasions God brings a work of justice or salvation to completion in a hidden manner. God's dwelling in history is not simple and obvious, so that it may be found quickly, directly, and unmistakably. God is present in human history with its tensions, successes, and conflicts, but finding God requires a search.

Searching, as I said earlier, is a profound spiritual theme in every discussion of the way to reach God, in every reflection on the always unprecedented ways of coming to this hidden God, who most often accomplishes the work of salvation in ways that are not ours, as Isaiah says (Is 55:8). Consequently, if we are to find God acting in history, we must have an attitude of faith that is open to novelty and mystery. The Lord cannot be manipulated, nor can we invent a God who will meet our expectations. On the contrary, we must agree to be constantly challenged by God.

3. EVERYTHING BEGINS WITH AN ENCOUNTER

God's dwelling in history reaches its fullest form in the incarnation in Jesus the Galilean, the poor man of Nazareth. A verse in the Prologue of John's Gospel puts it in a warm-blooded, concrete way: "And the Word became flesh and made his dwelling among us" (Jn 1:14). The *Biblia Española* version reads: "And the Word became a man and camped among us." These are different ways of expressing the same certainty: the dwelling of God in history. This central theme of the Bible finds its fullest implementation in the incarnation. Matthew stresses this point by applying the prophecy of Isaiah: Jesus is Emmanuel, a name which, as the evangelist specifically points out, means "God with us" (Mt 1:23; see Is 7:14).

In the Word Was Life

The Gospel of John is determined to bring home to us the importance of this encounter. His Prologue touches on all the major themes of his work; it resembles a symphonic overture announcing the material that will be developed in the body of the work. In these eighteen opening verses of the Gospel we find in fact the dialectic of death-life, light-darkness, truth-lie, grace-sin, the theme of witnessing, and the alternatives of freedom and slavery; all this in addition to the historical perspective, which is more important in John's Gospel than is commonly thought. The essence of the passage consists in the repeated assertion of various ways in which the word became flesh and pitched his tent in our midst. All this has its source in the primordial experience of John, the beloved disciple and author (though not necessarily the redactor) of this Gospel — that is, in his personal encounter with Jesus (see Jn 1:35–42). The lines of force in the Prologue cross at this point.

The first thing that calls for our attention and is of major importance for understanding John's theological purpose is the opening words: "In the beginning was the Word" (1:1). The Bible as a whole opens with the words "in the beginning" (Gn 1:1), as it speaks of God the Creator, whose Spirit "swept over the waters" (Gn 1:2). John uses the same words for the opening of his Gospel: "In the beginning was the Word, and the Word was with God" (Jn 1:1). The Greek words *en pros*, which are translated "was with," signify a direction and movement: "was directed toward." For this reason, some have given the translation: "was face to face with God." The words are a way of expressing the divinity of the word.

Verse 2 repeats, in a kind of summary, the idea of the divine origin of the word: "He was in the beginning with God."

Verse 3 again forcefully brings out the divinity: "All things came to be through him, and without him nothing came to be." The word is not created but creative.

The next verse adds an important idea to that of creation: "In him was life" (REB). The God who is revealed in the Bible is radically life. This is the main characteristic of God in the Bible and a fruitful theme of the fourth Gospel. A little further on, John will say to us: "Just as the living Father sent me and I have life because of the Father, so also the one who feeds on me will have life because of me" (Jn 6:57). Jesus transmits the Father's life to us; possession of this life is the purpose of God's creative work and salvific action. "And this life was the light of the human race" (v. 4). The word is life and it is light. The perspective of life sheds light on the message. This was John's own experience: his meeting with Jesus was a source of illumination for him. The option for life becomes the definitive criterion for being and acting as Christians. Everything that involves giving life in various ways is characteristic of the followers of the Lord. By contrast, everything that entails rejection, poverty, exploitation, and contempt for life means a covenant with death and a denial of the God of Jesus.

When I speak of life, I mean all life. At the new beginning of creation that follows the flood, God says to Noah and his family that the covenant is "with you and your descendants after you and with every living creature that was with you. ... This is the sign of the covenant I have established between me and all mortal creatures that are on earth" (Gn 9:9–10, 17). The covenant is with the various forms of life, which all come from God. The important and pressing concern for ecology in our day finds in the Bible, as I said earlier, a solid and fertile basis, provided we set aside an exclusively anthropocentric interpretation of ecology. From the standpoint of the poor of this world we ought to pay increasing attention to this subject.

The Book of Job teaches us a major lesson in this regard when it reminds us that not everything was created for the service of human beings; there are many things in the natural world that human beings may consider "useless" but in which God finds delight.[6] Human beings, made as they are in the "image and likeness of God," occupy a privileged place among living things and are called to the grace of full communion with God. But Paul reminds us that the whole of creation waits for its liberation through the children of God (Rom 8:21–22). The activity of Jesus is directed toward communicating this fullness of life: "I came so that they might have life and have it more abundantly" (Jn 10:10).

Life is light, and darkness is what hinders it. The contrast between light and darkness is a theme that runs throughout the Gospel of John. Thick darkness is to light what death is to life. This idea has various roots. In Genesis, darkness precedes light; it "covered the abyss" (Gn 1:2) and is a component of chaos; but there is an important nuance here, as compared with John: the darkness is not actively opposed to the light. In John, on the other hand, the image of darkness is laden with hostility: the darkness is expressly opposed to the acceptance of the word. The reign of death is opposed to the reign of life. Darkness in John is connected with the world of falsehood, which, as we know, is another major theme of his Gospel. The world of falsehood is the work of human beings or, more accurately, the result of the refusal to accept the Lord, who is truth (see Jn 14:6). Darkness stands for sin, opposition, hostility. Light, on the other hand, is the milieu of love. There is antagonism between the darkness and the light, but John tells us that "the light shines in the darkness, and the darkness has not overcome it" (v. 5). The Lord is the light of the world: "Whoever follows me will not walk in darkness, but will have the light of life" (Jn 8:12). To follow Jesus means to set free and to give life.

In this setting of creation, life, and light a prophet makes his appearance: John the Baptist, "a man . . . sent by God" (v. 6); in him we begin contact with the history of a people. The precursor came to bear witness to the light; but only they who have experienced it can be witnesses. This is a thought that John repeats in the prologue of his first Letter: "What we have seen and heard we proclaim now to you" (1 Jn 1:3). Here, at the beginning of John's Gospel, another John, the Baptist, is presented to us as a witness. His light is a reflected light; he is a man who has received the light he needs in order to help others and illumine the way that leads to the Lord. John the Evangelist knew the Baptist and had been his disciple;

that is why he knew that the Baptist "was not the light, but came to testify to the light" (v. 8).

The word alone is "the true light, which enlightens everyone" (v. 9), but makes himself known through messengers. All are called to believe; as soon as they enter this world, the light is present to them, because it is God's intention that human beings should reach the fullness of life. By a free act, which no one else can do by proxy, every person must choose light or darkness. And this freedom itself is the result of life received.

It is in the world of history that we accept or reject the word. The decision we make is heavy with consequences. The word made the world; if the world does not know him — that is, does not accept and love him — it denies its very self. Its refusal amounts to rejecting the life that gave it its beginning, and therefore to fall back into darkness and chaos, this time definitively.

Beginning in verse 11 the author introduces the central theme of the Prologue: the dwelling and reception of the word in history: "He came to what was his own [or: to his own home], but his own people did not accept him." In his own journey of faith, how often had John the Evangelist himself failed to "accept" the Lord? Behind the seemingly abstract language of the Prologue stands living experience.

Those who accept the word receive the gift of becoming children of God; this is one way of bringing out the life that was in the word. The gift here given signifies a power or force: God makes us sons and daughters. We respond actively to this gift by ourselves in turn accepting the daughters and sons of the Father whom we meet on our journey to him.

He Made His Dwelling among Us

"He came to what was his own" (v. 11); he "became flesh" (v. 14): these are expressions showing the word's entrance into history. In the Bible "flesh" means the human being, sometimes with the connotation of weakness. In this short phrase John sums up the theme of emptying to which Paul will give sublime development in the second chapter of Philippians. The word entered history and accepted the human condition, including what makes it most fragile: "For your sake he became poor although he was rich" (2 Cor 8:9).

"He made his dwelling among us" (v. 14): this fine image is taken from the Old Testament. We are told in Exodus that "the tent, which was called the meeting tent, Moses used to pitch at some distance away, outside the camp" (Ex 33:7). The tent played a very important role for the Israelites during their crossing of the wilderness toward the promised land. The shadow of this tent of repose, which gave meaning and energy for the long journey, provided an anticipated taste of the goal reached after forty years of journeying. The presence of the tent transforms an experience of desolation into the beginning of a strengthening encounter with God, just as, according to Saint-Exupéry, the existence of a well in the middle of a desert transforms it into a life-giving space that gives us courage and spurs us on our quest.

According to John, the flesh that the word assumes is the new tent of meeting. We are called to become one in it; to be a disciple of Jesus means to live, believe, and hope under this tent. Paul expresses the same idea when he says that Christians are members of the body of Christ. The word "camped" among us and then, laden with humanity, rose once more to the Father: "And we saw his glory, the glory as of the Father's only Son" (v. 14). John traces a thought-provoking pattern: the word was with God in the beginning; he enters history to bring life; and he returns to the Father. Christ becomes one of us and then raises us up to contemplation of the glory he has received from the Father. That is why the evangelist says in verse 16: "From his fullness we have all received, grace in place of grace." The incarnate word gives us a share of the life he has in himself; he communicates a share in his own fullness by making us daughters and sons of the Father: "grace and truth came through Jesus Christ" (v. 17).

The Prologue ends with a restatement of the transcendence of God: "No one has ever seen God" (v. 18). The incarnation does not strip God of holiness, radical otherness. God is completely different; God does not belong to this world. That is what is implied in invisibility. But the Son sees God and therefore can reveal God: "The only Son, God, who is at the Father's side, has revealed him" (v. 18). John is here reverting to his claim that if one is to give testimony, to reveal, one must have seen and experienced. The Son, who is face to face with the Father, is the only one who can reveal him.

4. An Irruption Smelling of the Stable

Despite appearances, the Gospel of John, including the Prologue, is steeped in concrete history and personal experience. But the more narrative language of the other Gospels undoubtedly provides us with a different and complementary approach to the presence of the Lord.

A Historical Faith

The Gospel of Luke tells us that "in those days a decree went out from Caesar Augustus that the whole world should be enrolled. This was the first enrollment, when Quirinius was governor of Syria" (2:1–2). The Gospel of Matthew adds that Jesus was born "in Bethlehem of Judea, in the days of King Herod" (2:1).

These simple texts convey a profound message: Jesus was born in a particular place at a particular time. He was born under Emperor Octavius, who had himself named Augustus when he reached the pinnacle of power; when Quirinius was governor of Syria; during the reign of Herod, who was traitor to his people and had sold out to the occupying power. It was during this time that Jesus was born, a man of no importance in the eyes of the cynical and arrogant authorities as well as in the eyes of those who disguised cowardice as peace and political realism.

He was born in Bethlehem, "one of the little clans of Judah" (Mi 5:1 NRSV), where at his birth he was surrounded by shepherds and their flocks. His parents had come to a stable after vainly knocking at numerous doors in the town, as the Gospels tell us; we are reminded of the popular Mexican custom of *las posadas*. There, on the fringe of society, "the Word became history, contingency, solidarity, and weakness; but we can say, too, that by this becoming, history itself, our history, became Word."[7]

It is often said at Christmastime that Jesus is born into every family and every heart. But these "births" must not make us forget the primordial, massive fact that Jesus was born of Mary among a people that at the time were dominated by the greatest empire of the age. If we forget that fact, the birth of Jesus becomes an abstraction, a symbol, a cipher. Apart from its historical coordinates the event loses its meaning. To the eyes of Christians the incarnation is the irruption of God into human history: an incarnation into littleness and service in the midst of the overbearing power exercised by the mighty of this world; an irruption that smells of the stable.

Christian faith is a historical faith. God is revealed in Jesus Christ and, through him, in human history and in the least important and poorest sector of those who make it up. Only with this as a starting point is it possible to believe in God. Believers cannot go aside into a kind of dead-end corner of history and watch it go by. It is in the concrete setting and circumstances of our lives that we must learn to believe: under oppression and repression but also amid the struggles and hopes that are alive in present-day Latin America; under dictatorships that sow death among the poor, and under the "democracies" that often deal unjustly with their needs and dreams.

The Lord is not intimidated by the darkness or by the rejection of his own. His light is stronger than all the shadows. If we are to dwell in the tent the Son has pitched in our midst, we must enter into our own history here and now, and nourish our hope on the will to life that the poor of our continent are demonstrating. If we do so, we shall experience in our flesh the encounter with the word who proclaims the kingdom of life.

This proclamation calls believers together as a "church," as a community whose vocation it is to continue the mission of the word. At the end of the first chapter of his Gospel, John tells us of the meeting of two disciples of John the Baptist with the word made flesh, and how these two straightaway went and told others what they had seen and heard. Andrew says to his brother Simon: " 'We have found the Messiah' (which is translated Anointed). Then he brought him to Jesus" (Jn 1:41–42).[8] Thus the passing on of the good news gave birth to the community of the disciples of Jesus, men and women destined to bear witness to the God of history.

In an earlier section I reminded the reader that according to the Bible nothing can contain God. The same cannot be said without qualification of Jesus. Yet, while bearing in mind this new situation, the corrective offered by the prophets can open up meaningful ways of understanding God's relation to history. The New Testament speaks of the fullness of time in connection with Christ, but at the same time it tells us that Christians who are incorporated into the body of Christ by baptism have a historical journey to make.

This body, the head of which is Christ, is required for the fullness (*plēroma*) of Christ, of which the Apostle speaks. Given this perspective, it becomes possible to understand one focus of the prophetic concern mentioned above. In the present situation, this concern is focused rather on the body of Christ, the *ekklēsia*, which is a pilgrim in history and whose visible boundaries are nevertheless not those of God's presence in the world. This means that God is not contained within these boundaries. The *parousia* or return of the Lord will seal the completion of the fullness of time.

Hope of the *parousia* is an integral element in our life of faith. The Lord's second coming, to which little thought is given, is not a marginal question nor can it be dealt with in passing. Before it happens, there is a journey to be made, a march toward the full implementation of the promise. With the incarnation we have entered into the fullness of time, though we still have a distance to go; the body of Christ is now present in history. The time of the church is that of the process whereby God dwells in history.

The Faces of the Lord

The Son of God was born into a little people, a nation of little importance by comparison with the great powers of the time. Furthermore, he took flesh among the poor in a marginal area—namely, Galilee; he lived with the power and emerged from among them to inaugurate a kingdom of love and justice. That is why many have trouble recognizing him. The God who became flesh in Jesus is the hidden God of whom the prophets speak to us. Jesus shows himself to be such precisely in the measure that he is present via those who are the absent, anonymous people of history—those who are not the controllers of history—namely, the mighty, the socially acceptable, "the wise and the learned" (Mt 11:25).

In the Old Testament God is manifested as defender of the poor. This fact leads to the assertion that mistreatment of the deprived is an attack on God. The Book of Proverbs, for example, says: "He who oppresses the poor blasphemes his Maker, but he who is kindly to the needy glorifies him" (Prv 14:31; see also Prv 17:5; Lv 19:14; Sir 34:20). But Jesus' identification of himself with the least members of society is unparalleled and original (see Mt 25:31–46).

Several other passages bring us close to the same idea. For example: "Whoever receives one child such as this in my name, receives me" (Mk 9:37). In this context, we should not forget that in the culture of that time children were among those to whom no heed was paid.[9] But no passage of the Gospel has the power of the always startling text of Matthew on the final judgment. A good deal might be said of it, and in fact I shall return to some aspects of it further on. For the moment, I am interested in calling attention to what it says about the presence of God among us.

This well-known passage, Matthew 25:31–46, sheds light on two important identifications. The one coming to judge is the Son of man who "will sit on his glorious throne" (v. 31). A great deal has been written on the expression "Son of man," which Jesus uses so often to designate his mission. Let us note that in Matthew's own Gospel it is found several times in various contexts: Jesus' suffering and surrender of his life (17:22; 26:2), his service (24:28), and the eschatological judgment (25:31). The present passage goes on to say that it is the king who will judge (v. 34). Son of man and king, then, signify the same person.

The Gospel of John makes the same identification in one of its most substantial and profoundly theological passages (18:28–19:22). Here John focuses on the kingship of Jesus (kingship and king are mentioned here twelve times, out of sixteen occurrences in the Gospel as a whole). Before Pilate, who represents the most powerful government of that age, the Lord acknowledges that he is a king, but also that his kingdom is of a different kind. "So Pilate said to him, 'Then you are a king?' Jesus answered, 'You say I am a king'" (18:37). A moment before, Jesus had made the point that "my kingdom does not belong to this world" (18:36); that is, the power exercised in it is used not to dominate, as was the case with the Roman authorities, but to serve. Jesus is a king who identifies with the least members of society, those whom society scorns. That is why they make fun of his claim to kingship (see 19:2–3). This king is then led forth and presented as "the man" (or: the Son of man)(19:5).[10]

A passage in Mark explains power that is used for service:

Then James and John, the sons of Zebedee, came to him and said to him, "Teacher, we want you to do for us whatever we ask of you." He replied, "What do you wish [me] to do for you?" They answered him, "Grant that in your glory we may sit one at your right and the other at your left." Jesus said to them, "You do not know what you are asking. Can you drink the cup that I drink or be baptized with the baptism with which I am baptized?" They said to him, "We can." Jesus said to them, "The cup that I drink, you will drink, and with the baptism with which I am baptized, you will be baptized; but to sit at my right or my left is not mine to give but is for those for whom it has been prepared." When the ten heard this, they became indignant at James and John. Jesus summoned them and said to them, "You know that those who are recognized as rulers over the Gentiles lord it over them, and their great ones make their authority over them felt. But it shall not be so among you. Rather, whoever wishes to be great among you will be your servant; whoever wishes to be first among you will be the slave of all. For the Son of Man did not come to be served but to serve and to give his life as a ransom for many." [Mk 10:35–45]

Here two of Jesus' closest followers show their lack of understanding by asking for places of honor. The Lord answers their petition with (once again!) a question: Are they able, like he, to pay the price in suffering and death that the proclamation of the kingdom of life demands? The announcement that Jesus himself must suffer and die has already elicited a first reaction of rejection from Peter (see Mk 8:31–32). Self-surrender to others and not personal glory is the lot Christ sets before his servants. The disciples are indignant at James and John, not because the latter are mistaken regarding the message of Jesus but because they have stolen a march in asking for what all of them want. In point of fact, it is not easy to understand what it means to receive the kingdom; one of the most serious misunderstandings disciples can have is to think that our status as Christians or our responsibilities in the church make us "absolute lords" over others. That is, that these give us a right to personal glory as understood according to the categories prevailing among the great of our society.

Jesus, the Messiah, turns the reigning order upside down. In his effort to help his disciples advance along the way they have entered upon, he tells them that the truly great one among them is the one who serves and that he who would be first must be "the slave of all." This is the "messianic inversion" that is a central element in the gospel message. The inversion begins with the Lord himself who, when he became one of us, intended not to be served but to serve. Service does not mean passively accepting the present state of affairs. Rather it implies initiative and creativity, the knowledge and strength needed to build a human, just, and fraternal world. What the Gospel rejects is power viewed as domination, as the quest to have others acknowledge us as "rulers"; it does not reject power understood as service.

This distinction helps us to understand better the second identification. Ten of the sixteen verses in Matthew's story of the judgment speak of the Lord identifying himself with the least, with the unimportant. To give life (or refuse it) to the poor is to encounter (or reject) Christ himself. This is the point being made in the Greek word used here: *elachistos* ("least"). Matthew uses the same word to describe the littleness of Bethlehem (Mt 2:6), which is nonetheless destined for greatness because from it will come the Messiah.[11] Every person who is poor and forgotten is, like Bethlehem, unimportant, but from this person the Lord comes to us.[12] It is in commitment to the marginalized that we find the meaning of our lives as believers and as human beings. When we serve the poor we serve the Christ in whom we believe; when we are in solidarity with the neediest we discern the lowly reality of the Son of man. There is no other way of "inheriting the kingdom."

Some years ago, John Paul II provided a forceful and creative commentary on this important passage:

> Christ stands before us our judge. He has a special right to make this judgment. Indeed he became one of us, our brother. This brotherhood with the human race—and at the same time his brotherhood with every single person—has led him to the cross and the resurrection. Thus he judges in the name of his solidarity with each person and likewise in the name of our solidarity with him, who is our brother and redeemer and whom we discover in every human being.[13]

The pope goes on to say:

> The Second Vatican Council, following the whole of tradition, warns us not to stop at an "individualistic" interpretation of Christian ethics, since Christian ethics also has its social dimension. The human person lives in a community, in society. And with the community he shares hunger and thirst and sickness and malnutrition and misery and all the deficiencies that result therefrom. In his or her own person the human being is meant to experience the needs of others.

The pope then situates the Lord's words in a broad but specific historical context and says that Christ "is speaking of the whole universal dimension of injustice and evil. He is speaking of what today we are accustomed to call the North-South contrast. Hence not only East-West, but also North-South: the increasingly wealthier North and the increasingly poorer South."

John Paul II ends by drawing stern (and chilling) conclusions for the wealthy nations:

> Nevertheless, in the light of Christ's words, this poor South will judge the rich North. And the poor peoples and poor nations—poor in different ways, not only lacking food, but also deprived of freedom and other human rights—will judge those people who take goods away from them, amassing to themselves the imperialistic monopoly of economic and political supremacy at the expense of others.

The surprise that both the just and the condemned express shows us that this meeting with the Lord is highly unexpected. Christ hides himself behind the faces of those whom we tend to avoid because they have little importance in the eyes of society. The difficulty of recognizing the Lord becomes even greater when the poor organize to defend their rights and deepen their faith. At this point they show themselves ready for conflict and therefore elicit resistance and hostility in the privileged members of our society. The latter prefer a religion that justifies inequality and protects their interests.[14] To the extent that the oppressed fight for their rights and enter upon what the popes have called "the noble struggle for justice," it becomes more difficult for many people to see in their faces "the suffering features of Christ our Lord," to use the words of Puebla (31) in a fine passage that I think it worthwhile to excerpt here.[15] These faces, says Puebla, include:

— the faces of young children, struck down by poverty before they are born, their chance for self-development blocked by irreparable mental and physical deficiencies; and of the vagrant children in our cities who are so often exploited, products of poverty and the moral disorganization of the family;
— the faces of the indigenous peoples, and frequently of the Afro-Americans as well; living marginalized lives in inhuman situations, they can be considered the poorest of the poor;
— the faces of the peasants; as a social group, they live in exile almost everywhere on our continent, deprived of land, caught in a situation of internal and external dependence, and subjected to systems of commercialization that exploit them;
— the faces of laborers, who frequently are ill-paid and who have difficulty in organizing themselves and defending their rights;
— the faces of old people, who are growing more numerous every day, and who are frequently marginalized in a progress-oriented society that totally disregards people not engaged in production. [Puebla 32, 34, 35, 36, 39]

There, in the poor, the "hidden God" questions and challenges us, especially if, like Puebla, we put ourselves in the presence of today's concrete poor, without indulging in any fantasies about them. God became flesh and is present in history, but because God is identified with the poor of the world, God's face and action are hidden in them. The Lord hides his presence in history, and at the same time reveals it, in the life and suffering, the struggles, the death, and the hopes of the condemned of the earth. But we must also bear in mind that this condemnation, this rejection of the kingdom of life, is what motivates God's absence. The dialectic of God's transcendence and God's presence in history, as well as the dialectic of revelation and hiddenness, are set forth in the Bible in a complex and fruitful way that calls for historical discernment and attention to what that unforgettable pope, John XXIII, called the signs of the times.

Vallejo with his poetic intuition spoke to us of this God who is hidden in the wretched:

The lottery ticket seller who cries "A thousand-dollar
    winner!"
contains I know not what depths of God. . . .
And I wonder on this tepid Friday that

struggles on beneath the sun:
Why should the will of God be dressed
as a seller of lottery tickets?
[César Vallejo, "La de a mil," in his *Los Heraldos Negros*]

The lottery ticket seller passes by and offers us "a thousand-dollar win-ner." We will never know whether if we had bought the ticket we would have won the lottery. But this tattered fellow, who shows us "I know not what depths of God" and who despite his seeming inability to love, can, like God, "give us heart," is thereby able to revive our lost hopes and shatter our boredom. Fortune, which is fickle, uncontrollable, impossible to subdue, seems to elude even the farsightedness of "this bohemian god." We do not know whether in meeting this crier of lottery tickets we might run into fortune and encounter God. That is why the poet asks about the will of God, about this God who so mysteriously is linked to the marginalized of history and who is hidden, dresses as a seller of lottery tickets, a crier and itinerant vender.[16]

CHAPTER VI

THE TIME CAME

The heart of the message of Jesus is the announcement of the kingdom. The Old Testament had already proclaimed a hope focused on the day when the mercy and justice of God would reign unopposed. Jesus begins his ministry among the poor and marginalized of his people. To seek the kingdom and justice is to launch out on the way of encounter with God; it is to inquire after "Jesus of Nazareth, the crucified, [who] has been raised" (Mk 16:6). This theme urgently turns our attention to those who are the privileged persons in the kingdom—namely, the least regarded of history—and helps us to understand the hope of, and search for, the kingdom in a continent that is poor.

1. THE DAY OF YAHWEH

One of the main lines of force running through the Old Testament is the eschatological hope of the day on which Yahweh will become fully present. The term "eschatological" does not refer solely to the end of history; it also implies a clear-sighted attention to the present and to the historical changes in which we try to discover the will of God.[1] The Bible has many ways of presenting this "day of Yahweh" that ought to guide our present commitment. I shall single out two beautiful and important passages.

Like a Sunday in the City Streets
Chapter 8 of the Book of Zechariah gives us an interesting handful of promises having to do with Yahweh's intention of becoming present in the midst of the people and, ultimately, of all the nations of the earth. Like Haggai, Zechariah (chapters 1–6) exercises his prophetic ministry after the destruction of Jerusalem by the Babylonians and at the time when his people are returning from exile and are in a situation still filled with uncertainties. "Thus says the Lord of hosts: Old men and old women, each with staff in hand because of old age, shall again sit in the streets of Jerusalem. The city shall be filled with boys and girls playing in her streets" (Zec 8:4–5).[2]

Old people and children—the weak extremes (physically speaking) of humanity—will be able to be at ease in the streets of Jerusalem. Nothing will threaten them, no one will take advantage of their weakness. The elders will be able to sit on the benches along the streets with their staffs in their hands and quietly recall the good times; the children will play happily and without risk. They will not have to work or beg for their livelihood as do the elderly and the children of our countries. The passage says that there will be no exceptions to this situation. It speaks of old men and old women, of boys and girls; it is significant that the author explicitly refers to women, who experience greater mistreatment and oppression; old women and girls will be free also to work according to their age and will be able to enjoy the freedom of repose. That is what it will be like some day in Jerusalem, which, in accordance with a promise prior to the one on which I am commenting, is called to be converted into a "faithful city" (or: city of truth) (Zec 8:3). This "holy mountain" will become the place where Yahweh's plan is carried out.[3] "Jerusalem shall abide in security!" (Zec 14:11).

This passage must be contrasted with another that we find in the Lamentations of Jeremiah. Here the author describes a situation that is the very opposite of the one shown in Zechariah. The wickedness that prevails in Jerusalem has led to its ruin; the destruction affects everyone: "Dead in the dust of the streets lie young and old" (2:21). A few verses earlier the writer has said: "On the ground in silence sit the old men of Daughter Zion" (2:10). Children and the elderly here stand for the weak members of society, for all the needy and unimportant individuals. These are the first victims of injustice and exploitation. Yahweh wants this state of affairs to be reversed. "Thus says the Lord of hosts: Even if this should seem impossible in the eyes of the remnant of this people, shall it in those days be impossible in my eyes also, says the Lord of hosts?" (Zec 8:6).

There are some who may think that the promise of life in fullness cannot be carried out, but God is not one of them (see also Jer 31:12–13). That future state is not an illusion but a utopian vision that sets history in motion. The powerful, those who do not want things to change because their privileges are based on the status quo, are skeptical about any plan to establish a different social order. They are the ones who ask: "Do you really believe that a state of affairs in which there are no injustices, in other words, a perfect society, is possible?" The supposed realism of the question is nothing but a smoke screen disguising the unacceptableness of the situation in which the poor and the oppressed are living *today*. In the face of this skepticism and of the possible discouragement of those who see themselves being crushed by the forces of injustice, the Lord says that his will to life for all can indeed take flesh in history.

At the same time, however, the gift of life makes clear demands of those who receive it; the gracious gift implies a covenant: "They shall be my people, and I will be their God, with faithfulness and justice" (Zec 8:8). In this context Zechariah offers a brief code of ethics in verses 16–17, but for the moment I shall defer commentary on it. I shall limit myself to saying here that, as always in the Bible, moral behavior has its place in the framework of the eschatological hope for a different world that is at once God's gift and the result of human work.

This passage of Zechariah reminds us in a simple and beautiful way that on the day of Yahweh life, justice, and joy will reign. Everything will happen in full daylight: "There shall be one continuous day, known to the Lord, not day and night, for in the evening time there shall be light" (Zec 14:7). The weak of the entire human race (see Zec 8:23–24) shall cease to be marginalized and exploited. All will be able to come together and meet in order to relax and congregate as do the inhabitants of any little town in the main square on Sundays.

None Shall Live by the Work of Their Hands

The last section of the Book of Isaiah (chapters 56–66) is attributed to one or several followers of the prophet known as Second Isaiah (chapters 40–55). In these later chapters the theme of justice and salvation holds the central place in the message to those among the Jewish people who are trying to live by the master's teachings during the difficult and unsettled decades of Israel's history at the end of the sixth and the beginning of the fifth century before Christ. The opening words of Third Isaiah are programatic:

> Thus says the Lord:
> Observe what is right, do what is just;
> for my salvation is about to come,
> my justice, about to be revealed. [Is 56:1]

The salvation that Yahweh brings is inseparable from the practice of justice. The author is trying to raise his people's hopes of a better world in which God's will to life will be triumphant over the forces of destruction and death. Toward the end of the book the "day" of Yahweh's full sovereignty is depicted as a new creation:

> Lo, I am about to create new heavens
> and a new earth;
> The things of the past shall not be remembered
> or come to mind.
> Instead, there shall always be rejoicing and happiness
> in what I create;
> For I create Jerusalem to be a joy
> and its people to be a delight;
> I will rejoice in Jerusalem
> and exult in my people.

No longer shall the sound of weeping be heard there,
or the sound of crying. [Is 65:17–19]

Yahweh promises to make everything new; the past shall be completely erased. The expression "new heavens and a new earth" occurs frequently in the Bible and is intended to bring out the radicalness of the change that will take place. The author repeats the same idea in the next chapter, but with the interesting addition of the element of permanence:

As the new heavens and the new earth
which I will make
Shall endure before me, says the Lord,
so shall your race and your name endure. [Is 66:22]

That is the important thing. The establishment of justice is one of the great themes of the Bible; it cannot fail to be part of the new world that the Lord will create.

The depth of the transformation proclaimed will be a source of joy for those who believe in Yahweh. This joy is a messianic blessing and therefore accompanies both the promise and the fulfillment of the promise regarding the day on which the Lord will reign. The text of Isaiah emphasizes this point. Thus in Isaiah 65:18–19, cited above, there are six references to joy and delight. It is even said that these words will be the new names of the city of Jerusalem and its inhabitants. So great will the joy be that all suffering will be done away with (the same idea is echoed in Rv 21:4). This will happen because the day of the Lord is a response to a profound longing and legitimate human right: the longing for and the right to happiness, which is the manifestation of life fulfilled.

The passage in Isaiah 65 goes on to specify the content of the promise:

No longer shall there be in it
an infant who lives but a few days,
or an old man who does not round out his full lifetime;
He dies a mere youth who reaches but a hundred years,
and he who fails of a hundred shall be thought accursed.
[Is 65:20]

The prophet is speaking of the gift of life. Once again, the two opposite ends of life, children and the elderly, serve to show that today's weak and oppressed will be able to live an unhindered and undiminished life. Their right to life and happiness will be ensured and respected. In these new conditions, infants will not die prematurely; these premature deaths are surely one of the cruelest signs of poverty and injustice. We know this from our experience of premature and unjust death on this continent and in our own country, which has one of the highest infant mortality rates in Latin

America. At the same time, longevity will be the ordinary thing; we know how the Old Testament esteems a long life and sees it as a blessing from God.

The gift of life necessarily finds expression in just social relationships. Such relationships suppose that a proper value is set on human labor:

> They shall live in the houses they build,
>   and eat the fruit of the vineyards they plant;
> They shall not build houses for others to live in,
>   or plant for others to eat.
> As the years of a tree, so the years of my people;
>   and my chosen ones shall long enjoy
>   the produce of their hands.
> They shall not toil in vain,
>   nor beget children for sudden destruction;
> For a race blessed by the Lord
>   are they and their offspring. [Is 54:21–23]

All have a right to enjoy the results of their labor. Enemies or hoarding strangers will not take for themselves what someone has sown and harvested (see Is 62:8–9). No one will work for other individuals or authorities, but each will decide how to use their own energies and will be able to live by their own efforts; no one will wrest from them the wealth created by their hands. No work will be useless; no longer will parents beget children who are to be subjected and plundered. In this way the most serious causes of premature death will be eliminated.

The final verses of the passage tell us that everything previously described is the result of union with God. It is on this basis that fellowship among human beings will be established:

> Before they call, I will answer;
>   while they are yet speaking, I will hearken to them.
> The wolf and the lamb shall graze alike,
>   and the lion shall eat hay like the ox.
> None shall hurt or destroy
>   on all my holy mountain, says the Lord. [Is 65:24–25]

Communion with God is something that God brings into being in an utterly free way; it finds expression in the Lord's readiness to hear and respond to the petitions of the people. Chapter 65, on which I have been commenting, begins with a tender, almost breathless, declaration of this readiness:

> I was ready to respond to those who asked me not,
>   to be found by those who sought me not.

I said: Here I am! Here I am!
    To a nation that did not call upon my name. [Is 65:1]

Here is a faithful love that is persistently offered, but by one in whom no one is interested, as these verses of Vallejo say:

No one has come to ask me today;
nor have they asked me for anything this evening. . . .
This evening all, all pass by
and do not ask or request anything. . . .
I go to the door,
and they make me want to cry to all:
If they are short of anything, let them stay here![4]

If God has been able to go in search of those who do not come to God and to say to them almost timidly: "Here I am," God will surely be responsive to those who address God and tell God of their desires.

In describing human brotherhood and sisterhood, the author here (65:25) harks back to a well-known and beautiful prophecy of First Isaiah, which we recall during the season of Advent. It describes the peace of the messianic age, that time when God's envoy will make justice reign. Our actions will be judged by the standard of righteousness:

Not by appearance shall he judge,
    nor by hearsay shall he decide,
But he shall judge the poor with justice,
    and decide aright for the land's afflicted.
He shall strike the ruthless with the rod of his mouth,
    and with the breath of his lips he shall slay the wicked.
Justice shall be the band around his waist,
    and faithfulness a belt upon his hips.
Then the wolf shall be a guest of the lamb,
    and the leopard shall lie down with the kid;
The calf and the young lion shall browse together,
    with a little child to guide them.
The cow and the bear shall be neighbors,
    together their young shall rest;
    the lion shall eat hay like the ox.
The baby shall play by the cobra's den,
    and the child lay his hand on the adder's lair.
There shall be no harm or ruin on all my holy mountain;
    for the earth shall be filled with the knowledge of the
        Lord,
    as water covers the sea. [Is 11:3–9]

On that day the age-old enmities seen in nature shall cease. Wolf and lamb, leopard and kid, calf and lion, cow and bear, lion and ox, child and serpent shall cease to be enemies. What will thus be found in the world of nature will also, and with greater reason, be found in the world of human beings.[5] The holy mountain shall be everywhere, and on it shall reign the knowledge of the Lord—that is, love of the Lord.

A passage in the Second Letter of Peter echoes this vision. On "the day of the Lord" (3:10) everything that is shall vanish and give place to something new. The author asks how believers should behave: "Since everything is to be dissolved in this way, what sort of persons ought [you] to be, conducting yourselves in holiness and devotion?" (3:11). Faithful Christians wait for and hasten "the coming of the day of God" (3:12). The author says more specifically that "according to his promise we await new heavens and a new earth in which righteousness dwells" (3:13). That is the important point. The "dwelling of righteousness" is one of the great themes of the Bible; it will characterize the new world that the Lord is going to create.

The Apocalypse picks up the theme and develops it in a forceful and ample way. This book, which was written in order to support the hope of Christian communities that were being subjected to persecution and death, reminds us that the main battle has already taken place and has been won. The sufferings of Christians today are simply a consequence, with no aftermath, of that battle, for in fact the risen Lord has won a definitive victory, and it is our role to make that victory present in history. We will do this by our actions; "I know your works," the author says repeatedly to the seven churches (see chapters 2–3), and by these works we shall be judged. If we are to bear witness to the Lord's definitive victory, we must keep alive our hope in God's will to create a new world in which life shall reign.

The new state of things that the Lord will create is described in the Apocalypse as "a new heaven and a new earth" (21:1). Then "God's dwelling . . . with the human race" will be established. Using the language of covenant, John tells us that God "will dwell with them and they will be his people and God himself will always be with them [as their God]" (21:3). The Lord, God-with-us, will console—that is, liberate—the people. " 'He will wipe every tear from their eyes, and there shall be no more death or mourning, wailing or pain, [for] the old order has passed away.' The one who sat on the throne said, 'Behold, I make all things new' " (21:4).

The day of Yahweh will, in the final analysis, be a state of communion with God and of fellowship among human beings; these two conditions are two aspects of the one reality. No suffering, no death; only joy, as the passage in Isaiah had said. This new world reflects the gratuitousness of the love of the God who even now is present to the history of the human race.

2. THIS IS THE TIME OF FULFILLMENT

At the beginning of his Gospel, Mark gives us a summary of the preaching of Jesus: "After John had been arrested, Jesus came to Galilee proclaiming the gospel of God: 'This is the time of fulfillment. The kingdom of God is at hand. Repent, and believe in the gospel' " (Mk 1:14–15). The scene is a short one, as all are in Mark, but every word counts. Let me follow it step by step.

From Galilee

John, "the voice . . . crying in the desert," had announced the coming of the Messiah and preached "a baptism of repentance" (Mk 1:3–4). For his preaching he was arrested by King Herod, a collaborator with the Roman occupation who saw it as a challenge to his power and privileges. Mark connects the mission of Jesus with that of the Baptist: "After John had been arrested. . . ." The Evangelist wants to let us know, in an unobtrusive way, that the work of Jesus will likewise meet with resistance from the powerful of his time. He too will encounter hostility leading to the arrest and death of the Messiah. The Evangelist is giving notice in advance of the price to be paid for a mission that has hardly begun.[6]

"Jesus came to Galilee." That is where Jesus has lived, and it is from there that he preaches the reign of God to the entire world.[7] Galilee was an unimportant region of the country. All but ignored in the Old Testament, it is called "the District of the Gentiles" in Isaiah 8:23 (a text cited in Mt 4:15–16); the Gospels, however, will speak of it often. It was a region looked down upon by the inhabitants of Judea, where Jerusalem was located. Galilee was a provincial area, close to pagan populations, which influenced its speech and distinctive accent (later on, the bystanders in the high priest's courtyard will say to Peter: "Surely you too are one of them; even your speech gives you away": Mt 26:73), its customs, and its quite unorthodox religious practices. Nothing good could come from Galilee: of this all good Jews were convinced. When Nicodemus tries to defend Jesus, the Pharisees say to him: "You are not from Galilee also, are you? Look and see that no prophet arises from Galilee" (Jn 7:52). Thus Jesus, a Galilean (Nazareth was in Galilee), proclaims his message in a place that was unimportant and marginal. It is from among the poor and despised that the message comes of the universal love that the God of Jesus Christ has for humankind.[8]

This mission brings Jesus into confrontation with the great men of his people, who live in Judea and specifically in Jerusalem. They are worried by this preacher who goes about in the peripheral areas of their land, and have sent spies to listen to what he says and observe what he does, and also to oppose him (see Mk 2–3).[9] Jesus is aware that this confrontation is unavoidable and that Jerusalem, the center of religious and political power in his nation, will be the place where he is to suffer. There, in Judea, they will use violence in their effort to prevent him from spreading his proclamation of the kingdom: "From that time on, Jesus began to show his disciples that he must go to Jerusalem and suffer greatly from the elders, the chief priests, and the scribes, and be killed and on the third day be raised" (Mt 16:21). Pilate will call attention to the Galilean origin of Jesus by having the inscription on the cross read "Jesus the Nazorean, the King of the Jews" (Jn 19:19).

"The gospel [or: good news] of God" is what Jesus preaches. Only in the light of who this man is is it possible to grasp the scope of his message; that is, only in light of the fact that the Son of God himself has taken flesh in the midst of human history (see Jn 1:14). In the history that Jesus makes his own, the proclamation of the kingdom is heard from the lips of those who are not listened to and who struggle for life and for recognition as human beings: the lips of the poor and the marginalized. Jesus begins his mission in Galilee; it is there that he recruits his closest followers. In Galilee, too, the risen Christ makes his appearance (see Mk 16:7), and from there his witnesses go forth to make "disciples of all nations" (Mk 16:15–16 and Mt 28:19).[10]

In this same history, which we share with Jesus, the powerful and the privileged resist hearing the call and suppress those who, like John or Jesus and his followers, bear witness to "the kingdom [of God] and his righteousness" (Mt 6:33). And they have continued to bear witness. In our own time we remember, every March, the murder of Bishop Oscar Romero, a witness to the God of life. Since that day, his death has become an integral part of our celebration of the Lord's resurrection in Holy Week.

Bishop Romero's testimony helps us to understand that we must seek and proclaim life and liberation in Christ by walking the same stony and muddy paths that are walked by the marginalized and oppressed of Latin America. When the Lord comes to wipe away the tears (see Is 25:8 and Rv 7:17 and 21:4) we have shed because of our desire to share the sufferings of the poor, we will be able to show him that our feet too are dirtied. He will understand us, because even today, as he sits at the Father's right hand, some of Galilee's dust must still be on his feet.

The Kingdom Is at Hand

When Jesus comes to give his witness, "the time of fulfillment" has come. The day of the Lord has arrived.

The Bible uses mainly two Greek words for time: *chronos* and *kairos*. The first, in addition to being the name of a Greek divinity, came to signify the quantitative, measurable, controllable aspects of time. The reference was to temporal succession as a dimension of things that was dependent on the movement of the stars. The reality meant could be measured by the calendar and the clock: "on this date, at this hour." This is the aspect of time to which we are most accustomed and which we have made part of our everyday lives; it is chronological time. Our diaries remind us of it, sometimes painfully.

The second Greek word for time refers to something more complex. *Kairos* corresponds to a more qualitative outlook. It refers, that is, not so much to an hour or a date as to the element of human density, or, in other words, to historical significance, which is here in question. Something of this aspect of time also shows up in our everyday language, as, for example, "everyone's time comes," or when the military spoke of "D Day" just before the Allied invasion of Europe during the Second World War. In the Bible, *kairos* signifies a propitious moment, a favorable day, a time when the Lord becomes present and manifests himself. "Behold, now is a very acceptable time" (2 Cor 6:2; see also 1 Tm 6:15; Heb 1:7).

In the passage on which I have been commenting, Mark refers to this understanding of time and speaks therefore of *kairos* and not of *chronos*. In the sentence, "this is the time of fulfillment," the meaning is that a *kairos* has arrived and not simply that a date set in advance has been reached. The implication of *kairos* is that God is now being revealed in a special way in the history in which Jesus has involved himself. The revelation is the revelation of the kingdom. Nor is the kingdom something purely interior that occurs in the depths of our souls. No, it is something planned by God that occurs at the heart of a history in which human beings live and die and welcome or reject the grace that changes them from within. The reality of the kingdom manifests itself by way of a difficult process to which Jesus alludes with his mention of John and which, more importantly, is present today in the person of Jesus the Messiah. The kingdom of love and justice is God's plan for human history; it speaks, therefore, to the whole person.

Being a Christian means being attentive to this *kairos*, this special moment of God's self-manifestation in our here and now. It means discerning the signs of the times, as John XXIII called upon us to do on the eve of the Second Vatican Council. At issue here is the authentically prophetic dimension of all Christian life. The *kairos* calls upon us to heed the judgment of God on the situation in which the great majority of people live in Latin America and in our own country [Peru]. It calls upon us to be aware that a reaction against a state of things contrary to the kingdom of life is being signaled today by gestures of solidarity among the poor, by the testimony of Christian communities that are arising among the poor and marginalized people of this world, by expressions of respect for all dimensions of the human person, by the joy and hopefulness of the poor amid their suffering, by the way men and women are learning profound prayer amid the struggle for liberation. All these phenomena are signs of the presence of the kingdom in our own history.

The kingdom is a gift, a grace of God, but also a demand made upon us. Its nearness makes these two dimensions of it all the more urgent. The two together constitute what Mark elsewhere calls "the mystery of the kingdom of God" (4:11). "Mystery," here, does not mean something enigmatic and hidden, but an enveloping reality that cannot be manipulated and within which we determine the character and meaning of our lives.

The kingdom, which is the object of God's free and unmerited plan, is a dynamic reality that, for the followers of Jesus, gives history its final meaning. "Final meaning," however, does not mean that the kingdom is located at the chronological end of the historical process. Rather, it is something that is, if I may coin a word, "kairologically" at hand and in process of being brought to completion. This twofold aspect is captured in the term "eschatology," which refers both to the future and to the historical present or, in other words, to an event that is already present but has not yet attained to its full form. There is at work here a dynamic vision of history as set in motion by the gift of the kingdom.

On the other hand, and closely connected with the point just made, the kingdom of God brings with it the demand for certain kinds of behavior. The disciples of Jesus who accept the gift of the kingdom respond to it by a specific conduct. This is the ethical dimension of the kingdom. "Repent" is the demand that accompanies the gift of the kingdom and leads to a new kind of activity in relation to God and one's brothers and sisters. Repentance, or conversion, supposes a break, but above all it means entering upon a new, and indeed constantly new, way: "Believe in the gospel." To believe is to say "Amen" to God; it is to declare our fidelity and our acceptance of the kingdom and its demands.[11] The acceptance finds expression both in thanksgiving to God and in deeds done for our brothers and sisters. It is in this dialectic that the meaning of the kingdom emerges. The kingdom requires us to change our present reality, reject the abuses of the powerful, and establish relationships that are fraternal and just. When we behave thus, we are accepting the gift of the Lord's presence.

The "eschatological" perspective (understood simply as a reference to future realities) strips ethics of its historical density and leaves it occupied with formalities that have no concrete meaning in relation to others. Here an apparently exclusive concern with God in our lives masks a forgetfulness of the demands that the God of the Bible makes upon us in relation to our brothers and sisters. This was precisely Jesus' objection to the conception of the law represented by the Pharisees, those who at that time, as today, "strain out the gnat and swallow the camel" (Mt 23:24). The "Pharisees" are, for practical purposes, those who claim to comply with formally religious demands while at the same time exploiting and marginalizing the poor; who say they love God but do not take the side in history of those who are the privileged members of God's kingdom: the have-nots and the needy. St. John calls them liars (see 1 Jn 4:20)—that is, deniers of the Lord who told us that he is "the truth" (Jn 14:6).

A moralist approach, meanwhile, puts the emphasis on the rights that works give in relation to God. This is a position that can at best lead to a moral humanism again alien to the teaching of Jesus, for whom thanksgiving for the gift of the Father's love is at the center of his disciples' lives and expands their vision of history. Only when the gratuitousness of this love has been grasped is it possible to understand the imperious demand for works in behalf of the neighbor.

Accepting the kingdom of God means refusing to accept a world that instigates or tolerates the premature and unjust deaths of the poor. It means rejecting the hypocrisy of a society that claims to be democratic but violates the most elementary rights of the poor. It means rejecting the cynicism of the powerful of this world. To be a disciple one must proclaim the liberation of captives and good news to the poor (Lk 4:18–19); one must raise the hopes of a people that suffer age-old injustice. To accept the kingdom is to turn Mark's statement that "this is the time of fulfillment; the kingdom of God is at hand" into an inchoative historical reality. It is to find God in the dynamism that this *kairos* infuses into human history.

3. SEEKING THE KINGDOM AND THE RIGHTEOUSNESS OF GOD

At the heart of the chapters of Matthew that we know as the Sermon on the Mount, there is an exhortation that underscores the unqualified place of the kingdom in the lives of believers: "Seek first the kingdom [of God] and his righteousness, and all these things will be given you besides" (Mt 6:33). The God of whose kingdom and righteousness the text speaks is the heavenly Father, as he is called in verse 32, whose providential love takes care of our lives: "Your heavenly Father knows that you need them all." We seek, then, the kingdom and righteousness of *God*; to seek them is to try to find the Father who dwells in them.[12]

The Signs of God's Presence

The words "seek" and "find" go logically together. In the Bible they are used chiefly in relation to God. Of the various nuances that the term "seek" has in the Old Testament, one is especially important: "seeking" is not a purely intellectual act but an existential attitude that involves the different dimensions of the human person.

The prophets often use the image. In their indictments we frequently meet both the complaint that Israel has not sought its God and the exhortation to do so. But in the view of the prophets there is no seeking of God without a determination to establish what is right and just. Jesus adopts the same perspective when he calls upon his hearers to seek God by accepting God's kingdom and practicing God's justice or righteousness. The same word that was used for the anxious search of the pagans for temporal goods (see Mt 6:32) is now used for the joyful and resolute longing for the kingdom that should characterize the disciples. The latter are not engaged in a vague and restless quest, for in the person of Jesus the kingdom and righteousness of God are offered to human beings.

When Jesus speaks in Matthew's Gospel of seeking the kingdom and righteousness of God, he is calling attention to the demand that the seeking implies. I refer to the effort required for all attentive and responsive waiting. Watchfulness marks the attitude of the disciple who looks for the Lord's return. In Matthew watchfulness expresses an active, responsible hope; it is a characteristic element of his thinking. The parables of the steward (Mt 24:45ff.), the ten virgins (Mt 25:1ff.), and the talents (Mt 25:14ff.) emphasize the same theme. In addition, watchfulness implies an active generosity that causes the blessings of the kingdom to bear fruit.

To seek the kingdom and righteousness means, then, to wait for it, but to wait for it actively. Thus the significance of righteousness or justice is reinforced, since the disciple, while waiting, practices justice and attentiveness to the poor. Such a practice is seen as the attitude proper to the disciple who accepts the kingdom.

In Matthew's Gospel we find a strong emphasis on the demands of the kingdom. This is not because Matthew fails to recognize the element of gratuitousness proper to the kingdom (the parable of the merciless servant, for example, brings out the two aspects—gift and demand—of the kingdom; see Mt 18:23–35); rather it is because he is so concerned with the active fidelity of the disciples in the church and in the world.

Seeking and waiting look forward to finding. In Matthew, what is found is the kingdom of God, and when this happens it is always a gift that relativizes the importance of other aspects of our lives (Mt 13:44–46). The kingdom that is sought is already present among us, not fully, however, but in an inchoative form that makes us hungry for the full reality. The signs of the kingdom speak to us of the historical presence of the kingdom but at the same time they open us to a future.

Signs have two aspects to which it is worth calling attention. On the one hand, they invite us to know the reality signified; through signs a revelation reaches us, in this case the revelation of the kingdom. On the other hand, signs are a call to commitment, a summons to make our own the demands of the kingdom. Both aspects make clear the historical dimension of the kingdom. The kingdom becomes known as already present in history and at the same time it challenges us by calling us to conversion.

In the New Testament one sign of the kingdom is the community that develops around Jesus, for the existence of this believing people is evidence that God is acting in history. The community is a sign inasmuch as it is a messianic people, the people of the Messiah who on his historical journey makes the kingdom known through what has been called the "messianic inversion." Let me explain this.

The messianic inversion finds expression in, for example, the statement of the gospel that "the last shall be first" (Mt 20:16).[13] Such an assertion contradicts the value system of this world, in which the poor and the little folk do not count. The ecclesial community, the messianic people, show forth the gratuitousness of God's love precisely in the measure that they promote in history the creative presence of the poor. The freely given and unmerited love of God is proclaimed by speaking of the poor and their needs, their rights and dignity, their culture, and, above all, of the God who wants to place them at the center of the history of the church.

Paul brought out this truth with incomparable power. In his first letter to the community in the wealthy city of Corinth, the Apostle explains that neither "the wisdom of the wise" nor "the learning of the learned" (1 Cor 1:19) will enable human beings to grasp the plan of God. What is being rejected here is the claims of the experts, who are proud of their knowledge. Matthew (11:25–26) would later echo the same passage from Isaiah (29:14) that Paul is citing here. What is needed, instead, is a genuine understanding of the word; by God's grace, this will come from a Christian community made up of the least members of society. Paul appeals to the experience of those to whom he is writing: "Consider your own calling, brothers. Not many of you were wise by human standards, not many were powerful, not many were of noble birth" (1 Cor 1:26).

We need to look into one another's faces to grasp the truth of Paul's assertion. It is due not to random chance but to a calling, a grace of the Lord, that we realize that "the last shall be first." "Rather, God chose the foolish of the world to shame the wise, and God chose the weak of the world to shame the strong, and God chose the lowly and despised of the world, those who count for nothing, to reduce to nothing those who are something" (1 Cor 1:27–28).

This only emphasizes the fact that everything comes from God. It is to this that the church is called, for it is made up of the unimportant folk of history and is committed to them. "So that no human being might boast before God. It is due to him that you are all in Christ Jesus, who became for us wisdom from God, as well as righteousness, sanctification, and redemption, so that, as it is written, 'Whoever boasts, should boast in the Lord'" (1 Cor 1:29–31).

Being a creative sign of the kingdom is a permanent requirement of the church's spirituality and pastoral method. To the extent that the church creates room for freedom and participation, respect and dialogue, committed love and shared forgiveness, the defense and care of life, it gives birth to a new people, a new creature; it acts as the leaven that, placed in the world, causes the new creation to come into being.

But this birth is not a painless one. If we are to make our way today in the history of our country, we must rebuild it starting from Ayacucho in the forgotten mountain country and marginalized jungle; from the alleys and slums of Lima; from the desperation of the poor and their lack of resources; from their right to life and to a peace that is based on justice; from the creativity of the poor and their power in history. All this confronts the ecclesial community with an increasingly radical demand that it be a sign of the kingdom of life, and this in a shifting and confused setting in which violence and terror, repression and affliction, but also hope and prophetic energy, are intermingled.

The Kingdom Judges the Church

The struggle against death in which the Lord engages in his risen life holds a central place in the Apocalypse. It is the setting in which the church carries out its mission as a sign of the kingdom. Death and its servants have already been conquered: "They did not prevail and there was no longer any place for them in heaven" (Rv 12:8). The contest continues on earth during the time of the Christian community, but it must be inspired by the conviction that victory has already been won:

> Then I saw a new heaven and a new earth. The former heaven and the former earth had passed away, and the sea was no more. I also saw the holy city, a new Jerusalem, coming down out of heaven from God, prepared as a bride adorned for her husband. I heard a loud voice from the throne saying, "Behold, God's dwelling is with the human race. He will dwell with them and they will be his people and God himself will always be with them [as their God]. He will wipe away every tear from their eyes, and there shall be no more death or mourning, wailing or pain, [for] the old order has passed away." [Rv 21:1–4]

It is the task of the church to bear witness to this dwelling and this new world; in this way it proclaims the kingdom in which the Lord makes himself present in human history. It is in the carrying out of this mission that the community of Jesus' disciples is built up. As the bishops said at Puebla:

> The core of Jesus' message is the proclamation of the Kingdom, which is coming and is rendered present in Jesus himself. Though it is not a reality detachable from the Church (LG:8), it transcends the Church's visible bounds (LG:5). For it is to be found in a certain way wherever God rules through his grace and love, wherever he is overcoming sin and helping human beings to grow toward the great communion offered them in Christ. This activity of God is also in the hearts of human beings who live outside the perceptible sphere of the Church (LG:16; GS:22; UR:3). But that definitely does not mean that membership in the Church is a matter of indifference. [Puebla 226]

This action of the Lord is also the reason for the believer's hope in times of crisis. The church, which is the community of Christ's disciples, is a sign of the kingdom to the extent that it allows its historical activity to be judged by the kingdom. This judgment is not rendered only at the end of history. It begins now.

The judgment passed by God shows clearly that the gift of the kingdom creates demands upon us. The object that is judged is in practice a conduct. "I know your works," says the Lord to each of the seven churches of the Apocalypse (see chapters 2 and 3). The criteria of God's judgment are provided by the nature of the kingdom, which is a kingdom of peace, love, and justice. Matthew reminds us of the christological and historical dimensions of the judgment (see his chapter 25). Like each individual, the church as a whole is judged by its relation to Christ. And it is works of justice, solidarity, and love that give content to this relation.

The kingdom urges the church to move constantly forward, for it is a utopia that has already begun to become a reality but has not yet attained its full form. The process goes on in history, but its completion will come beyond history. The deepest meaning of historical events for believers is that in and through them they receive the kingdom of God. This reception builds up the community of the followers of Jesus.

Skepticism and submissive resignation in the face of historical events are not Christian attitudes, because they take no account of hope. One of the tasks of the prophets was to feed the hopes of the people in times of crisis. This tradition was continued by the author of the Apocalypse, which is addressed to Christian communities that are bowed under the weight of persecution and of the death that the great empire of the day was entering. The church has a like duty today during this difficult time for Latin America and our country. The challenge to the church is to live by a hope that is rooted in the concrete history of a people who are at once oppressed and believing, and that is inspired by the plan of the kingdom, which urges us on to something new and different.

If the church breaks its links with the kingdom, it will by that very act lose its transcendent purpose and its ability to be critical of the present. It will submissively adapt itself to situations or will try to come to grips with them in terms of its earthly interests and not of the demands of God or the needs of the poor. In other words, it will lose its hope in the God who "makes all things new" (Rv 21:5).

The cultivation of the required critical attitude to all historical fulfillments prevents the intended kingdom from being watered down into history. The steady assertion of hope at ill-omened junctures justifies our faith in life as the final word in human development. The church is not identical with the kingdom, but it must bear witness to the kingdom by forming and organizing itself as a community; that is, by committing itself in the light of the kingdom, so that in that light it can pass judgment on history and also upon itself. For the Christian community and not simply for individual Christians, seeking the kingdom and righteousness means two things: trying to be a sign of the kingdom and accepting to be judged by the kingdom.

To the extent that the ecclesial community begets new persons thanks to a different kind of interrelationship—that is, to the real participation of all and to the respect for the life and freedom of the weakest that it promotes in its own midst—it creates a new style of human community marked by radically different ways of experiencing and understanding power. The domination and oppression that characterize power as exercised in this world are called into question by the attitude of service and the freedom that are signs that the kingdom of God has been received. The teaching of their master provides Christ's disciples with very demanding criteria for life within the community: "Whoever wishes to be first among you will be the slave of all. For the Son of Man did not come to be served but to serve and to give his life as a ransom for many" (Mk 10:44–45).

The text just cited is a further expression of what I called earlier the "messianic inversion." The Lord proclaimed freedom by serving, life by overcoming death. Christians, and the church as a whole, are to seek the kingdom and righteousness of God by entering into human history, lining up with the poor and oppressed, and finding the Lord in the faces of the most needy. Seeking the kingdom means being a sacrament of life amid the death that is among us today as a result of persistent structural violence, terrorist violence of various kinds, and the violence of indiscriminate repression. It means waiting for the definitive meeting with the God of life.

4. THE INTENDED RECIPIENTS OF THE KINGDOM

The God of the kingdom comes to meet us in history. Jesus proclaims him from Galilee and calls upon us to be converted and become seekers. If we know to whom this proclamation is addressed, it will be easier for us to find the God who is revealed in the will to life and love.

All Nations

As the reader may know, the expression "kingdom of God" occurs only late in the Old Testament, whereas the assertion that "Yahweh reigns" goes back to ancient times. The earliest psalms attest its use:

> God mounts his throne amid shouts of joy;
>   the Lord, amid trumpet blasts.
> Sing praise to God, sing praise;
>   sing praise to our king, sing praise.
> For king of all the earth is God;
>   sing hymns of praise.
> God reigns over the nations,
>   God sits upon his holy throne.
> The princes of the peoples are gathered together
>   with the people of the God of Abraham.
> For God's are the guardians of the earth;
>   he is supreme. [Ps 47:6–10; see Ps 24]

God's reign is universal, over the cosmos (see Ps 19 and 93) and over history (see Ps 44, 47, 95, 99). God reigns over all the nations; the reference here is not to a limited geographic area but to God's sovereignty throughout history. The prophets emphasized the ethical demands imposed by this reign, first on Israel and then gradually on all peoples. Jeremiah calls Yahweh "king of the nations" (Jer 10:7), and Second Isaiah becomes champion of God's universal will to salvation as evidenced in the mission of the servant of Yahweh: "I will make you a light to the nations, that my salvation may reach to the ends of the earth" (Is 49:6).

It is for this very reason that the prophets oppose the institution of kingship. The controversy over the monarchy became violent at times; the reason for the opposition of the prophets is that in the eyes of those who represent the tradition of Israel, Yahweh alone is king. The Jewish people acquires the monarchy it asks for (see 1 Sm 8:1–9), but the opposition of the prophet nonetheless achieves one undeniable result: the kings of Israel are never divinized like those of neighboring peoples.

In the Bible God is repeatedly called Lord of the entire universe. In the prayer that Jesus teaches his disciples, after the petition "your kingdom come" Matthew adds words that reinforce the idea of that petition: "Your will be done on earth as it is in heaven" (Mt 6:10). The sovereignty of Jesus Christ has the same range: "All power in heaven and on earth has been given to me" (Mt 28:18).

The preaching of the gospel is directed to all without exception: "Go into the whole world and proclaim the gospel to every creature" (Mk 16:16). The Gospel of Matthew puts it forcefully: "Make disciples of all nations" (Mt 28:19). Conversion to the kingdom reaches the four corners of the world: "People will come from the east and the west and from the north and the south, and will recline at table in the kingdom of God" (Lk 13:29). All nations will be subjected to the judgment of the king.

There are many texts in the gospel like the ones I have just cited. The message is clear: the proclamation of the kingdom of God is directed to all; no one is excluded from either the gift or its demands. Therefore the Samaritan woman, who does not belong to the Jewish people, bears witness to the Lord before her own people: "Come see a man who told me everything I have done. Could he possibly be the Messiah?" (Jn 4:29). Luke, in whose gospel Samaritans play an important part, tells us that only one of the ten lepers healed by Jesus returned to give thanks; Jesus says to him: "Your faith has saved you" (Lk 17:19). The love of the Lord embraces even those scorned by the Jewish people.

Paul is the apostle of the universality of the message. The basis of this universality is the resurrection of Christ. If the Lord's message is universal, if it acknowledges no boundaries, it is because its starting point is the conquest of death, which is the greatest limitation set on human beings. The resurrection is thus an affirmation and promise of life for all human beings without exception. At the bottom of it all is the gratuitous love of God, which manifests itself in the gift of definitive life:

But if Christ is preached as raised from the dead, how can some among you say there is no resurrection of the dead? If there is no resurrection of the dead, then neither has Christ been raised. And if Christ has not been raised, then empty [too] is our preaching; empty, too, is your faith. Then we are also false witnesses to God, because we testified against God that he raised Christ, whom he did not raise if in fact the dead are not raised. For if the dead are not raised, neither has Christ been raised, your faith is vain; you are still in your sins. [1 Cor 15:12–17]

The followers of Jesus are witness to the resurrection. It was this testimony that brought together, and still brings together, the ecclesial assembly. That is why it is so important for our faith and our preaching. It is important to observe that the passage just cited is addressed to the community of Corinth, which was influenced by the dualist mentality of the Greeks, according to which the body is of no great importance because it is simply as it were a casing for the soul. People with this outlook regarded any talk of the resurrection of the body as absurd. Paul responds forcefully: if Christ did not rise from the dead, we are false witnesses. Furthermore, the resurrection of Christ is not an isolated occurrence, but has as its consequence the resurrection of every other human being. Paul's argument is an affirmation of life. Solidarity in the resurrection includes solidarity in the body. This is a basic insight in Paul's thinking, and he sets it down with the authority of a witness and an apostle.

The theme of the risen Christ is so central in Paul that some have thought to see in him a lack of concern for the historical Jesus. This is incorrect. Although Pauline references to the historical Jesus are brief and restrained (perhaps because in dealing with these communities he did not have to mention details, these being already sufficiently familiar), the importance that the idea of the body has for Paul shows that this point is essential to his message and to the connection with the historical Jesus. Christ rises with the body of the historical Jesus. Jesus was the Son of God made flesh—that is, a human being, or a "body" in the biblical understanding of the word.[14]

The idea of body is important if we are to grasp the scope of resurrection in Paul. It is the reason why in his view to be a Christian means being incorporated into Christ and why he calls the church the body of Christ. This accurate, concrete language shows how and under what conditions Christians are witnesses to the resurrection. Paul's is a message of life for every human being and for the whole of creation, which groans in its longing for the freedom of the children of God (see Rom 8:20–21). Because it overcomes the bounds set by death, the resurrection of Christ is a message of life that carries the stamp of universality. This universality is a basic characteristic of witness given to the resurrection of the Lord.

The Last Will Be First

In a parable that he alone gives us (20:1–16), Matthew contrasts the first and the last, and in so doing highlights the utter freedom of God's love over against a narrow conception of justice. The decision of the landowner to pay a full day's wages to those who come to work in the vineyard only as the day is ending, at the eleventh hour, elicits a reaction from those who had been there from early morning: "They grumbled against the landowner, saying, 'These last ones worked only one hour, and you have made them equal to us, who bore the day's burden and the heat.' " To them, equal treatment smacks of injustice. The landowner rejects the accusation: "Did you not agree with me for the usual daily wage? Take what is yours and go." The justice of God transcends the established practice in human justice. It takes into account the deeper needs of human beings, of those who against their will "stood all the day idle" because no one had hired them. The workers who came at the eleventh hour had, after all, the same right to work as the first ones hired and to support themselves and their families by their toil. This is something we can readily understand in a country like ours, which has so many unemployed and underemployed.

But there is more to the parable. The Lord says: "What if I wish to give this last one the same as you?" He then asks the grumblers some pointed questions: "Am I not free to do what I wish with my own money? Are you envious because I am generous?" This is the real issue. A literal translation of "are you envious?" would be "is your eye evil?" The phrase is revealing, for in the Semitic mentality it means a look that is grim and envious (the phrase occurs in Mt 6:23 and Mk 7:22 with the same meaning). This is a look that turns reality to stone, that has no place for anything new, leaves no room for generosity, and, above all, claims to set bounds to God's goodness. It is the look we cast around us to protect our property and prerogatives, even if this means impoverishing and marginalizing others. This outlook makes us think that what is just for others is unjust for us if it affects our privileges. Believers in a good God who loves without limits must avoid the "evil eye." The parable contains a clear teaching about the heart of the biblical message: the utter freedom of God's love. This freedom alone can explain his preference for the weakest and the oppressed.

"Thus"—in the way just described in the parable—"the last will be first, and the first will be last" (v. 16).[15] Often, only half the sentence is quoted: "The last will be first"; we forget that for the same reason the first will be last. We have here an idea that is couched in the form of an antithesis; the terms of the contrast shed light on each other and therefore cannot be separated. The Gospels constantly speak in this fashion when referring to those for whom the kingdom is intended; they speak of those who will enter the kingdom proclaimed by Jesus, but at the same time they tell us who cannot enter. This kind of antithesis conveys a profound revelation of the God of the kingdom. Let me go more fully into this point by citing some examples.

1) In Luke the beatitudes are followed by a set of woes. Everyone is familiar with the text:

> And raising his eyes toward his disciples he said:
> "Blessed are you who are poor,
>   for the kingdom of God is yours.
> Blessed are you who are now hungry,
>   for you will be satisfied.
> Blessed are you who are now weeping,
>   for you will laugh. . . .

But woe to you who are rich,
  for you have received your consolation.
But woe to you who are filled now,
  for you will be hungry.
Woe to you who laugh now,
  for you will grieve and weep."
        [Lk 6:20–21, 24–25][16]

According to the majority of exegetes, the words "his disciples" should be taken in a broad sense and not restricted to the twelve. The exegetes appeal to, among other things, what Luke says at the end of the Sermon on the Plain: "When he had finished all his words to the people, he entered Capernaum" (7:1).

Isaiah provides an important source for the first three beatitudes in Luke, namely, 61:1–2, a text that, as we saw earlier, has inspired other passages of the gospels (see Lk 14:16–20; 7:18–23; Mt 11:2–6).[17] Woes, or curses, for their part, occur frequently in the Old Testament and help us to comprehend the demands made by God[18] (see, for example, Is 1:4–9; 5:8–23; Am 5:7–6:14).

The Greek word used here for the "poor" is *ptochoi*, and its meaning is not in doubt. Etymologically, *ptochos* means "one who is stooped," "one who is frightened"; the word is used to signify the needy, those who must beg in order to live and whose existence, therefore, depends on others; these are defenseless people. The connotation of social and economic inferiority is already present in the Hebrew words that *ptochos* translates in the Septuagint. Scholars who have studied the matter agree that *ptochos* is used in fundamentally the same sense in the New Testament.[19]

The situation of the rich, who have already received their consolation, is quite different.[20] Here again, the meaning of "rich" is clear: they are the possessors of substantial material goods. Luke often contrasts them with the poor: in the parable, for example, of the rich man and poor Lazarus, in which, as I observed, it is not the rich man but the representatives of the nameless folk of history who are given a name (16:19–31); or in the passage on the vanity of important people and their oppression of the poor (20:46–47).

Among the passages that make use of this contrast it will be worth our while to call attention to the exquisite one that speaks of the widow's mite:

When he looked up he saw some wealthy people putting their offering into the treasury and he noticed a poor widow putting in two small coins. He said, "I tell you truly, this poor widow put in more than all the rest; for these others have all made offerings from their surplus wealth, but she, from her poverty has offered her whole livelihood" [Lk 21:1–4].

Jesus is in the temple, the heart of religious, economic, and political power in Jerusalem. In this place ("he sat down opposite the treasury," says the parallel passage in Mk 12:41), the Lord proceeds to watch the believers who come to the temple to pray, as they place their alms in the box. The wealthy put a great deal in (see Mk 12:41); a widow (we are reminded of the three types of poor in the Old Testament: widows, orphans, strangers) puts in "two small coins." In the eyes of this acute observer who looks beyond appearances, this is not an everyday event. He reads reality in light of the message about the kingdom that he himself proclaims. The master then shows his disciples the meaning of what is happening. The widow's action seems insignificant to eyes not illumined by faith, but in Jesus' eyes her alms is worth more than that of the ostentatious rich, who give only of their surplus. For the widow gives what is in fact necessary for her livelihood. God is more important to her than to the wealthy.

Let me return to the beatitudes. We also find there a contrast between the hungry and the satisfied. The Greek word that Luke uses for "hungry" (*peinountes*), like the Hebrew terms that this Greek word translates in the Septuagint, shows that not just any hunger is meant but rather a hunger that takes possession of persons like a deep-seated and prolonged illness. The lack of food here is chronic. "Starving" would therefore be a better translation than "hungry." The starving will be satisfied (Matthew uses the same verb as Luke to express this satisfaction or satiety). The satisfied, on the other hand, those who are fully satiated, are the equivalent of the rich in the first beatitude. For this reason, the song that Luke puts on Mary's lips sets up an expressive contrast between the rich and the hungry (Lk 1:53). In fact, Luke often associates poverty and hunger, on the one hand, and wealth and abundance of food, on the other (see Lk 16:19–31).

Those who weep (in the third beatitude) are people who experience a grief keen enough to force its outward expression. Tears are an expression of feeling to which Luke is especially sensitive (he uses the verb "to weep" eleven times). Here again, we are not dealing with a passing distress but with profound suffering resulting from a permanent marginalization. On the other hand, the New Testament makes few references to laughter. Laughter can be a legitimate expression of joy (6:21), but it can also manifest a prosperity that forgets the sufferings of others and is based on privilege (6:25).

The situations reflected here are real situations (including social and economic situations) of poverty and wealth, hunger and satiety, suffering and self-satisfaction. The kingdom of God is promised to those who live in conditions of weakness and oppression (and to those also who share their lives out of solidarity with them). The entrance of others into the kingdom will be more difficult than "for a camel to pass through the eye of a needle" (Lk 18:25).[21]

2) The Gospels tell us of various ways in which the despised and unim-

portant people gain access to the kingdom and to knowledge of the word of God.

When the Lord cautions his disciples: "Let the children come to me . . . for the kingdom of heaven belongs to such as these" (Mt 19:14), we quickly think of the docility and trustfulness of children. If we do, we fail to see how radical the message of Jesus is. In the cultural world of Judaism at that time, children were regarded as incomplete human beings; along with the poor, the sick, and women, they were counted among the unimportant folk. This outlook shocks our modern sensibilities, but there is a great deal of evidence that it existed.[22] To be "such as these," like children, meant therefore to be insignificant, to be someone on whom society set no value. Children are close neighbors to the little ones and the ignorant to whom God the Father has willed to be revealed (Mt 11:25) and in whom we meet Christ himself (Mt 25:31–46).

Over against these stand "the wise and the learned" (Mt 11:25). These are the people who have taken possession of "the key of knowledge" (Lk 11:52) and are contemptuous of the common people, the *'am ha-ares*, whom they regard as ignorant and immoral ("this crowd which does not know the law": Jn 7:49). The gospel describes these people as "simple" (Mt 11:25 REB), using the Greek word *nepioi* (literally: little children), which clearly connotes ignorance and lack of sophistication.

Here again we are in the presence of real social situations, of levels of religious knowledge. To be ignorant is not a virtue; to be wise is not a fault. The preference for the simple is not due to their moral and spiritual dispositions but to their human weakness and to the scorn of which they are the object.[23]

3) The parable about the guests invited to the banquet, which is recorded by Matthew (22:2–10) and Luke (14:15–24), would better be called the parable of the uninvited, since these are in fact the focus of its message. The exegetes are increasingly abandoning what used to be a common interpretation of the passage, according to which it is about Israel that was called and then rejected because of its sins and about the non-Israelites who are called in its stead.

The tendency today is to see in those first called the important folk who combined social position and knowledge of the law, and in the second group those to whom Jesus prefers to address his message—namely, the poor and needy—whom the religious leaders of the Jewish people regard as ignorant and sinful.[24] Matthew even says something surprising: "The servants went out into the streets and gathered all they found, bad and good alike, and the hall was filled with guests" (22:10). "*Bad* and good," in that order. Once again, there is no question of moral deserts, but only of the objective situation of "the poor and the crippled, the blind and the lame," as Luke describes them (Lk 14:21). The same list of persons was mentioned a little earlier in the advice Jesus gave to "one of the leading Pharisees" (Lk 14:1) who had invited him to dinner—namely, that in giving his invitations he should prefer the least of society, those "far off," those who are "unable to repay" (14:14).

4) Jesus insists that he has come not for the righteous but for sinners, not for the healthy but for the sick (see Mk 2:17 par.). Once again we see an antithesis used in describing the addressees of his message. On this occasion he speaks ironically, for are there in fact any upright and healthy people who do not need his saving love?[25] The "righteous" here are those who claim to be sinless, the "healthy," those who think they do not need God. In fact, despite the show of respect they receive in society, these people are the greatest sinners, filled as they are with pride and self-sufficiency. Who, then, are the sinners and the sick for whom the Lord comes? In keeping with what has just been said about the righteous and the healthy, the sinners and the sick are those despised by the important people of the social and religious world.[26]

As I said earlier, those who suffered from some serious illness or some bodily deformity were regarded as sinners (see John 9). This is why lepers, for example, were cut off from the life of society; Jesus reincorporated them into that life when he restored their physical health. On the other hand, public sinners, such as tax collectors and prostitutes, were also regarded as the scum of society. This status of theirs, and not their moral or religious character, is what gave them priority in the love and affection of Jesus. This is why he tells the mighty among his people: "Tax collectors and prostitutes are entering the kingdom of God before you" (Mt 21:31). The gratuitousness of God's love constantly surprises.

The Motive for God's Preference

We must acknowledge that this antithetical presentation of those for whom the kingdom is intended disconcerts us. Accustomed as we are to a religious perspective based on merits and rewards, sins and punishments, the God who loves the poor because they are poor bewilders us. And yet the Gospels are clear on this point: the despised of this world are the ones whom the Lord prefers. The way in which God's gratuitous love manifests itself transforms our norms and values.

The proclamation of the kingdom is a revelation about God; it is a message about God's free and unmerited love, which does not depend on the moral and religious dispositions of its addressees.[27] At Puebla the bishops echoed this outlook when they wrote: in Christ "the poor merit preferential attention, whatever may be the moral or personal situation in which they find themselves" (1142). This perspective has deep biblical roots,[28] and sets us before the mystery of God and God's will to life.

God's preference for the poor, the oppressed, the unimportant runs throughout the Bible. A few years back, L. Alonso Schökel gave us a searching and beautiful interpretation of a biblical passage that we thought we knew well. I am referring to the relationship between Cain and Abel. Starting with a key question, which the text itself already suggests: "What did

Cain do to explain God's attitude toward him?" the author proposes that Genesis 4:4–5 is not correctly understood as meaning an acceptance of the sacrifice of Abel and a rejection of that of Cain. The harsh turn of phrase used here occurs frequently in the Bible, but it would be accurate to say the following:

> The Hebrew expression translated as "looked with favor/did not look with favor" here conveys a comparison and a preference. The issue is not acceptance and rejection, but simply a preference for the younger brother. . . . And if we insist on asking: "Why does God prefer Abel?" we must perhaps fall back on a constant principle which God applies freely: he prefers Abel precisely because he is the younger. The same is true of Isaac and Jacob and Joseph and David. The motive is in fact one found in the Bible, even though many purely human considerations might be adduced against it. God wanted to establish and reveal this pattern right from the beginning.[29]

God looked with favor on Abel (whose name means "vapor," "something light"), not in order to spurn Cain, but rather to force the latter to think about his younger brother, communicate with him, and protect him.[30] It is clear that Cain did not accept this preference for Abel. The rejection of the free and unmerited love of God, who prefers the poor, and thus turns into the attitude of a Cain.

God's preferential option for the poor, the weak, the least members of society, runs throughout the Bible and cannot be understood apart from the absolute freedom and gratuitousness of God's love. The ways of God are not our ways (see Is 55:8). For God, therefore, "the last will be first, and the first will be last." The God of biblical revelation is not satisfied to ask for a righteousness that is legal or formal. God's love, and therefore what God demands of us, leaps over these boundaries and goes out in a free and generous search of those whom society marginalizes and oppresses. We must be always open to the freshness and creativity of God's love. Gratuitousness is not the realm of the arbitrary or the superfluous; it is not opposed to, nor does it denigrate the search for righteousness; on the contrary, it gives this search its true meaning. There is nothing more demanding than freely given, unmerited love.

Universality and preference mark the proclamation of the kingdom. God addresses a message of life to every human being without exception, while at the same time God shows preference for the poor and the oppressed. God's "unconditional and passionate" option "always against the proud, always in favor of those to whom these rights are denied or from whom they are taken" (the words are those of Karl Barth, one of the great theologians of the twentieth century[31]), must not make us forget that God's love is limitless and reaches to all. It is not easy to preserve both universality and preference, but that is the challenge we must meet if we would be faithful to the God of the kingdom that Jesus proclaims—namely, to be able to love every human being while retaining a preferential option for the poor and the oppressed.[32]

The gratuitous love of God requires that we establish an authentic justice for all, while giving privileged place to a concern for the unimportant members of society—that is, for those whose rights are not recognized either in theory (by a set of laws) or in practice (in the way society conducts itself).

Do we not witness this in, for example, the scandalous treatment of the poor peasants of Ayacucho? They are a population that not only lives in cruel poverty but is caught in the crossfire of terrorist violence on the one side and repressive violence on the other. Their bodies disappear, be they themselves still alive or already corpses; their families weep over these scandalous absences. Every day we see their faces, the mistreatment they endure, and their protests appearing in the newspapers or on the television screen, as though they belonged to a different world than ours. There is perhaps something valid in this feeling, for in reality they do form part of a universe that on alleged political grounds—terrorist subversion or the maintenance of "order"—has been declared a wasteland, a no man's land, a place where no laws hold and there is no respect for the most basic human rights. The inhabitants of this world meet with indifference, or scruples of conscience unaccompanied by any resolution to do better or the cynicism of the official world. The display of their sufferings makes up the most gruesome hour on national television.

"The last will be first," says the gospel. This is not a frivolous and manipulative political slogan; it sets before us a radical demand. It gives us to understand that our countries will not produce justice unless they take as their starting point compassion ("fellow feeling") for those who today are marginalized and oppressed by political structures and laws that are of benefit to, and defend, the privileges of the "first" of society. Without justice there is no true peace.

The unemployed, the poor, the blind, the crippled, public sinners, Ayacuchan Indians, landless peasants, populations looking for shelter: these are the least members of history. Therefore they are the first objects of the tender love of the God of Jesus Christ. The justice of God is deep and true because it is steeped in gratuitousness. It is this justice that demands an authentic justice of us today.

CHAPTER VII

THE ETHICS OF THE KINGDOM

The kingdom is a gift but also a demand. It is a freely given gift of God and it calls for conformity to God's will to life. This is what is asked of disciples, that they live a life situated between gratuitousness and demand. The way to the Father requires that we make others our brothers and sisters. We receive the gift of sonship or daughterhood only when we create an authentic brotherhood and sisterhood among ourselves. The beatitudes in Matthew are therefore the Magna Carta of the congregation (the church) that is made up of the disciples of Jesus. Our following in his footsteps finds expression in actions toward our neighbor, especially the poor, in life-giving works; in these, love of God and love of neighbor are intertwined and call each for the other.

We shall not be able to shed light on the question: Where is God? unless we are able to answer the Lord's challenge: "Where is your brother?" (Gn 4:9). In this way we hasten history, as Hugo Echegaray put it[1]; that is, we cause the kingdom to come; we cause the *kairos* to arrive, not as something fated but as the result of the free acceptance of God's gift. Acting "as free people" (1 Pt 2:16 REB), by our behavior we "wait for and hasten the coming of the day of God" (2 Pt 3:12).

1. KINGDOM AND JUSTICE

After Peter's first sermon, on Pentecost, with its focus on the death and resurrection of the Lord, his hearers spontaneously ask: "What are we to do, my brothers?" Peter answers: "Repent" (Acts 2:37–38).[2] The Gospels lay down this same requirement from the first moment of the proclamation of the kingdom. Conversion means a change of behavior, a different approach to life, the beginning of a following of Jesus.

Between Gift and Demand

Discipleship is a central theme in the Gospel of Matthew; it is the central idea to which many of the actions and sayings of Jesus refer. Adding various traits, brightening the picture at one point, issuing warnings at another, Matthew sketches a portrait of those who follow the Lord.[3] In my view, this

118

characteristic of his Gospel is a key to understanding the meaning of his version of the beatitudes. This difference between his version and Luke's (which, as I mentioned, is regarded by scholars as closer to the words of Jesus) is commonly attributed to his effort to "spiritualize" the beatitudes, in the sense that he allegedly takes statements that in Luke were a concrete, historical expression of the coming of the Messiah and turns them into purely interior, unincarnated dispositions.

I do not think that this was the case. One reason, among others: it is undeniable that the Gospel of Matthew is especially insistent on the need of concrete, "material" actions toward others and especially the poor (see Mt 5:13–16; 7:15–22; and, beyond a doubt, 25:31–46). The least that can be said is that this insistence is incompatible with an alleged Matthean "spiritualism." The obvious contradiction between these two approaches would seem to be the result not of anything in Matthew but of applying to the first Gospel categories inconsistent with its real outlook. Let us try to enter into this outlook.

The beatitudes open the section of the Gospel known as the Sermon on the Mount, a lengthy, polemical presentation of the new law in its relationship to the old. The sermon sets down the main ethical demands a Christian must meet. It does not limit itself to a wearisome reminder of the law in which "it was said" (see Mt 5:21, 27, 31, 33, 38, 43), but puts the disciples on notice that they must continually seek new forms of loving others — that is, that they must fulfill the new law: "I say to you." Continuity, therefore, and newness. The Lord speaks here with the full authority with which he is invested. An ethics that has its roots in the gratuitousness of God's love is always creative. Christian Duquoc is right when he says that in the sermon "righteousness is linked to the order of gift and gratuitousness."[4]

The righteousness in question, which "surpasses that of the scribes and Pharisees" (Mt 5:20), is not limited to obeying precepts but draws its inspiration from an ever new and imaginative love. It leads us to the kingdom and makes the kingdom present even now in history. Kingdom and righteousness (gift and task) are the two key words that enable us to see the basic structure of the carefully constructed text that is the beatitudes. The first and last of these speak of the promise of the kingdom here and now (the other six beatitudes use the future tense). Each block of four beatitudes (containing thirty-six words in the Greek text) ends with the mention of righteousness or justice:

to the poor in spirit	belongs the kingdom of heaven
the meek	will inherit the earth
they who mourn	will be comforted
they who hunger and thirst for righteousness	will be satisfied
the merciful	will be shown mercy

the clean of heart	will see God
the peacemakers	will be called children of God
to them who are persecuted for	
the sake of righteousness	belongs the kingdom of heaven

The kingdom is the center of Jesus' message, the utopia that sets history in motion for Christians. As everyone knows, Matthew speaks of "the kingdom of heaven" in order to avoid mentioning the name of God, out of a respect that is inborn in the Jewish mind. Righteousness or justice is a theme closely connected with that of the kingdom.[5] I have already had occasion to point out its scope, and shall limit myself here to emphasizing its importance especially in the Sermon on the Mount but also throughout the Gospel of Matthew, which is alert to the duties of the followers of Jesus.

Matthew retains the richness and complexity of the term "justice" (= righteousness) in the Bible. Justice is the work of God and therefore must also be the work of those who believe in God. It implies a relationship with the Lord—namely, holiness; and at the same time a relationship with human beings—namely, recognition of the rights of each person and especially of the despised and the oppressed, or, in other words, social justice. In various ways, even when he is not using the word justice, Matthew reminds us of this demand of the kingdom: to do what is right and just. In a pithy summarizing statement, already cited, which comes right in the middle of the sermon, Matthew says forcefully: "Seek first the kingdom of God and his righteousness" (6:33).

The kingdom and its six specific descriptions are the reason for the happiness to which the beatitudes bear witness; in all of them this reason is clearly asserted: the people described are blessed or happy "because" the promise is fulfilled now and will be in the future. The gift of the Lord produces happiness in those who dispose themselves to receive it and who act accordingly. The beatitudes are clearly located in the dialectic of gift and demand.

Discipleship

The Matthean passage on the beatitudes can be said to have two distinct parts, although there are, of course, other ways of dividing the text.

1) The first group of beatitudes in Matthew is close to Luke's version, but in my opinion it attenuates somewhat the contrast found in Luke. The reason for this is a change of perspective.

A lot of ink has been lavished on the first beatitude. Matthew's addition "in spirit" has always been a subject of controversy. In both Matthew and Luke the word "poor" represents the Greek *ptochoi*. In Luke the persons referred to are—it is often said—poor in the literal, material sense. The Greek word used already points in this direction. Whom does Matthew have in mind when he adds "in spirit"?

In the biblical mind (and indeed the Semitic mind generally) the words "in spirit" are used to indicate a dynamism at work; the spirit is breath or vital force. It is something that manifests itself in knowledge, understanding, virtue, and decision-making. "Spirit" is the dynamic aspect of human existence.

The addition "in spirit" is often used in the Old Testament to change the original meaning of certain words, thereby giving them a figurative sense. For example, "lofty in spirit" (Prov 16:18) means "a haughty spirit" (NAB) or "arrogance" (REB); "lofty" or "high" describes a bodily condition, but the addition of "in spirit" directs our attention to a different human dimension. In like manner, "err in spirit" (Is 29:24) is to be understood as meaning that someone is on the wrong road; the strayer is a person who does not find the proper path. The addition, in this context, suggests someone who does not observe the commandments of God.[6]

"Poor in spirit" is an expression of that kind; it points to something more comprehensive than an attitude of detachment from material possessions. "In spirit" transforms an economic and social condition into a readiness to accept the word of God. We are, in fact, in the presence of a central theme in the biblical message: spiritual childhood.[7] The reference is to living as people fully open to the will of God; to making God's will our food, as Jesus says in the Gospel of John. This is the attitude of those who know that they are sons and daughters of God, and brothers and sisters to one another. To be poor in spirit is to be a disciple of Christ. This is the basic meaning.

I shall return to this point after briefly reviewing the other beatitudes. It is expedient, however, that I make one point right now. It has been suggested that Matthew's text be translated: "Blessed are they who choose to be poor."[8] The purpose is to preclude the spiritualist interpretation to which I referred earlier. The intention is praiseworthy, but the translation (apart from criticisms that might be made of it from the viewpoint of a literal analysis of the text) is somewhat inadequate and leaves an ambiguity. The choice of poverty underscores a dynamic aspect of Christian life and of solidarity with the least important persons of history (in this respect, the translation is successful). In my opinion, however, spiritual poverty refers to a more comprehensive and more radical outlook than the acceptance of real poverty or the cultivation of an attitude of interior distance from material possessions.

Accepting poverty is indeed a manifestation, and a very important one, of spiritual childhood, but discipleship is not limited to this. Discipleship means, above all, an openness to the gift of God's love and a preferential solidarity with the poor and oppressed; it is in this context, and in this context alone, that it makes sense to choose a life of poverty. Real poverty is, after all, not a Christian ideal but a condition required today of those who seek to be in solidarity with the really poor, with the unimportant folk—that is, those who lack the necessities of life, which their dignity as human beings and children of God requires. As Medellín reminded us, real poverty is, according to the Bible, an evil, a situation not intended by the God of life, an acceptance of means seeking to eliminate the injustice that causes the spoliation and mistreatment of the poor.[9] This effort necessarily presupposes a solidarity with their hopes and interests, friendship with them, and a sharing both of their lives and of their struggle for justice. This commitment and quest manifest an acceptance of God's will, and this acceptance in turn is the core of spiritual poverty or spiritual childhood; in other words, it is the essence of discipleship.

The second beatitude ("blessed are the meek"; in some versions, this is the third beatitude) is sometimes regarded as an elucidation of the first. Be that as it may, it is certain that the Hebrew words *'anaw* and *'ani'* (both meaning "poor") are also translated by the Greek word *praeis* (used here), which means "humble, meek." The source of this Matthean beatitude seems to be Psalm 37:11: "The meek shall possess the land." Let me specify more fully the meaning of the word "meek," which, it must be admitted, jolts us somewhat.

According to J. Dupont, we have here a nuance of the phrase "poor in spirit"; the emphasis in "meek" is on the ability to deal with others. The meek are those who are able to accept others; meekness, then, is a human quality (the Bible never speaks of the meekness of God). Even Jesus uses the term of himself: "Come to me, all you who labor and are burdened, and I will give you rest. Take my yoke upon you and learn from me, for I am meek and humble of heart" (Mt 11:28–29). In another passage of Matthew, Jesus applies to himself the prophecy of Zechariah about the king who comes "meek and riding on an ass" (21:5).[10] To be meek, then, is to be like the master.[11] As Romano Guardini aptly says, meekness is "not . . . weakness, but . . . strength become mild."[12]

To the meek is promised the land, which, in addition to being the object of profound hope on the part of the Jewish people, conveys strong overtones of stability, of something permanently acquired. "Land" is the first description of the kingdom in the beatitudes, and in the Bible it clearly connotes life.[13] Even among us today, the promise of land continues to be a promise of life for so many peasants and aborigines who have for centuries been dislodged from their own land.[14] To them the land is what Bishop Luis Dalle used to call "the place of communal brotherhood." In their struggle for land they find in the Bible a source of inspiration and in the kingdom a utopia that sets history in motion.[15] The beatitude speaks of "inheriting" the land, and the same verb will be used in Matthew 25:34, where the kingdom is inherited by those who feed the hungry and give drink to the thirsty.

In his third beatitude ("blessed are they who mourn") Matthew uses a different verb than Luke does in the parallel text, but the meaning is similar. Here too there is question of an affliction that causes one to weep. The word used suggests suffering due to bereavement, catastrophe, or oppression (see 1 Mc 1:25–27). In another passage of his Gospel, Matthew uses a different form of this verb to convey the feelings of the disciples regarding the presence of Jesus in their midst: "Can the wedding guests mourn as long as the bridegroom is with them?" (Mt 9:15). It is the absence of the Lord that causes the disciples to mourn. They desire and wait for his bodily presence, as they do for the accomplishment of God's will and kingdom. Blessed, therefore, are they who do not resign themselves to having injustice and aggression prevail in the world; for, as Medellín says, "where ... we find social, political, economic, and cultural inequalities, there will we find rejection of the peace of the Lord, and a rejection of the Lord himself" (*Peace*, 14).

They will be comforted. The word "comforted" is a strong one, and rich in meaning. The Greek verb *parakalein*, "to console," takes us back to Second Isaiah: "The Lord comforts his people and shows mercy to his afflicted" (Is 49:13). The comfort here connotes a liberation: the Hebrew verb translated by the Greek *parakalein* means literally that God will enable the people to give a deep sigh of relief (*naham*, to restore breathing) — that is, that God will deliver them from Babylonian domination. Luke shows Jesus fulfilling the promise of consolation for Israel (see Lk 2:25). This will also be the mission of the Spirit, the Paraclete (comforter), who "will guide" us "to all truth" (Jn 16:13) and whose presence ensures our freedom (see 2 Cor 3:17). Happy are they who have learned to share the sorrow of others, even to the point of weeping with them. For the Lord will comfort them, drying their tears and removing "the reproach of his people ... from the whole earth" (Is 25:8; see Rv 21:4).

The fourth beatitude adds a new touch to the basic text (that is, the first beatitude), again in the perspective of discipleship. Here there appears for the first time a theme that I have shown to be central in Matthew: justice or righteousness. The addition of "thirst" to "hunger" lends the statement a greater urgency and gives a more religious nuance. The object of this aching desire is justice or righteousness, both as a gift from God and a human task; it specifies the conduct required of those who want to be faithful to God. To be just means to recognize the rights of others, especially of those who are most destitute. For the same reason, to be just also supposes a relationship with God that can be described as holiness. Such is, in fact, the behavior of the Lord. The Lord:

> Shall judge the poor with justice,
>> and decide aright for the land's afflicted.
> He shall strike the ruthless with the rod of his mouth,
>> and with the breath of his lips he shall slay the wicked.
> Justice shall be the band around his waist,
>> and faithfulness a belt upon his hips. [Is 11:4–5]

These verses are part of a passage that the New Testament applies to Jesus; justice done to the oppressed is an essential element of the messianic message. The establishment of "what is right and just" is the mission that the God of the Bible entrusts to the people, and the task in which God is revealed as the God of life. Those who hunger and thirst for justice await it from God, but their waiting is not passivity; it implies a determination to bring about what they desire. Their desire—like the "seeking of justice" (see Mt 6:33)—will be satisfied; this satisfaction will be an expression of the joy that the coming of the kingdom of love and justice produces.

2) The fifth beatitude begins the second group in Matthew, which is made up for the most part of beatitudes proper to this Gospel. The mercy of God is a favorite theme of Matthew, and the parable he reports in 18:23–35 illustrates the fifth beatitude. The mercy shown by the king in the parable is completely gratuitous (as can be seen from, among other things, the fact that the debt forgiven was for a huge amount, so that it was in practice unpayable). The very gratuitousness, however, requires all the more that the servant behave in like manner. Luke expresses the very same idea in his Sermon on the Plain: "Be merciful, just as your Father is merciful" (Lk 6:36).[16] His exhortation is in the same line as that of Leviticus: "Be holy, for I, the Lord, your God, am holy" (Lv 19:2).

Mercy is a behavior required of the followers of Jesus. Matthew links this call with the Old Testament when he cites Hosea 6:6: "I desire mercy, not sacrifice" (Mt 9:13; 12:7). The mercy called for is a deep-seated attitude and not a mere formality. It is what makes us disciples of Jesus. In the final analysis, it is upon this that judgment will be passed. Matthew 25:31–46 talks of the works of mercy (the word is not used, but the reality is clear) and tells us that those who do these works will enter the kingdom of heaven. Those, on the other hand, who refuse to practice solidarity with others will be rejected. The deciding point will be the practice of mercy. The beatitude in Matthew declares happy those who will receive God's love, which is always a gift. But this gift demands in turn that the recipients be merciful to others. They will obtain mercy because God will make their hardships as God's own and will regard as done to God their gestures of solidarity with others.

Who are the clean of heart? The common tendency to identify religion with interior and cloistered attitudes can make it difficult to understand the sixth beatitude. Or, rather, it can make this understanding too easy, but mistaken. Psalm 51 puts us on solid ground here: "You are pleased with sincerity of heart, and in my inmost being you teach me wisdom. . . . A clean heart create for me, O God, and a steadfast spirit renew within me" (vv. 8 and 12). Cleanness of heart presupposes sincerity, wisdom, and steadfastness; there is no question, therefore, of anything ritual or external. As Joel says, conversion means rending hearts; not garments:

> Yet even now, says the Lord,
>   return to me with your whole heart,
>   with fasting, and weeping, and mourning;

Rend your hearts, not your garments,
and return to the Lord, your God.
For gracious and merciful is he,
slow to anger, rich in kindness,
and relenting in punishment. [Jl 2:12–13]

It is interior attitudes that count. This is the reason for the disagreements with the Pharisees, which Matthew presents in such a forceful way. One of these disagreements has to do with cleanness of heart and ends with this clear statement: "For from the heart come evil thoughts, murder, adultery, unchastity, theft, false witness, blasphemy. These are what defiles a person, but to eat with unwashed hands does not defile" (Mt 15:19–20).

In the Gospel of Matthew the word "Pharisee" does not refer only to the historical enemies of Jesus; it also signifies a mistaken way of understanding fidelity to God and the commandments. Phariseeism is a danger that lies in wait for every Christian; it consists in saying or professing one thing and doing another, separating theory from practice, doctrine from everyday behavior. This is why Jesus calls these persons hypocrites. Matthew is trying to warn the disciples of Jesus not to succumb to a similar frame of mind.

The Letter of James (which is close to Matthew on many counts) uses a very meaningful expression. It twice rejects those who are of "two minds" (Greek: *dipsychos*).[17] The context is significant in both instances:

That person must not suppose that he will receive anything from the Lord, since he is a man of two minds, unstable in all his ways. [Jas 1:7–8]

Draw near to God, and he will draw near to you. Cleanse your hands, you sinners, and purify your hearts, you of two minds. [Jas 4:8][18]

Those who are of two minds cannot hope for anything from God; they are not steadfast in God's service because they have set their hearts partly on something or someone other than the Lord.[19] The Old Testament likewise rejects this kind of split, which is also a lack of decisiveness ("unstable in all his ways"). Let me recall a text already cited: "How long will you straddle the issue? If the Lord is God, follow him; if Baal, follow him" (1 Kgs 18:21). The God of the Bible demands a complete surrender; to straddle the issue is to be an idolater. Matthew, for his part, says in a passage I have already examined: "No one can serve two masters. He will . . . hate one and love the other" (Mt 6:24). If we are to draw near to God, we must "cleanse our hearts," unify our lives, and be single-minded. "You shall love the Lord, your God, with all your heart, and with all your soul, and with all your strength," commands Deuteronomy (6:5) in a text that Matthew repeats (Mt 22:37).

To be clean of heart, then, means not being of two minds, not being a hypocrite. In the Quechuan language the word for "hypocrite" is a person "of two hearts" (*iskat sonkko*). The reference is to a person who tries to do justice simultaneously to two loves, each of which because of its comprehensiveness and radicalness excludes the other. If we are to be disciples of the Lord, we must be consistent, like the master. Therefore the clean of heart, those who are whole, will see God "face to face," as Paul says (1 Cor 13:12). This promise is a source of joy to the followers of Jesus.

Peacemaking is an essential task of Christians.[20] But if we are to grasp the scope of "peacemaking" we must set aside a narrow view of peace as simply the absence of war or conflict. This is what the seventh beatitude calls upon us to do. The familiar Hebrew word *shalom* has a rich content.[21] The word refers to a state of wholeness and integrity, a condition of life that is in harmony with God, other people, and nature. *Shalom* is opposed to all that militates against the well-being and rights of persons and nations. In a denunciation of those who act unjustly, Jeremiah says: "Small and great alike, all are greedy for gain; prophet and priest, all practice fraud. They would repair, as though it were naught, the injury to my people: 'Peace, peace!' (*shalom, shalom*), though there is no peace (*shalom*)" (Jer 6:13–14; the *Nueva Biblia Española* translates: " 'Things are going well, very well.' But they are not going well"; the NEB has: " 'All is well.' All well? Nothing is well!"). The real meaning of peace is the establishment of authentic justice and salvation, in this case for an entire people, and not the issuance of formal proclamations. The word "injury" translates a Hebrew word used in the Bible (see Jer 8:10; Ez 22:27; Prov 1:19) to signify a life spent in quest of profit by means of oppression and theft.[22] When Isaiah describes the Messiah as "Prince of peace," the words he uses are "Prince of *shalom*"; the Messiah brings wholeness of life.

It is not surprising, therefore, that justice and peace are closely linked in the Bible. "Justice and peace (*shalom*) shall kiss" (Ps 85:11). Both are denied to the poor and oppressed; therefore they are meant especially for those robbed of life and well-being. Psalm 72 sums up this outlook in a forceful and beautiful way:

> O God, with your judgment endow the king,
>   and with your justice, the king's son;
> He shall govern your people with justice
>   and your afflicted ones with judgment.
> The mountains shall yield peace (*shalom*) for the people,
>   and the hills justice.
> He shall defend the afflicted among the people,
>   save the children of the poor,
>   and crush the oppressor.
> May he endure as long as the sun,
>   and like the moon through all generations.

He shall be like rain coming down on the meadow,
    like showers watering the earth.
Justice shall flower in his days,
    and profound peace, till the moon be no more. . . .
For he shall rescue the poor man when he cries out,
    and the afflicted when he has no one to help him.
He shall have pity on the lowly and the poor;
    the lives of the poor he shall save.
From fraud and violence he shall redeem them,
    and precious shall be their blood in his sight.
          [Ps 72:1–7, 12–14]

Such is the peace that must be established. It must be actively sought; the text refers to *makers of* peace and not to what is usually meant by "peaceful" and pacifists.[23] Medellín points out quite aptly that "peace is not found, it is built. The Christian man is the artisan of peace. This task, given the above circumstances, has a special character in our continent; thus, the People of God in Latin America, following the example of Christ, must resist personal and collective injustice with unselfish courage and fearlessness" (*Peace*, 14). This passage provides a perspective for giving meaning to the terms mentioned a moment ago and differentiating among them. "The Christian man is peaceful and not ashamed of it. He is not simply a pacifist, for he can fight" (*Peace*, 15). The peaceful can fight for life and justice.

Those who build this peace—which implies being attuned to God and God's will in history, as well as a wholeness of life, both personal (health) and social (justice)—"will be called children of God"; this means that they will *be* children of God. Acceptance of the gift of being sons and daughters of God necessarily implies building brotherhood and sisterhood in history. Children of God: such is the title of the followers of him who has sent the Spirit to enable us to say: "Abba, Father" (Gal 4:6). "Children of God" is the "new name" that, according to one of the letters to the seven churches, is inscribed on the "white amulet" that those faithful to the Lord will receive as an identification (see Rv 2:12–17).

The eighth beatitude brings together the two key terms: "kingdom" and "justice" (or: righteousness). Those who live by, and establish, justice (= have a hunger and thirst for it) bring upon themselves the opposition of the powerful, as is attested by the prophets and the life of Jesus himself. Those who have made the decision to be his disciples cannot be above their master (see Mt 10:24). Matthew is very aware of this risk that disciples run; consequently, the theme of persecution appears at various points in his Gospel (5:44; 10:23; 23:34). This is an experience with which he is familiar.

Luke's fourth beatitude likewise takes into account the difficulties that disciples face: "Blessed are you when people hate you, and when they exclude and insult you and denounce your name as evil, on account of the

Son of Man" (Lk 6:22). Matthew explicitly adopts, for all his beatitudes, this focus of discipleship, which is not directly present in the basic text of the beatitudes and is only hinted at in Luke's first three beatitudes.[24] Furthermore, Matthew lends greater force to his statement about persecution "for the sake of justice" by adding, in the next verse, a promise of happiness for those who are insulted "because of me." Matthew 5:11 is therefore quite close to Luke 6:22, which speaks of persecution "on account of the Son of Man," while at the same time he establishes an equivalence between justice and Jesus as motives for the hostility experienced.[25] In this way Matthew prepares the way for the surprising identification in chapter 25 between love-inspired actions done for the poor and actions done for the son of man who has come to judge all the nations. To give one's life for the sake of justice is to give it for Christ himself. The christological perspective at work in the beatitudes is clear.

The kingdom is promised to those who suffer for justice. By repeating the term "kingdom," which he has already used in the first beatitude, Matthew seeks to round off and lend force to his text by means of the literary device known as inclusion. The promises in the six beatitudes enclosed between the first and the last are specifications that help us grasp the meaning of the kingdom. Land, comfort, satisfaction, mercy, the vision of God, and divine sonship or daughterhood spell out the life, love, and justice produced by the reign of God.

These promises are gifts of the Lord, fruits of his gratuitous love, and therefore call for a certain kind of behavior. The beatitudes tell us of the attitudes proper to the followers of Jesus. It is to the latter that the beatitudes are addressed: "When he saw the crowds, he went up the mountain, and after he had sat down, his disciples came to him. He began to teach them, saying . . ." (Mt 5:1-2). The attitudes prescribed in this teaching must be translated into acts of solidarity with others, especially the poor and helpless, so that Father may be glorified (see Mt 5:16).

In my opinion, therefore, Matthew is not offering us a spiritualized (in a onesided and even pejorative sense) version of the original beatitudes, to which Luke's version is closer. His perspective is quite different; his interest is in discipleship. The followers of Jesus must feed the hungry and visit those in prison. Such actions are expressions of their longing for justice; therefore they will be misunderstood and persecuted (see also Lk 6:22-23). On the part of the disciples, the need is for concrete, material acts of solidarity, which are important to Matthew throughout his Gospel. The church's experience, which is the backdrop of his text, leads him to these specifics. Let me go more deeply into the meaning of these "works," before I draw some conclusions about the scope of the beatitudes and the relation between the versions of Luke and Matthew.

2. THE WAY OF WORKS

Christ, who is also "the truth and the life," is the disciples' way to the Father (Jn 14:6). The Lord's life in us finds expression in works; these are the fruit of the presence of the Spirit. As Samuel Rayan says: "The followers of Jesus, those who are open to the Spirit, to the values of God and to an appreciation of life, those who are committed to affirming life in all its human fulness, whatever be their grasp of their faith, are bringers of life for the world."[26] Works express this life, mark out the way, and "do the truth" (Jn 3:21)—that is, the love of God in history.

Bringers of Life

Above (chapter 5) I commented on a prophecy of Zechariah concerning the day of Yahweh. A few verses further on, Zechariah places the following exhortation on the lips of Yahweh: "These then are the things you should do: Speak the truth to one another; let there be honesty and peace in the judgments at your gates, and let none of you plot evil against another in his heart, nor love a false oath. For all these things I hate, says the Lord" (Zec 8:16–17).[27]

"The things you should do": there is here an ethical requirement that is to be concretized in a certain kind of behavior. If human beings speak the truth to one another, they will create a climate of credibility and will make Jerusalem truly a "faithful city" (Zec 8:3). The next part of the sentence brings together two key words: *mishpat* (judgment) and *shalom,* the rich and complex meaning of which I have already discussed. The reference is to judgments that are capable of establishing peace, harmony between persons, happiness, and life. It is to this end that behavior is directed that is in keeping with the gift of the day of Yahweh. Evil plots against others are contrary to *shalom* and opposed to the will of Yahweh.

A little earlier in his book, Zechariah himself gives us a very brief but meaningful code of ethics that is drawn up in the same perspective. "Thus says the Lord of hosts: Render true judgment, and show kindness and compassion toward each other. Do not oppress the widow or the orphan, the alien or the poor; do not plot evil against one another in your hearts" (Zec 7:9–10).

On the positive side, true, genuine judgment, and the practice of love and mercy.[28] The passage then describes in negative terms the behavior of believers in Yahweh. The verb used here for "oppress" (*'shq*) has the connotation of economic exploitation.[29] Believers are not to violate the rights of the poor or take from them the necessities of life. Widows and orphans are among the weak and uncared for members of society; the compassionate love prescribed in the preceding verse must be shown especially to them. The foreigners often found living in the midst of the Jews were temporary workers, hired day by day. Having no permanent jobs and owning no property in a country that was not their own, they were a pool of cheap labor and open to exploitation (see Deut 24:14). Widows, orphans, and foreigners are the main trio often used in the Old Testament as a synonym for the poor. Rarely, however, do we find what we see here: the prophet adding the redundant word "poor" (here: *'ani*) to the list. By adding it, he reinforces and summarizes his references to those who are abused and unimportant and without legal protection.

Acceptance of the gift of the day of Yahweh, which Zechariah announces, supposes actions done for others, especially the most needy. To the prophets, the establishment of justice means respecting the rights of all and especially the needs of the poor. Acceptance of God's merciful love requires that we commit ourselves to others; our acceptance of life from God should motivate us to create justice and peace, happiness and life, or, in a word, *shalom*, around us.

On the other hand, to oppress the poor means to take away their life, to murder them. Biblical texts on this point are very numerous. I shall cite a few from the New Testament:

Behold, the wages you withheld from the workers who harvested your fields are crying aloud, and the cries of the harvesters have reached the ears of the Lord of hosts. You have lived on earth in luxury and pleasure; you have fattened your hearts for the day of slaughter. You have condemned; you have murdered the righteous one; he offers you no resistance. [Jas 5:4–6]

Injustice is murder; the oppressor is a murderer. The passage echoes one we saw earlier, in Sirach 34:18–22. It is not clear to what James is referring when he speaks of the "day of slaughter." The common view is that he is speaking of the "day of judgment" on which the rich will be punished; he may also, however, be rebuking those who feast and amuse themselves while oppressing the poor and shedding their blood. The words are harsh but well aimed. Unfortunately, they fit situations that have recurred throughout the history of Christianity, including our own day. The Letter of James allows no loopholes or excuses. Bread is bread, and wine wine.[30] The Christian message seeks to overcome the conflict; therefore it does not deny its existence.

In the preceding section I said that the beatitudes pinpoint the attitudes proper to disciples. The verses that follow upon the beatitudes in the Gospel of Matthew are completely attuned to them and thus form with them a single text that ought to be interpreted as a whole:

You are the salt of the earth. But if salt loses its taste, with what can it be seasoned? It is no longer good for anything but to be thrown out and trampled underfoot. You are the light of the world. A city set on a mountain cannot be hidden. Nor do they light a lamp and then put it under a bushel basket; it is set on a lampstand, where it gives light to all in the house. Just so, your light must shine before others, that they may see your good deeds and glorify your heavenly Father. [Mt 5:13–16]

Verses 11–12, which are an explication of the eighth beatitude, shift from the third person plural to the second, and the text now continues to refer to the second person plural. The disciples are said to be ("you are") the salt of the earth and the light of the world; the images embody a call for an identity and a visibility. Salt gives flavor and must do this permanently; if it becomes itself tasteless, it loses its specific function and can only be thrown out. The task of the disciples is to make known the message of Jesus; this is knowledge that must be made flavorful, for then people will appreciate the teaching and want to grasp it more fully. If the followers of Jesus do not put the commandments of their master into practice, they lose their identity and betray their mission; they become fools.[31]

The visibility that light creates is confirmed by the images of the city on a mountain and the lamp that cannot be hidden. The phrase "light of the world," which is parallel to "salt of the earth," brings out the universal scope of the responsibility disciples have. The followers of Jesus cannot hide or conceal the message they bring. Only a personal and Christian identity will allow a genuine dialogue with others ("the earth," "the world").

Disciples are therefore called upon to bear witness through concrete actions. The entire opening section of Matthew 5 is directed toward verse 16, and the evangelist emphasizes the movement by connecting the verse with what has gone before: "Just so"—marked by the identity and visibility of true disciples—their conduct is to shine before others. "Good deeds" refer to concrete behavior that is in accord with God's will; they refer especially to works of mercy, a classical list of which is given in Matthew 25:31–46.

Reference is also made to good deeds in the first Letter of Peter: "Maintain good conduct among the Gentiles, so that if they speak of you as evildoers, they may observe your good works and glorify God on the day of visitation" (1 Pt 2:12).

The witness, here as in Matthew, is not in the service of self-glorification but is to be given for the glory of God, as Jesus did who was "eager to do what is good" (Ti 2:14). This is the ultimate purpose of the commitment of disciples, that through it human beings may be led to the Father. To glorify the Father means to acknowledge the primacy of love for him, to adhere to his will, and to be faithful to his plan for the human race.

The works of the disciples are a way to the Father; by doing them, the disciples make the way of Christ their own. The passage that begins in Matthew 5:1 and ends at verse 16 may be regarded as the introduction to the Sermon on the Mount; it shows us the part played by deeds in the attitudes befitting a disciple. "Blessed are the poor in spirit," and so on, means "blessed are the disciples." Disciples are those who practice justice or righteousness through life-giving works of love and thereby glorify the Father.

The focus seen here makes it possible to connect chapter 5 of Matthew, with which the preaching of Jesus begins, and chapter 25, with which this preaching concludes. In the course of my comments on the text of the beatitudes I have pointed out its links with the passage on the final judgment. The proclamation of the kingdom begins with the promise made to the poor in spirit and ends with the gift of the kingdom to those who come to the aid of the materially poor. The disciples are said to be blessed, or happy, because they give life by giving food to the hungry and drink to the thirsty, by clothing the naked and visiting prisoners, or, in other words, by concrete actions; in this way they proclaim the kingdom and enter into it. This is what St. James calls "the law of the kingdom" (2:8; translated from the Greek).

All these considerations enable me now to establish a fruitful relation between Matthew and Luke. The beatitudes of the third evangelist emphasize the gratuitous character of the love shown by the God who has a preferential love for the materially poor. The beatitudes in Matthew complement those in Luke by bringing out the ethical demands made of the followers of Jesus, demands that flow from the loving initiative taken by God. The difference between the two evangelists is thus one of emphasis (both aspects are present in each version of the beatitudes); their approaches are complementary. Matthew is therefore not "spiritualizing" the beatitudes; rather he is "discipleizing," if I may coin a word. Matthew's perspective thus proves especially demanding. The followers of Jesus are those who translate the grace they have received—a grace that makes them witnesses to the kingdom of life—into works done for the neighbor and especially for the poor; disciples are those who enter into solidarity, even at the "material" level, with those for whom the Lord has a preferential love. That is why they are declared "blessed" and suited for entrance into the kingdom that has been "prepared . . . from the foundation of the world" (Mt 25:35).

The life of disciples runs its course between gratuitousness and demand, investiture as witnesses and mission. In his version of the beatitudes Matthew emphasizes the need of behavior oriented to others. This is a requirement that flows from the gift of the kingdom. Nothing makes greater demands for solidarity with others than the gratuitousness of God's love.

Do Even More Than I Say

The outlook and attitude I have been evoking is summed up in a simple but profound way in a short and infrequently cited book of the New Testament. The Letter of Paul to Philemon contains greater pastoral and theological riches than is commonly thought.[32] I shall limit myself here to a reading of the letter from the viewpoint of the relation it sets up between grace and task, faith and works.

Paul addresses his letter to Philemon and, with him, the entire Christian community of which he is a member. "Paul, a prisoner for Christ Jesus, and Timothy our brother, to Philemon, our beloved and our coworker, to

Apphia our sister, to Archippus our fellow soldier, and to the church at your house" (vv. 1–2).

This is, then, not a private letter, since the ultimate addressee is the church that meets in Philemon's house. Philemon may not keep the letter in his pocket and run the risk of forgetting its content. Instead, the community will keep an eye on his conduct, once they have read this letter, which involves them, too, since it is addressed also to them.

The "prisoner for Christ Jesus" quickly gets to the point:

> I give thanks to my God always, remembering you in my prayers, as I hear of the love (*agape*) and the faith (*pistis*) you have in the Lord Jesus and for all the holy ones, so that your partnership (*koinonia*) in the faith may become effective in recognizing every good there is in us that leads to Christ. For I have experienced much joy and encouragement from your love (*agape*), because the hearts of the holy ones have been refreshed by you, brother. [vv. 4–7]

The pairing of love and faith is central to the letter, since it is through these that we are united to God and to our neighbor. Paul usually mentions faith first, then love[33]; here he does the opposite, and the change is not without meaning. Philemon makes an honest effort to combine love and faith, and Paul gives thanks for this. In Christ we have received many blessings; the gift of our partnership in the faith must be translated into effective action, into works and solidarity with others, because what counts in the final analysis is "faith working through love" (Gal 5:6). Paul rejoices because this is the case with his friend, since love has led Philemon to meet the needs of his brothers and sisters. It is in this that his solidarity with them consists.

In the passage cited, Paul uses a word that he will use twice more in this short letter; this suggests that it is important to him. The word is "heart" (= Greek *splangchna*, i.e., the "inward parts," especially the heart).[34] The word is used for the entirety of the person in all its dimensions, spiritual and material, with the connotation of what is fundamentally necessary. Philemon has been sensitive to the pressing needs of others and has been able to make his love for others effective, to be in true solidarity with them. This is a comfort to Paul, who gladly calls him "brother."

But Paul, now "an old man," wants more of Philemon and his community. The theme of gratuitousness has already been hinted at when Paul speaks of what we have received in and through Christ. The love of the addressee of this letter has been tested, but love knows no limits:

> Therefore, although I have the full right (*parrhesia*) in Christ to order you to do what is proper, I rather urge you out of love, being as I am, Paul, an old man, and now also a prisoner for Christ Jesus. I urge you on behalf of my child Onesimus, whose father I have become in

my imprisonment, who was once useless to you but is now useful to [both] you and me. I am sending him, that is, my own heart, back to you. I should have liked to retain him for myself, so that he might serve me on your behalf in my imprisonment for the gospel, but I did not want to do anything without your consent, so that the good you do might not be forced but voluntary. [vv. 8–14]

The passage plays on the opposition between useful and useless and between obligatory and voluntary. In Greek, the name Onesimus means "useful." In the past and in his status as slave, this man was perhaps useless to Philemon; henceforth, now that he has been begotten as a Christian by the imprisoned Paul, he will be useful to Philemon in a new and authentic way, just as he has been to Paul. In fact, Paul would have liked to keep Onesimus with him as a substitute for Philemon himself. Onesimus has been for Paul a companion in labor. Therefore, just as Paul received him as if he were Philemon himself, so Philemon should accept him as Paul's "own heart."[35]

The second opposition (between obligatory and voluntary) has to do with a major theme in Paul's writings. The author of the letter has authority (*parrhesia*, the competence to speak forthrightly) to give orders, but he prefers to appeal to the freely given love of his correspondent. This shows finesse and tact on Paul's part, but also a profoundly true sense of the Christian message, for the love of Christ present in each Christian plays a more important role than any external authority. The letter makes its appeal to this gift of love. Paul wants Philemon's action to be "not . . . forced but voluntary."

Perhaps this is why he was away from you for a while, that you might have him back forever, no longer as a slave but more than a slave, a brother, beloved especially to me, but even more so to you, as a man and in the Lord. So if you regard me as a partner (*koinonon*), welcome him as you would me. [vv. 15–17]

The emphasis here is on equality and brotherhood. Brotherhood, first, with Onesimus "as a man," as a human being. This outlook leads to social solidarity and does away with slavery at its root. There can be no love except between equals. The warmth of friendship implies a sharing that creates an equality and breaks out of the categories of master and servant. Our Christian life is judged by our ability to make others our friends. We are not committed to the poor and oppressed, for example, unless we are friends with them.

In addition, however, Philemon is to look upon Onesimus as something more and other than a slave; he is to regard him as "a brother, beloved . . . in the Lord," and must welcome him as he would Paul himself. Onesimus the slave was Philemon to the apostle and must be Paul to his friend; these identifications create a framework of solidarity. Philemon has great esteem for Paul, the spiritual father of his community as well as his own spiritual father; he is to welcome Onesimus with the same respect and love. Such is the wish of Paul, in whose eyes communion (*koinonia*) is forged both at the human level and in the Lord, and is therefore to be expressed in concrete actions.

Paul continues the theme of his identification with Onesimus by harking back to the contrast between obligatory and voluntary:

> And if he has done you any injustice or owes you any thing, charge it to me. I, Paul, write this with my own hand: I will pay. May I not tell you that you owe me your very self? Yes, brother, may I profit from you in the Lord. Refresh my heart in Christ. With trust in your compliance I write to you, knowing that you will do even more than I say. [vv. 18–21][36]

If Onesimus owes a debt, it is to be charged to the account of one to whom Philemon owes a far greater debt. Payment will be made, but Paul will still have credit remaining. After making this point with some degree of fraternal irony, Paul returns to his more personal style and asks: "Do me this service." The service is to Paul himself, to his heart, the deepest part of himself. Philemon's love has found expression in actions that have refreshed "the hearts of the holy ones" (v. 7); he will now be in a position to do the same for Paul by declaring his solidarity with Onesimus. Communion at the level of the heart must be translated into new social relationships. As we learn to treat one another as brothers and sisters, as friends, the structures supporting inequality begin to collapse. The transformation of these will in turn promote personal exchanges. I am referring not to mechanistic processes but to a reciprocal relationship in which hearts and structures make demands upon each other.

This part of the letter ends with the most important statement in the entire document, a statement that sums up the message of Paul to Philemon and his community. Philemon is a good Christian, one who observes the commandments of the Lord. Paul knows this, but he also knows that it is not enough. The master told us to "be perfect as your heavenly Father is perfect" and to "give freely what you have freely received." Therefore he issues a challenge that is at the same time an expression of confidence in Philemon: "knowing that you will do even more than I say." This assumption arises from a deep conviction of the apostle, and if we interpret the letter in a legalistic way we will fail to recognize it. Christian love must necessarily and inevitably lead to the elimination of slavery and every other form of oppression, but love must go further than that. The call for gratuitousness is not added on to an already existing Christian life that is built on an almost exclusive basis of duties and rewards; rather it is at the heart of the behavior of a follower of Jesus. It is not an addition but the foundation.

In Paul's view, Christians must daily "invent" their life of love and commitment. This is the viewpoint Paul adopts in his polemic against the law; it is the outlook that is at the very heart of his theology. "Do even more than I say" is a formula for limitless demands. The point is that Christian love is to find expression in works without limitation. "Knowing that you will *do*": love must be efficacious; communion with the Father requires solidarity with others.

This is a call to freedom and creativity. We find Paul expressing the same outlook when he asks the Corinthians to help other Christian communities. His approach is a skillful one:

> Now as you excel in every respect, in faith, discourse, knowledge, all earnestness, and in the love we have for you, may you excel in this gracious act also. I say this not by way of command, but to test the genuineness of your love by your concern for others. For you know the gracious act of our Lord Jesus Christ, that for your sake he became poor although he was rich, so that by his poverty you might become rich. [2 Cor 8:7–9]

Paul does not give an order; he urges his readers to generosity, to a completely free gesture. He knows, moreover, that what he is asking goes far beyond what is strictly due. Christianity has norms and precepts, but the thing that ought to characterize Christians is that they go beyond what norms and precepts require. Only through works done in generosity (by grace) will the sincerity of our love be proved. This outlook has its source in the example of Christ.

In his Letter to Philemon, Paul conveys the whole of his message: his readers are to do more that he says. This "more" sums up all the demands made by Christian life and the entire challenge to exercise our creativity in the present juncture of our people, in the today of God's word, in the current situation of the poor in our country and in all of Latin America. By our commitments and solidarity as Christians and as a church we will prove that we have truly received the gift of love.

Where Are the Poor to Sleep?

The Gospel of Matthew reports a conversation of Jesus with a Pharisee who puts a question to him with the intention of testing him:

> "Teacher, which commandment in the law is the greatest?" He said to him, "You shall love the Lord, your God, with all your heart, with all your soul, and with all your mind. This is the greatest and the first commandment. The second is like it: You shall love your neighbor as

yourself. The whole law and the prophets depend on these two commandments." [Mt 22:36–40]

By "the law and the prophets" Jews meant the entire Bible. Matthew uses the phrase here because he is writing in a Jewish setting. The two loves referred to in the two citations from the Old Testament (Dt 6:5 and Lv 19:18) sum up the commandments of God. In the parallel passage in Luke, the person who refers to the two loves is the same scholar of the law who asks the question, while Jesus limits himself to saying at the end: "You have answered correctly; do this and you will live" (Lk 10:8). The practice of these two commandments is the way to life and brings us near to the kingdom (Mk 12:34).

Love of God and love of neighbor are the two basic dimensions of the gospel of Christ. Some of the tensions we experience in the church are due to the skewed way in which we interpret the relation between these two demands. There are those who emphasize love of God in a way that makes it appear that our relation to our neighbor is something secondary, added on to what is truly important. Given this perspective, it is difficult to show the relevance of Christians' work in history and of the demands made on them by the orphan, the widow, and the foreigner.

On the other hand, there are those who imply that Christian existence finds its almost exclusive manifestation in commitment to and solidarity with others. The pressures of inhuman and deeply unjust situations seem to lead them to act, rather than to think, in this way. But then prayer, celebration, the knowledge of God's word and a taste for it—all of them vital expressions of the world of gratuitous love in which our relationship with the Lord has its setting—lose their full meaning and are narrowed in their scope.

We are not dealing here with two forms of service: one of God, the other of wealth, such as characterizes those who are "of two minds." No, there is but a single love, the different expressions of which cannot be separated, because when we clothe the naked we clothe the Lord himself. Only the clean of heart, those who live out their faith in an integral way, can grasp this identification of Christ and the poor.

It is important to note, moreover, that those who claim to find God while being uninterested in their neighbor will not find the God of the Bible. They will perhaps find a God who is first mover of all being or the explanation of creation, but they do not find the God whom Jesus Christ proclaimed, for he is inseparable from his kingdom—that is, from his will to love and justice for all human beings. The acknowledgment of God as Father inevitably leads to forming true fellowship among ourselves. Those, on the other hand, who in practice limit themselves solely to commitment to others run the risk of seeing these others, who are beings of flesh and blood and not abstractions, slip from their hands. Gratuitousness is the framework not only of our encounter with God but also of reciprocal recognition among human beings.

There is no middle ground. If we try to stop at one of these two loves, we lose both. When this kind of choice is made, there is not in fact a reduction of one of them to the other, but rather the disappearance of both. "Whoever is not with me is against me," says the Lord. To choose between the two dimensions of Christian life is to be against God.

One thing is certain: the tension between these two requirements exists more at the practical level than the conceptual. At the level of ideas it is perhaps possible to reach agreement on the unity to be maintained. The difficulty is greater in the sphere of action; it is action that determines our real orientation.

A simple question in Exodus calls upon us to make a very concrete choice. It reminds us of what we must be concerned about: "This cloak of his [your neighbor's] is the only covering he has for his body. What else has he to sleep in?" (Ex 22:26). Are we concerned in this way? Are we anxious to know how the poor of our country will cover themselves and where they will spend the night? What happens within the intimacy of each home expresses, perhaps better than any other indicator, the deep differences there are among us. Will they sleep beneath a roof? On the ground, on a mat, or on a bed? One, two, five, six to a room? In an apartment from which they shall soon be evicted?

Those who would be Christians in present-day Latin America must be concerned about where the poor are to sleep. Given this kind of concrete problem, does it make sense to get into intellectual discussions about priorities or about the balance between love of God and love of neighbor? Precisely because it is concrete, this demand makes us realize what we have right in our own hands: the inseparable connection between the two loves. The question of where the poor are to sleep is important to God, as we are told in the same passage of Exodus: "If he cries out to me, I will hear him; for I am compassionate" (Ex 22:26). Therefore it ought to be important to us as well. The Lord wills that the act of helping the poor be an encounter with him.

The challenges posed by concrete human situations take us to the sources of Christian life. Conceptual distinctions and theological developments do not there disappear, as a pedantic anti-intellectualism would have it; on the contrary, they take on meaning and vitality. A concern for where the poor are to sleep will make us realize that it is in fact not possible to separate love of God and love of neighbor; that is, that we must live both aspects as intertwined with each other. When we experience things at their root, we are helped in seeing that the unity of our life is not created by a fine, balanced formulation of ideas, but by taking the path of practicing love of God and love of neighbor in one and the same action. This alone will lead us to life. The journey is a costly one but also full of hope, because on it we gradually become compassionate as the God in whom we believe is compassionate. "Compassionate" means to be capable of "feeling with" God and other human beings. Feeling, and not just thinking. When we situate ourselves at the sources, we seek unity as something new and creative, and not as a nicely balanced synthesis.

A final thought. There are those who feel a certain uneasiness when they hear: "Love your neighbor *as yourself*"—a command also found in the passage that has served as my guiding thread in these last few pages. They think they see in this admonition a lack of radicalness or perhaps an excessive self-regard. These dangers do exist, but they do not exhaust the interpretation of the statement.

The Gospel clearly calls upon us, in many passages, to forget our own interests as we commit ourselves to others. At the same time, the passage of Matthew, with its Old Testament roots, reminds us of something fundamental: we must also be able to love ourselves. We can undoubtedly distort this requirement and make it the justification for a more or less subtle self-centeredness. We may ask ourselves, nonetheless, whether self-neglect on the grounds that we are serving others allows this commitment to be, as it should, joyful and friendly, a service done by men and women who do not expect it to compensate them for what they have denied to themselves. The practice of righteousness should bring joy (see Is 64:4).

I am not here rejecting the traditional ascetical call for a necessary moderation in all areas of Christian life. Rather I am trying to convey an understanding that solidarity with others does not demand an imbalance in personal life. We must love "Brother Body," we are told by Francis of Assisi, an eminently evangelical saint. There is indeed a risk of distortion in this love, but there is also the risk of distortion in the opposite direction.[37]

Love of God and commitment to the poor (including love of ourselves) are central elements in the experience of those who believe in the God of life. The proper interrelating of these elements turns our faith into a journey, accomplished in solidarity, as followers of Jesus.

PART THREE

UNDER THE INSPIRATION OF THE SPIRIT

God is love, as Jesus shows us when he addresses God as his Father. God is present wherever the gift of the kingdom and its demands are welcomed into our lives and activities. Consequently, we find the Father by following Jesus.

Such are the conclusions I have reached in trying to answer the first two of the questions I raised at the beginning: Who is God? Where is God? Now I must ask: How are we to talk of God? Of a God who is love and inseparably connected with the kingdom of justice? How are we to find adequate words and the courage to speak? The prophets felt this problem:

> The word of the Lord came to me thus:
> Before I formed you in the womb I knew you,
>> before you were born I dedicated you,
>> a prophet to the nations I appointed you.
> "Ah, Lord God!" I said,
>> "I know not how to speak; I am too young."
> But the Lord answered me,
> Say not, "I am too young."
>> To whomever I send you, you shall go;
>> whatever I command you, you shall speak.
> Have no fear before them,
>> because I am with you to deliver you, says the Lord.
> Then the Lord extended his hand and touched my mouth,
>> saying,

> See, I place my words in your mouth!
>   This day I set you
>   over nations and over kingdoms,
> To root up and to tear down,
>   to destroy and to demolish,
>   to build and to plant. [Jer 1:4–10]

Fear assails Jeremiah. The words that Yahweh speaks to him are especially demanding. He must accept them in full freedom. He was chosen from his mother's womb and is therefore predestined, but not predetermined. The Lord reassures him: the Lord will tell Jeremiah what he is to preach; the Lord will put the words in his mouth. The language to be used about God and God's message comes, in the final analysis, from God. That is why the words of the prophets confront and destroy what is opposed to the Lord's will; primarily, however, they build up and give life.[1]

God's word must be communicated in everyday language. To evangelize is to transmit to others the joy of knowing that we are loved by God; it is to share with others the experience of the gratuitous character of God's love. Evangelization is the basic demand of the gospel: "The gospel must . . . be preached to all nations" (Mk 13:10).

The Bible connects this preaching with the presence of the Spirit. Jesus foresees the difficulties his disciples will face and therefore he tells them: "When they lead you away and hand you over, do not worry beforehand about what you are to say. But say whatever will be given to you at that hour" (Mk 13:11).

Christians find the right language under the inspiration of the Holy Spirit. The story of Pentecost shows that this is characteristic of the proclamation of the Lord's message. What is needed is not to speak the same tongue but to be able to understand one another. In the story of Pentecost we are told that each of the people who had come from various places heard the disciples of Jesus "speaking in his own language. They were astounded, and in amazement they asked, 'Are not all these people who are now speaking Galileans? Then how does each of us hear them in his own native tongue?' " (Acts 2:6–7). Each speaks one's own language, but all understand one another. The language to be used about God comes from the Christian message but also, and inseparably, it comes from the manner in which the message is brought to life. This depends in turn on very particular historical circumstances. There is no theology that does not have its own accent in speaking about God. These different accents must be respected; otherwise we risk sinning against the Spirit. What is needed is not an imposed uniformity but fidelity to the message and an understanding of diversity.

On the other hand, the tongues of fire on Pentecost signify the power that the Spirit—Father of the poor, as the liturgy calls the Spirit—places in our mouths so that we may speak of the God of life. It is for this reason that Peter invokes the prophecy of Joel: "I will pour out a portion of my spirit upon all flesh. Your sons and your daughters shall prophesy, your young men shall see visions, your old men shall dream dreams. Indeed, upon my servants and my handmaids I will pour out a portion of my spirit" (Acts 2:17–18).

Without dreams, without plans, without a utopia, history remains motionless, dead. The Spirit is life; the Spirit's presence in believers will enable them to speak in God's name — that is, to prophesy:

> And then, on that day,
>   the mountains shall drip new wine,
>   and the hills shall flow with milk;
> And the channels of Judah
>   shall flow with water:
> A fountain shall issue from the house of the Lord
>   to water the Valley of Shittim. [Jl 4:18]

This is the God in whom we believe: the God who gives life in abundance. It is in terms of this life that our existence is defined: "Before man are life and death, whichever he chooses shall be given him" (Sir 15:17). This life is a gift of God, which we receive freely. It is the source of the joy we communicate when we speak of God. For this very reason the most profound and difficult question believers must face is: How are we to speak of the God of life and love in a situation of death and injustice? There are peoples and individuals who make us sharply aware of this contrast. Those who ask the question are to be found even in the Bible. The attempted answers do not gloss over uncertainties and protests, while at the same time they take us more deeply into our relationship with God. Gratuitousness and the demand for justice are two fundamental elements in the life of every believer.

On the threshold of the New Testament, the messianic hopes of the Jewish people, so ardently embraced by the poorest and least important of its members, render more intense the experience of joy that accompanies the fulfillment of the promises and enrich the vision of God. The words and witness of Mary regarding God continue still to evangelize us.

These approaches to the problem remind us that the God of the kingdom is proclaimed by actions and words: actions that bear witness to the resurrection of the Lord, and words that proclaim life to be the ultimate meaning of human history. The union of these two aspects gives power to the language of Jesus and is a major demand made of his followers.

A fine passage in Micah already serves as a model. What is asked of those who hear the word of God is "to do justice, and to love kindness, and to walk humbly with your God" (Mi 6:8 NREB).[2]

CHAPTER VIII

MY EYES HAVE SEEN YOU

I pointed out at the beginning of this book that talk about God presupposes practice, that is, the silence of contemplation and commitment. Let me now go into this matter more deeply with the aid of one of the most powerful books of the Bible: the Book of Job.[1] It is a book we cannot but love.[2]

How are we to speak of God in the light of poverty and suffering? This is the question raised by the Book of Job. The opening section, which is in prose, presents the question—in a dialogue between God and the satan (the adversary)—in the form of a test to which a man is put who is considered to be "a sound and honest man who feared God and shunned evil" (1:1). The test will consist in afflicting Job first with poverty (1:11) and then with sickness (2:7). Our question now becomes: How will Job speak of God in this new situation? Will he reject God? Will he curse God in this extreme situation? Will he speak ill of him? (1:11; 2:5).[3]

The real question, however, has to do with the possibility of believing "for nothing" (1:10). The satan challenges God: in his view, Job's religion is motivated by self-interest; Job says he believes, because his life is a prosperous one. Yahweh accepts the wager proposed by the satan, for he is convinced that faith can exist without thought of reward and that this is the case with Job. This wager provides the immediate context for what happens to Job. Is it possible for a person to have a disinterested faith under these conditions? Were Job's piety and righteousness perhaps due to his material well-being? The issue from the beginning, then, is the gratuitousness of love. How will Job speak of this?

Job, now a poor and sick man, is cast out by the society to which he belongs. He leaves the city and sits amid the rubbish, which his former neighbors cast away outside the walls. There, from the garbage heap, he will cry out at the pain he suffers; he will also give voice to his feelings for the sufferings of others, his protest against the injustice done to him, and, finally, his acknowledgment of God's gratuitous love. In sum, the author of the Book of Job, like Paul of Tarsus later on, reminds us in a forceful and penetrating way of the central theme of biblical revelation: the gratuitous love of God is at the origin of all things.

145

How can such an affirmation be reached in the extreme setting of the suffering of the innocent? In the book's final chapter, which reverts to prose after a very lengthy part in verse, Yahweh will say that his servant Job has spoken correctly of him (see 42:8). This judgment doubtless surprised the three friends who had been debating with Job. For this reason, the journey that led to this correct language about God will be enlightening for us.

On this journey, different kinds of theological discourse are used in an attempt to explain to Job what has happened to him; that is, various ways of accounting for faith in God are used. From this point of view, it is possible to distinguish in the Book of Job two languages about God: the prophetic and the contemplative. In offering this classification, however, I am not trying to "rationalize" a work so deeply poetic and so rich in nuances. The two languages are interwoven; the argument advances and at times retrogresses, but if we look at the book in its entirety progress and maturation can be seen.

1. THE CRY OF THE POOR

"The news of all the disasters that had fallen on Job came to the ears of three of his friends. Each of them set out from home — Eliphaz of Teman, Bildad of Shuah, and Zophar of Naamath — and by common consent they decided to go and offer him sympathy and consolation" (2:11). The purpose of the new arrivals is to share their friend's suffering and bring him some comfort. These are serious, learned men, perhaps a little overconfident of their knowledge; they intend to explain to Job the reason for what has been happening to him. When a misfortune is understood, it becomes easier to bear. Before the three friends could speak, however, they were so moved by Job's suffering that "they wept aloud" (2:12) and then fell silent: "they sat there on the ground beside him for seven days and seven nights. To Job they spoke never a word, for they saw how much he was suffering" (2:13). Their compassion and respect showed how seriously they took their friend's situation.

Job suffers and, like Jeremiah (20:14–15), he curses the day he was born: "Perish the day on which I was born and the night that told of a boy conceived" (3:3). He complains because of the pain of his misfortunes. "My only food is sighs, and my groans pour out like water" (3:24). He says, therefore, that he "long[s] for a death that never comes, and hunt[s] for it more than for buried treasure" (3:21). How is his suffering to be explained? What reason is there for so much suffering? Job cannot understand it. What role does God play in all this?

Two Ways of Thinking about God

These initial complaints are followed by the lengthy discourses of Job and his visitors. These will display two different ways of reasoning.

The friends of Job follow the prevailing theology of the age: a doctrine of temporal retribution, which says that the upright are rewarded with prosperity and health, while sinners are punished with poverty and sickness. The friends are fervent followers of this view, and in their name Eliphaz says very forthrightly: "Lo, this we have searched out and it is so! Hear and apply to yourself" (5:27).[4] Eliphaz rebukes Job: "Can you recall anyone guiltless that perished? Where then have the honest been wiped out?" (4:7).

Job is warned to apply this teaching to his own case: his poverty and sickness are a punishment for his sins. The matter is clear. Job's first obligation is to acknowledge his sins and ask God to forgive them. It is a harsh demand. Eliphaz realizes this and therefore says at the beginning of his discourse: "If we say something to you, will you bear with us?" (4:2). But he is convinced of what Job must do: that he must repent of his former wicked behavior: "If I were you, I should appeal to God and lay my case before him" (5:8).

This is a simple approach to morality, and one susceptible of a stubbornly individualistic interpretation. Its power is due precisely to its simplicity. It was prevalent in the period during which the author of the book was writing, and it has tenaciously retained its place in one type of religious mentality. It is, moreover, a convenient one for those who have great possessions in this world, while at the same time it elicits a culpable resignation in those who lack such possessions. Down through the ages certain tendencies in Christianity have repeatedly given new life to this ethical view, which sees wealth as a divine reward to those who are upright and work hard, and poverty as a punishment for sin and laziness.

On the other hand, it is a historical fact that the ideology of the capitalist system has made use of this doctrinal picture, at first openly but nowadays in more subtle forms.[5] This is a manipulation of religion that distorts a truth that nonetheless remains important—namely, that the Christian faith necessarily implies an ethic. I shall return to this point.

At the level of theory, Job shares the prevailing view to which his friends give expression, but he is not as sure of it as they are. Doubts assail him. What has happened is that when he examines his conscience, he sees no sin deserving of such a punishment; his experience therefore leads him to question the theological explanation. The arguments of his friends only heighten his awareness of his own innocence, for as he listens he becomes increasingly convinced that he is guiltless.

As he hears the arguments, Job gains a greater understanding of his situation and comes to a solid conviction: in this matter "I am upright" (6:29). He then develops his own reasoning: "Listen carefully to my words, and pay attention to what I am going to say. You see, I shall proceed by form of law, knowing that I am upright" (13:17–18). But such an attitude does not fit in with the ethical doctrine of retribution.[6] He has acted justly during his life: Why, then, has he been afflicted with poverty and sickness? Is God punishing him unjustly? The question is a tormenting one. Job has no clear answer; at times he seems to suggest that the Lord is indeed unjust, but he never says it in so many words. The one thing certain is that Job's consciousness of his innocence clashes with this ethico-religious doctrine, which until now he too has accepted.

Job's friends reproach him for being inconsistent; more than that, they try to prove to him that he is blaspheming. They realize all that is implied in Job's protestation of innocence, when this is judged according to their own categories of thought. Zophar says angrily:

> Is babbling to go without an answer?
>   Is wordiness a proof of uprightness?
> Do you think your talking strikes people dumb,
>   Will you jeer with no one to refute you?
> These were your words, "My conduct is pure,
>   in your eyes I am free of blame!"
> Will no one let God speak,
>   open his lips and give you answer? [11:2–5]

God, however, does not speak as yet. Eliphaz, meanwhile, tries to draw from Job's position a conclusion, which he regards as overwhelming: "You do worse: you suppress reverence, you discredit discussion before God . . . when you vent your anger on God and speeches come tripping off your tongue!" To extend his argument and reduce Job to confusion, he makes his question an even more general one: "How can anyone be pure, anyone born of woman be upright?" (15:4 and 13, 14).

A little earlier, cornered but still belligerent, Job had given his opponents a sarcastic answer:

> Doubtless, you are the voice of the people,
>   and when you die, wisdom will die with you!
> But I have a brain, as well as you,
>   I am in no way inferior to you,
>   and who, in any case, does not know all that? [12:2–3]

Now Job goes on the attack. Disillusioned with his friends and convinced that their arguments are worthless, he says:

> How often have I heard all this before!
>   What sorry comforters you are!
> "When will these windy arguments be over?"
>   or again, "What sickness drives you to defend yourself?"
> Oh yes! I too could talk as you do,
>   if you were in my place;
>   I could overwhelm you with speeches,
>   shaking my head over you,
> and speak words of encouragement,

and then have no more to say.
When I speak, my suffering does not stop;
if I say nothing, is it in any way reduced? [16:2–6]

Our language reflects the situation in which we find ourselves. Job's words are a critique of every abstract theology that is out of contact with reality and lacking in human compassion. Job finds it useless to talk about theological principles that are alien from life. A search in light of his human and religious experience enables him to glimpse other ways of talking (or being silent) about God.

Job's sarcasms do not, however, succeed in hiding the fact that he finds himself caught in the middle between, on the one hand, the ethico-religious doctrine of retribution and, on the other, his personal experience that convinces him of his innocence. Despite being thus caught, he does not allow himself to succumb to an easy formal logic: he never says that God is unjust. Before speaking ill of God, Job prefers to dispute the foundations of the prevailing theology.

The Suffering of the Poor

The dialogue between Job and his friends advances and matures. The friends repeat themselves and become more hostile. Job for his part goes more deeply into his experience and consolidates his thought.

As the friends keep insisting on the doctrine of temporal retribution, Job looks beyond his individual case and asks why the wicked enjoy prosperous lives. This extension of his own experience will serve him as an argument against the doctrine. It will demonstrate, from a different angle, the weakness of the arguments brought forward against him:

Why do the wicked still live on,
their power increasing with their age?
They see their posterity assured,
and their offspring secure before their eyes.
The peace of their homes has nothing to fear,
the rod that God wields is not for them. [21:7–8]

They lead prosperous lives, and yet these are people who neither serve God nor pray to God:

They end their lives in happiness
and go down in peace to Sheol.
Yet these are the ones who say to God, "Go away!
We do not want to learn your ways!
What is the point of our serving Shaddai?
What would we gain from praying to him?"...
Do we often see the light of the wicked put out,

> or disaster overtake him,
> or the retribution of God destroy his possessions,
> or the wind blow him away like a straw,
> and a whirlwind carry him off like chaff?
> [21:13–15, 17–18][7]

These instances show the emptiness of the arguments Job's friends offer in support of the theory of moral retribution. Job now sees that the question being debated does not concern him alone. This realization strengthens the protest of the supposedly patient Job who asks defiantly: "So God stores up punishment for his children?" (21:19). At each step Job moves further and further away from the doctrine of temporal retribution.

A second element that comes to light as Job broadens the range of his personal experience will hasten still more this self-distancing from the prevailing doctrine and turn Job's reasoning in a new direction. Poverty is a situation that affects more than himself; moreover, as Job sees it, poverty is not something fated but something caused by the wicked—that is, by those who say to the Lord: "Go away!" The wicked deny God and are the enemies of the poor. Their attitudes are but two faces of the same coin.

At this point, the author of the Book of Job is led to place on Job's lips the most painful and most effective description of the wretchedness of the poor that is to be found in the Bible, and also to level a bitter indictment against the powerful who deprive and oppress the poor.[8] It will be worthwhile to cite in its entirety this passage that is clearly prophetic in its inspiration:

> The wicked move boundary-marks away,
>   they carry off flocks and shepherd.
> They drive away the orphan's donkey,
>   as security, they seize the widow's ox.
> The needy have to keep out of the way,
>   poor country people have to keep out of sight.
> Like wild desert donkeys, they go out to work,
>   searching from dawn for food,
>   and at evening for something on which to feed their
>   children.
> They go harvesting in the field of some scoundrel,
>   they go pilfering in the vineyards of the wicked.
> They go about naked, lacking clothes,
>   and starving while they carry the sheaves.
> Two little walls, their shelter at high noon;
>   parched with thirst, they have to tread the winepress.
> They spend the night naked, lacking clothes,
>   with no covering against the cold.
> Mountain rainstorms cut them through,

unsheltered, they hug the rocks.
The orphan child is torn from the breast,
   the child of the poor is exacted as security.
From the towns come the groans of the dying
   and the gasp of the wounded crying for help.
Yet God remains deaf to prayer! [24:2–12]

Those who rob the poor are murderers. We have already met this theme that is so central to the Bible — namely, that injustice to the poor means their death. The cause of the poor is the cause of God. Job realizes, moreover, that his own situation is connected with the cause of the poor. That is why the passage just cited ends with a painful protest in God's presence: "Yet God remains deaf to prayer!"

The point of the debate has now shifted and broadened. There is no longer question only of the suffering of poor, sick Job; in his own consciousness the issue has become clearer. We are now confronted with the misfortunes of the innocent, of all who suffer unjustly. As a result, the question "why?," which this situation raises, becomes even more acute and painful.

The three friends have said what they have to say; they have used up all their arguments. They will not speak again. Job has debated with them and proclaimed his own integrity and uprightness. His defense now takes on sharper contours; the question now is no longer of his personal decency alone but of his behavior toward the poor, the favorites of the Lord. Job now rereads his life:

People deferred to me,
because I freed the poor in distress
   and the orphan who had no helper.
The dying man's blessing rested on me
   and I gave the widow's heart cause to rejoice.
Uprightness I wore as a garment,
   fair judgment was my cloak and my turban.
I was eyes for the blind,
   and feet for the lame.
Who but me was a father of the poor?
   The stranger's case had a hearing from me.
I used to break the fangs of the wicked,
   and snatch their prey from their jaws. [29:12–17]

"Father of the poor" and opponent of those who seek to devour: that is how Job sees himself, a man whose life is bound up with the poor and deprived of the world. Justice is established by liberating the poor. It is in this liberation that innocence consists, which Job has asserted throughout the heated debate with his friends. He will lay down a challenge, in the form of conditional sentence and questions:

> If I have ever infringed the rights of slave
>   or slave-girl in legal actions against me. . . .
> Have I been insensible to the needs of the poor,
>   or let a widow's eyes grow dim?
> Have I eaten my bit of bread on my own
>   without sharing it with the orphan? . . .
> Have I ever seen a wretch in need of clothing,
>   or the poor with nothing to wear,
> without his having cause to bless me from his heart . . . ?
> Have I raised my hand against an orphan,
>   presuming on my credit at the gate?
> If so, let my shoulder fall from its socket,
>   let my arm break off at the elbow!
>   [31:13, 16–17, 19–22]

If Job considers himself to be a just and upright man, it is because he has tried to take the side of the oppressed: "Have I not wept for those whose life is hard, felt pity for the penniless?" (30:25), and because he has always sought to establish "what is right and just." This commitment to the poor is connected in a significant way with a theme we saw earlier: the rejection of idolatry. Job will ask: "Have I put my faith in gold, saying to fine gold, 'Ah, my security'?" Money has not been his god; he has not been a greedy man, an idolater; on the contrary, he has wanted his life to be a surrender to the God of the poor.

Greatness of God and Justice for the Poor

At this point, Elihu unexpectedly appears. There has been no previous reference to such a person. Until now, he says, he has simply listened to what his elders have to say: "I am still young, and you are old, so I was shy and hesitant to tell you what I know" (32:6). He has been disillusioned, however, and after listening to the lengthy discourses of Job and his friends, he is convinced that "great age does not give wisdom, nor seniority fair judgment" (32:9). He has therefore decided to speak out, "for I am full of words and forced to speak by a spirit within me; within me, it feels like new wine seeking a vent, bursting out of new wine-skins" (32:18–19).

Elihu speaks with a certain degree of arrogance, but his arguments are, in their key points, the same as those we have already heard. The young theologian emphasizes two themes: "God is greater than any human being" (33:12) and God "does accord fair judgment to the afflicted" (36:6). He gives a more sophisticated presentation of the doctrine of temporal retribution, which has been defended by the three friends and against which

Job has rebelled. At certain moments, however, Elihu advances beyond this doctrine. He continues the criticism of Job and addresses him:

> How could you say in my hearing—
>   for the sound of your words did not escape me—
> "I am clean and sinless,
>   I am pure, without fault.
> But he keeps inventing excuses against me
>   and regards me as his enemy.
> He puts me in the stocks,
>   he watches my every path"?
> In saying so, I tell you, you are wrong:
>   for God is greater than any human being.
> Why then quarrel with him
>   for not replying to you, word for word?
> God speaks first in one way,
>   and then in another, although we do not realize it.
>   [33:8–14]

God uses different languages, and, contrary to what Job thinks, suffering can be one of them. Seeing Job's impatience, Elihu warns him that he must be attentive to the signs of God's action. These can take unexpected forms, such as a call to solidarity with those who suffer injustice.

Elihu then speaks of God's attitude to the poor and oppressed. Job had already emphasized the role of commitment to the poor in genuine righteousness. Elihu's contribution is the vigorous attribution of this same commitment to God. God is the one who "does accord fair judgment to the afflicted" (36:6):

> [God] is unimpressed by princes
>   and makes no distinction between rich and poor,
>   since all alike have been made by him.
> They die suddenly, at dead of night,
>   they perish—these great ones—and disappear:
>   it costs him no effort to remove a tyrant. . . .
> He breaks the powerful without enquiry
>   and sets up others in their places.
> He knows the sort of things they do!
>   He overthrows them at night, to be trampled on.
> He beats them like criminals
>   chained up for all to see,
> since they have turned their backs on him,
>   having understood so little of his ways
> as to make the cries of the weak rise to him

and let him hear the appeal of the afflicted.
[34:19–20, 24–28]

This link between God and the poor is at the very heart of the message of the prophets. Hearing the cry of the oppressed, the *go'el* breaks the mighty who part ways when they rob the poor. The Lord is always watchful, although this attentiveness takes unobtrusive forms. Therefore Elihu says to Job:

> If he is silent, who can condemn him?
> If he hides his face, who can see him?
> He is watching over nations and individuals
>   so that the wicked will not reign
>   and there be none to deceive the people. [34:29–30][9]

Solidarity with the poor provides a firm basis for talking about God. When seen from this vantage point, aspects of God that remain unseen from other viewpoints emerge. But new ethical demands likewise make their appearance: "he who mocks the poor blasphemes his Maker" (Prv 17:5). God is the ultimate, all-encompassing foundation of human behavior. The Lord requires solidarity with the marginalized and the oppressed; this is the ethic that derives from the exodus. God is present in the afflicted, as Matthew will tell us later on.

2. GRATUITOUSNESS AND FREEDOM OF GOD'S LOVE

The relationship between God and the poor that Job sketches and Elihu confirms retrieves the ethical perspective, but in a different context and with a different meaning than it had in the doctrine of temporal retribution. As a result, a face of the Lord is now seen that has not appeared previously. Belief in God certainly brings with it the demand for certain kinds of behavior, in particular a solidarity with the poor and the oppressed. But there is now another dimension of language about God that had been hinted at in the beginning and receives increasingly strong emphasis as the book moves through its course.

Blessed Be the Name of Yahweh

As the reader knows, the major part of the book on which I am commenting consists of a series of discourses by Job, his friends, and finally God. The theme of all the discourses is the meaning to be assigned to God's action in connection with what happens to the personage in question. But even before the discourses begin, Job himself has, in the prologue, given one interpretation of what has been happening to him. Having lost all his possessions, Job, now poor, accepts the situation, places himself in God's hands, and exclaims:

Naked I came from my mother,
naked I shall return again.
Yahweh gave, Yahweh has taken back.
Blessed be the name of Yahweh! [1:21]

So too, in a second stage in which Job suffers from a cruel illness and is reduced to sitting on a garbage heap, he refuses to accept the impatient view of his wife who rebukes him: "Why persist in this integrity of yours? Curse God and die." He answers her: "That is how a fool of a woman talks. If we take happiness from God's hand, must we not take sorrow too?" The paragraph ends with the author of the book saying of Job: "And in all this misfortune Job uttered no sinful word" (2:8–10). That is to say, he did not speak ill of God despite his poverty, isolation, and sufferings. "He uttered no sinful word"; on the contrary, he voiced a deep sense of the gratuitous love of God. Everything comes from God and is God's gracious gift; no one, therefore, has a right to make claims on God.

Job's language is of a kind often heard among poor but believing people. On so many occasions I myself have heard unsophisticated people talking like Job: "God gave him (or her) to me, God has taken him (or her) away." The words do not express a mere resignation; there is something deeper here that an enlightened faith finds it difficult to put a finger on. The faith of the people displays a keen sense of the lordship of God; it has a spontaneous awareness of what Yahweh says in the Book of Leviticus: "Land will not be sold absolutely for the land belongs to me, and you are only strangers and guests of mine" (Lv 25:23). The faith of the people is marked by a profound conviction that everything belongs to the Lord and everything comes from the Lord. This conviction is finely expressed in a beautiful prayer of David: "Everything is from you, and we only give you what we have received from you. For we stand before you as aliens: we are only your guests, like all our fathers" (1 Chr 29:15).

These initial reactions of Job contain, in inchoative form, the language of contemplation, which will take clearer shape as Job enters more deeply into his experience. It is certain, however, that if the language of the believing people remains at this inchoative level, it cannot successfully stand up to the onslaught of ideologized forms of talk about God. As a result, it is open to manipulation by theologies that are alien to the experience of ordinary folk. Furthermore, as in the case of Job, persistent poverty and suffering raises difficult questions; withdrawal and evasion in the face of these questions can end in an acceptance of evil and injustice, and even a resignation to it, which are in the final analysis contrary to faith in the God who liberates. It is necessary therefore to go more deeply into this intuition shown by the faith of the people and to strengthen it, but this process involves some ruptures.

These ruptures will come in Job's reaction to the efforts that his friends make to justify his sufferings.

Confrontation with God

The three friends argue from certain principles and endeavor to apply these to the case of Job: "Hear and apply to yourself" (4:27). These competent but mistaken theologians are sure of what they teach; Bildad will even say with a certain smugness: "Think—for it is our turn to speak!" (18:2). In the view of these men, Job is a stubborn and rebellious man who has failed to think (the idea that Job is "patient" will not stand up to a careful reading of the book).

Job too feels certain, not about a doctrine that he is perhaps unable to refute, but about his own experience of life: *he is innocent*. The arguments of his friends seem weak to him when set over against this deep conviction. On the other hand, Job experiences moments of hopelessness. He says, for example:

> If I prove myself upright, his mouth may condemn me,
>> even if I am innocent, he may pronounce me perverse.
> I am innocent; life matters not to me,
>> I despise my existence.[10]
> It is all one, and hence I boldly say:
>> he destroys innocent and guilty alike.
> When a sudden deadly scourge descends,
>> he laughs at the plight of the innocent.
> When a country falls into the power of the wicked,
>> he veils the face of its judges.
>> Or if not he, who else? [9:20–24]

Bold words, these, that have their source in unbearable suffering. But his complaint is directed to a God in whom he believes; thus he is paradoxically asserting God's presence. A few verses later, Job states his wish that some "arbiter" might intervene as mediator in his dispute with God:

> He [God] is not human like me; impossible for me to
>> answer him
> or appear alongside him in court.
> There is no arbiter between us
>> to lay his hand on both. [9:32–33]

This mediator, as will become increasingly clear in the course of the book, is God. Biting protest and unsteady confidence characterize the first phase in Job's spiritual struggle. The identity of the arbiter becomes clearer a few chapters further on:

> Cover not my blood, O earth,
>> and let my cry mount without cease!
> Henceforth I have a witness in heaven,

    my defender is there on high,
though my friends mock me
    and I must weep before God.
Let him judge between a man and God,
    between a man and his friend.[11]
For the years of my life are numbered,
    and I am leaving by the road of no return. [16:18–22]

While Job's friends mock him, suffering makes him "weep before God" with increasing intensity. On this occasion, he calls for a witness, someone to defend him in his suit against God—whom, be it noted, he calls his "friend." The identity of the witness remains unclear as yet, but, knowing himself to be innocent, Job demands that there be someone to testify to his integrity. He hopes that this person will appear soon, for his own years are numbered and, once they are finished, it will be too late to see justice done.

Nevertheless, doubts and uncertainties beset and torture him:

    Where then is my hope?
      Who can see any happiness for me?
    unless they come down to Sheol with me,
      all of us sinking into the dust together? [17:15–16]

Despite these doubts Job continues to insist on the same point of departure; that is, he tries to understand God's action in the light of his own experience and not of abstract principles. Amid his confusion (and in reaction to the friends who accuse him of blaspheming), amid his destitution and suffering, and despite the fact that he feels persecuted and wounded by "the hand of God," Job makes an act of faith that seems to be without any human support:

    I know that I have a living Avenger (*Gō'ēl*)
      and that at the end he will rise above the dust.
After they pull my flesh from me,
      and I am without my flesh, I shall see God;
I myself shall see him, and not as a stranger,
      my own eyes will see him. [19:25–27][12]

This famous and much scrutinized passage opens new perspectives. Job's experience of the Lord is becoming more profound. In a first phase, while rhetorically denying the possibility of an arbiter in his case against God, Job nonetheless called for such an arbiter to be present; he then drew a sketch of a mediator. Here this personage is called a *Gō'ēl*, an avenger or defender.[13] His advocate before God will be God.

A similar splitting of God can be seen in a passage of an author who had a keen awareness of human suffering and is representative in so many ways of the suffering people of Latin America. I am referring to César Vallejo, whose witness has helped me to understand the Book of Job and relate it more fully to my own experience. Shortly before his death, Vallejo dictated these dramatic and trust-filled lines to his wife Georgette: "Whatever be the cause I must defend before God after death, I myself have a defender: God."[14] In the language of the Bible he had a *gō'ēl*. This was a God whose fleeting presence he had felt at certain moments in his life. On this occasion, in a decisive hour of his life, he sees this God at his side as he faces the judgment that his life has merited from the same God.

At the Turning Point of the World: Gratuitousness

Job passionately longed for God to speak to him; now, despite Elihu's skepticism, God does address him. Tapping his deepest poetical vein, the author puts the heart of his message into the mouth of God. The claim has been made that God's words do not make reference to concrete problems and therefore do not respond to Job's distress and questions. This is not correct. God's discourse takes up the theme of his own greatness, to which Job had referred (while adding, to be sure, some complaints) and which Elihu had made one of the main ideas of his peroration.

The author, who begins once again to call God "Yahweh," as he had at the beginning of his book, shows God challenging Job: "Who is this, obscuring my intentions with his ignorant words?" (38:2). His first discourse is devoted specifically to setting forth the foundations of his plan for creation. God will overwhelm Job with a broadside of questions, but his real purpose is to show that his freely given, unmerited love is the foundation of the world:

> Where were you when I laid the earth's foundation?
>   Tell me, since you are so well informed!
> Who decided its dimensions, do you know?
>   Or who stretched the measuring line across it?
> What supports its pillars at their bases?
>   Who laid its cornerstone
> to the joyful concert of the morning stars
>   and unanimous acclaim of the sons of God?
> Who pent up the sea behind closed doors
>   when it leapt tumultuous from the womb,
> when I wrapped it in a robe of mist
>   and made black clouds its swaddling bands;
> when I cut out the place I had decreed for it
>   and imposed gates and a bolt?
> "Come so far," I said, "and no further;
>   here your proud waves must break." [38:4–11]

Yahweh goes directly to the source of all existing things, to the place and time when everything began. The friends, and to some extent Job himself, thought that the world had been made in order to be immediately useful to human beings and to be of service in temporal retribution: a reward for the just, a punishment for sinners. This they regarded as the ultimate reason for God's works; therefore his action in history is foreseeable:

> Have you been right down to the sources of the sea
>   and walked about at the bottom of the Abyss?
> Have you been shown the gates of Death,
>   have you seen the janitors of the Shadow dark as death?
> Have you an inkling of the extent of the earth?
>   Tell me all about it if you have!
> Which is the way to the home of the Light,
>   and where does the darkness live? —
> You could then show them the way to their proper places,
>   you could put them on the path home again! [38:16–20]

The questions are beyond the ability of our protagonist to answer. Yet, always in ironical tones, God pretends that Job has answers. Thus the series of questions ends with this statement: "If you do know, you must have been born when they were, you must be very old by now!" (38:21).

Other questions now follow, which make clearer what the Lord seeks to reveal. These questions play a key part in his discourse:

> Who bores a channel for the downpour
>   or clears the way for the rolling thunder
> so that rain may fall on lands where no one lives,
>   and the deserts void of human dwelling,
> to meet the needs of the lonely wastes
>   and make grass sprout on the thirsty ground?
>   [38:25–27]

Rainfall in the desert may seem useless to Job and his friends, but God is not a prisoner of their ways of thinking. Rain in the waste lands is beautiful, and this beauty is its "usefulness." The Lord sends rain because God freely desires to do so; because it pleases God to see the rain. The gratuitousness of God's love, and not retribution, is the hinge on which the world turns.

The same idea is further emphasized when God speaks of God's own freedom, which is mirrored in the freedom of animals, which human beings cannot tame:

> Who has given the wild donkey his freedom,
>   who has undone the harness of the brayer?

> I have given him the wastelands as his home,
> the salt plain as his habitat.
> He scorns the turmoil of the town,
> obeys no donkey-man's shouts.
> The mountains are the pastures that he ranges
> in quest of anything green.
> Is the wild ox willing to serve you
> or spend a night beside your manger?
> If you tie a rope around his neck
> will he harrow the furrows for you?
> Can you rely on his massive strength
> and leave him to do your heavy work?
> Can you depend on him to come home
> and pile your grain on your threshing-floor? [39:5–12]

Is everything that exists in the natural world really meant to be domes-
ticated by human beings and subjected to their service? God's speeches are
a forceful rejection of a purely anthropocentric conception of creation. The
idea of the human person as "lord of creation" has paradoxically caused
us to forget the meaning of creation and the respect we owe to it. Anything
nonhuman seems to lie outside the history of salvation. The poet-theologian
who wrote the Book of Job reacts against such a view. In his eyes, the world
of nature expresses the freedom and delight of God in creating. The divine
freedom refuses to be limited to the narrow confines of the cause-effect
relationship.

Job is conquered, but not convinced. He takes note of what God has
said to him, and he withdraws; he will not (he says) speak again:

> I feel my littleness: what reply shall I give?
> I had better lay my hand over my mouth.
> I have spoken once, I shall not speak again;
> I have spoken twice, I have nothing more to say.
> [40:4–5]

Job now knows more about God, but he does not yet know enough. The
light has still not fully dawned for him. His struggle has been too extensive
and too honest for him to change his opinion easily. The questions he had
remain and continue to disturb him. Yahweh knows this and, consequently,
shows that Yahweh is not satisfied with this first result. Moved, perhaps,
by Job's persistence, God begins a new discourse. This time the theme will
not be God's plan that springs from gratuitous love, but rather God's just
government of the world. This was what Job had questioned, but if God
was to deal with it in a fruitful way, God had first to situate it (as in the
first speech) within the overall plan of creation and of the gratuitous love
that motivates creation.

This time, despite the sarcastic tone, the Lord explains tenderly and, as it were, shyly, that he cannot simply destroy the wicked with a glance. He wants justice indeed, and desires that divine judgment reign in the world, but he cannot impose it, since he must respect what he has created. His power is limited by human freedom, for without freedom justice would not be present in history:

> Has your arm the strength of God's,
>   can your voice thunder as loud?
> Come on, display your majesty and grandeur,
>   robe yourself in splendor and glory.
> Let the fury of your anger burst forth,
>   humble the haughty at a glance!
> Bury the lot of them in the ground,
>   shut them, every one, in the Dungeon.
> And I shall be the first to pay you homage,
>   since your own right hand is strong enough to save you.
>   [40:9–14]

Between Gratuitousness and Justice

Not everything, but certainly a great deal, is now clear to Job. His second answer to God is quite different in tone from the first. His attitude has changed:

> This was the answer Job gave to Yahweh:
> I know that you are all-powerful and there is no plan you
>   cannot carry out.
> (You said:) "Who is this that blurs my plans with
>   ignorant words?"
>   —It is true: I spoke without understanding
>   marvels that are beyond my grasp.
> (You said:) "Listen to me, for I am going to speak;
>   I am going to ask the questions, and you are to
>   inform me."
> I once knew you only by hearsay,
>   now my eyes have seen you;
> therefore I repudiate and repent
>   of dust and ashes. [42:1–6][15]

Job's former knowledge of God was indirect, gotten through others (for example, through his friends). It is different now. In his worst suffering he had cried out: "I shall see God; I myself shall see him" (19:26–27). This hope has been fulfilled. The encounter is a logical step for a man with the outlook of Job, of Job the man of prayer. At the same time, however, the closeness to God that he now experiences is beyond all his hopes: "Now my eyes have seen you." We are in the presence of profound contemplation.

The experience leads Job, not to withdraw his words, but to set aside his lamentations and sadness; this is what is meant by "repenting of [changing his mind about] dust and ashes." Certain emphases in his protest had been due to the doctrine of retribution, which despite everything had continued to be his theological point of reference. Now that the Lord has overthrown that doctrine by revealing the key to the divine plan, Job realizes that he has been speaking of God in a way that implied God was a prisoner of a narrow way of understanding the doctrine.[16] It is this position that Job now says he is abandoning.

What is it that Job has understood? That justice does not reign in the world God has created? No. The truth that he has grasped and that has lifted him to the level of contemplation is that justice alone does not have the final say about how we are to speak of God. Only when we have come to realize that God's love is freely bestowed do we enter fully and definitively into the presence of the God of faith. Grace is not opposed to the quest for justice nor does it play it down; on the contrary, it gives it its full meaning. God's love, like all true love, operates in a world not of cause and effect but of freedom and gratuitousness. That is how persons successfully encounter one another in a complete and unconditional way: without payment of any kind of charges and without externally imposed obligations that pressure them into meeting the expectations of the other.

We saw earlier how in the debate with his friends Job came to see that he must transcend his individual experience. The dialogue brought home to him that his situation was not exceptional but was shared by the poor of this world. The new awareness in turn showed him that solidarity with the poor was required by his faith in a God who has a special love for the disinherited and exploited of human history. This preferential love is the basis for what I have been calling the prophetic way of speaking about God.

But the prophetic way is not the only way of drawing near to the mystery of God, nor is it sufficient by itself. Job has just experienced a second shift: from a penal view of history to the world of grace that completely enfolds and permeates him. In the first major step that Job had taken, he was not required to deny his personal suffering but to open himself to the suffering of others as well and to commit himself to its elimination. So in this second stage the issue is not to discover gratuitousness and forget the duty of establishing what is right and just, but to situate the quest for justice within the framework of God's gratuitous love. Only in the perspective of the latter is it possible to understand God's predilection for the poor.

This special love does not have for its ultimate motive the virtues and merits of the poor but the goodness and freedom of God, a God who is not simply the guardian of a rigid moral order. This preference for the poor—Job now realizes—is a key factor in authentic divine justice. Consequently there is no opposition between gratuitousness and justice, but there is indeed an opposition between gratuitousness and a conception of justice that can be translated into demands made of God by human beings and that renders God a prisoner of our deeds or our cultic actions. There is indeed a contradiction between the free, gratuitous, and creative love of God and the doctrine of retribution that seeks to pigeonhole God.

Inspired by the experience of his own innocence, Job bitterly criticized the theology of temporal retribution as maintained in his day and expounded by his friends. And he was right to do so. But his challenge stopped halfway and, as a result, except at moments when his deep faith and trust in God broke through, he could not escape the dilemma so cogently presented by his friends: if he was innocent, then God was guilty. God subsequently rebuked Job for remaining prisoner of this either-or mentality (see 40:8). What he should have done was to leap the fence set up around him by this sclerotic theology that is so dangerously close to idolatry, run free in the fields of God's love, and breathe an unrestricted air like the untamable animals described in God's argument. The world outside the fence is the world of gratuitousness; it is there that God dwells and there that God's friends find a joyous welcome.

The world of retribution—and not of temporal retribution only—is not where God dwells; at most he visits it. The Lord is not prisoner of the "give to me and I will give to you" mentality. Nothing, no human work however valuable, merits grace, for if it did, grace would cease to be grace. This is the heart of the message of the Book of Job. Paul will repeat it no less forcefully.

CHAPTER IX

HOLY IS GOD'S NAME

Devotion to Mary is one of the important characteristics of the faith of the Latin American people, as can be seen from the variety of names under which the Mother of the Lord is revered.[1] The faith of the Latin American poor helps us to understand that we cannot regard ourselves as disciples of Jesus unless we listen to what Mary tells us about God.

It is true, of course, that Marian devotion, like all important things, can give rise to excesses of various kinds or simply to unenlightened enthusiasms. Sometimes, too, it stimulates a prolixity that contrasts with the reserve that the gospels show in speaking of Mary.[2] But this reserve should not make us forget or overlook the supremely important message conveyed by her whom Karl Rahner rightly called "the perfect Christian."[3] It is significant that she was with the apostles when the Holy Spirit descended on them in the form of fiery tongues (see Acts 1:12–14; 2:1–4). From that moment on, those who had been the companions of Jesus began to proclaim his death and his resurrection; they began to speak of the God of love. Mary's silence as the Christian community took its first steps is no less eloquent than their preaching; her humble, intense presence ensures the continuity of the biblical revelation about God.

It is through Mary that important emphases in the word of the Lord have reached us. For in the Lukan infancy Gospel "the entire action" really "focuses on the word."[4] God speaks through messengers to the various individuals who make their appearance there, and these messages all have to do essentially with the coming of the Son, who is the Word of God made flesh. Mary, for her part, is presented to us as the one who meditates on everything referring to Jesus and stores it up in her memory. We are told that after the shepherds had "made known the message that had been told them about this child" (Lk 2:17), Mary "kept all these things, reflecting on them in her heart" (Lk 2:19). Further on, after the report of Jesus' words to his parents in the temple, we are told that "his mother kept all these things in her heart" (Lk 2:51).[5] She keeps alive within her the word that has taken shape in events and that speaks to us of God. For this reason, she is able to pass it on.

The Mother of the Messiah, a woman from the midst of the Jewish people, and "daughter of your Son," as Dante calls her in the final canto of his *Divine Comedy* (XXXIII, 1), holds a unique place in salvation history and in the proclamation of the kingdom of life. I am therefore especially interested in the paths taken by Mary's language—and silences—about God, for they will provide guidelines for the poor, and indeed for all believers, as they speak of, and keep silence about, God.

1. MARY THE WOMAN

It is as a woman that Mary tells us of God. She is female, one of those who are marginalized and looked down upon by the dominant male sex. It is obvious that Mary cannot be separated from her womanhood; she is called blessed not only as a believer but also as a woman, and is even called "most blessed . . . among women" (Lk 1:42). If we leave Mary's womanhood out of consideration, we keep ourselves from understanding what God wishes to reveal to us through her, and we miss the meaning of the Gospel passages in which Jesus addresses his mother and other women. The Lord's practice in this area plants a seed of transformation that has not always been recognized and properly valued by his followers.

This reminder of Mary's womanhood suggests some reflections on the situation of women in our midst today.

Doubly Oppressed and Marginalized

Puebla's chapter (part IV, chapter I) on "A Preferential Option for the Poor" attempts to specify from the outset what the term "poor" includes. It therefore begins with a description of the different aspects of poverty; one of these has to do with women. "The poor do not lack simply material goods. They also miss, on the level of human dignity, full participation in sociopolitical life. Those found in this category are principally our indigenous people, peasants, manual laborers, marginalized urban dwellers and, in particular, the women of these social groups. The women are doubly oppressed and marginalized" (Puebla 1135, note).[6] Women are thus the least of the least.

The label does indeed describe the situation of women in the various sectors of the people, for they are marginalized and oppressed not only because they are poor but also because they are women. Even within the social levels mentioned, the idea of masculine superiority prevails. Women are thus limited to household tasks and regarded as unfit for study. They receive a lower salary than men for the same work, and when they take on responsibilities, they find men reacting with skepticism or jokes in poor taste. Machismo reigns and has longstanding and strong historical roots; it is at the basis of an entire organization of society and has even penetrated to some extent into the consciousness of women, causing them to feel insecure in many ways.

Contempt for women sometimes takes misleading forms. Women are exalted in the abstract but undervalued in the concrete. Honoré de Balzac observed cynically that "women are slaves whom you must know how to put on thrones." No one can fail to see that the key words here are "know how to," with the opportunism and manipulation they imply in this context. That is why Kierkegaard could claim that "the misfortune of women is that at a given moment they are all-important, while the next day they are completely unimportant."

We have here a scale of values that displays a deep disdain for the condition of women, who see themselves subjected to shameful tricks for depriving them of their full rights as persons. They are given the low-grade jobs in the family, at work, in the organization of society, and in the church. Hegel describes women as "the repose of warriors," implying that it is men who are called to the important tasks and to the activities that shape history. This mutilation of women as persons also degrades men as human beings. Consequently, the human growth of both men and women demands that they rise above this state of affairs.

The special characteristics of the situation of women must not be overlooked in efforts to restore the rights of the poor. This is especially true and urgent when dealing with the various strata of ordinary people. There cannot, in fact, be a just struggle for the rights of those whom society marginalizes, unless the rights of women are included; if their rights are not recognized, the society we live in is sick. The poor belong to a social class, but also to a race, a culture, and a sex. These several aspects are not simply juxtaposed but form a complex totality that forbids our identifying the poor with only one of them.

The paradoxical result of all this is the disproportion we find in the church between the acknowledged place of Mary and the low value set on women. It will take a great deal of effort to overcome cultural ideas that are so deeply rooted and strongly present in society, especially when we ourselves have in one way or another helped give them their staying power. This has been true even of famous Christian thinkers whose thought was more in harmony with the prejudices of their age than with the judgment and attitude of Jesus. This is an area in which Christians must do penance; but they also face the task of overcoming social inertia, narrow outlooks, and concerns for power, and of deepening and developing the values that Christian revelation attaches to women. Thanks especially to the efforts of outstanding women, some of these values have risen to the surface at certain moments in the history of the church. Restrictions and putdowns, however, have set the dominant tone.

In this context, the experience gained from the participation of women in the Christian communities of Latin America seems to me to be of special interest. They play a role of the first importance there because of their sensitivity to the sufferings of others, their stubbornness in keeping commitments, their realism in approaching situations, and the room they find in these groups for developing their potentialities and charisms.

Jesus and Women

If we are properly to evaluate both the relationship of Jesus to women and the figure of Mary in the Gospels, we must bear in mind God's plan for human beings.

The first chapters of Genesis give us two accounts of the creation of man and woman. The first belongs to the priestly tradition, the second to the Yahwist. The first account emphasizes the fundamental equality of man and woman:

> God created man in his image;
> in the divine image he created him;
> male and female he created them. [Gn 1:27]

Man and woman alike are created in the image of God and for God. Humanity has two faces: male and female. Neither is subordinated to the other, both look to God as equals.

The second account, which presents woman as helper to man, emphasizes complementarity rather than equality.

> The Lord God said: "It is not good for the man to be alone. I will make a suitable partner for him." ... So the Lord God cast a deep sleep on the man, and while he was asleep, he took out one of his ribs and closed up its place with flesh. The Lord God then built up into a woman the rib that he had taken from the man. When he brought her to the man, the man said:
> This one, at last, is bone of my bones
> and flesh of my flesh. [Gn 2:18, 21–23]

The term "helper" (see also Gn 2:20; Hebrew: *'ezer*) is used a number of times to describe God as one who comes to the aid of individuals and of his people (see, e.g., Ex 18:4; Dt 7:26–29; Ps 20:3; 33:20; 70:5). The word used for the idea of helper or assistant means "to be joined to" and therefore does not imply any inferiority of woman. Thus when the man (Hebrew: *is*) says that the one taken from him shall be called *issah* ("woman"), he shows by the very name the equality of nature of these two who are to become "one body" (vv. 23–24). The two thus belong to each other by a double title.

The central message in these accounts is that man and woman alike are in the first place *beings for God*; this is their basic characteristic. At the same time, they exist for one another.[7] Human beings have an inescapable vocation to community. The equality and complementarity of man and woman follow from their more fundamental relationship to God. Man and woman together are the image of God, and this fact sets its imprint on the bond between them.[8]

Despite this, we find in the Bible stories of incidents that occurred among the Jewish people and of experiences and reflections of individuals in search of God, which reflect a particular culture and age. In these, masculine superiority is taken for granted. Various books of the Bible reflect this prejudice. And even though we also find in the Bible outstanding women who highlight the values proper to women, these do not succeed in breaking down the prevailing masculine mentality of the Jewish people and of the entire world in that age.

The attitude of Jesus to women represented, therefore, a real break with this distortion among his people and with the dominant categories of his time. His behavior elicited reactions of surprise and even scandal among his contemporaries, including his own disciples. Luke, who is especially alert to this aspect of Jesus' person, calls attention to the presence of women as companions and disciples of Jesus (see Lk 8:1–3; 23:49). The mere fact that women collaborated with Jesus shows how new and different his attitude to them was. But this only fed the prejudices and hostility of those who felt threatened by the ministry of the Galilean preacher.

The openness that Jesus showed to women was another thing his contemporaries found new and strange, since in their view women were unclean or were counted among those to be despised. His own disciples are scandalized to find him in conversation with a Samaritan woman:

> At that moment his disciples returned, and were amazed that he was talking with a woman, but no one said, "What are you looking for?" or "Why are you talking to her?" The woman left her water jar and went into the town and said to the people, "Come see a man who told me everything I have done. Could he possibly be the Messiah?" [Jn 4:27–29]

If people were bewildered to see a Jew talking to someone belonging to the despised people of Samaria, they were all the more bewildered when the Samaritan was a woman. Add to this that the woman becomes the bearer of the good news to her people; for Jesus to make the Samaritan woman an evangelizer is a bold and unorthodox step in his dealings with women. In so doing he adopts a position that is clearly opposed to the cultural and religious standards of his time.

He also acts against these standards in his treatment of the woman taken in adultery:

> Early in the morning he arrived again in the temple area, and all the people started coming to him, and he sat down and taught them. Then the scribes and the Pharisees brought a woman who had been caught in adultery and made her stand in the middle. They said to him, "Teacher, this woman was caught in the act of committing adultery. Now in the law, Moses commanded us to stone such a woman. So what do you say?" [Jn 8:2–5]

The Lord's answer, once again, shocks his questioners. He does not simply forgive the sinner. What he is really doing is challenging the double standard of morality (which, in its own way, is still present among us today) that inflicted the death penalty on an adulterous woman while applying lesser sanctions to a man in the same situation. Jesus' pardon thus expresses his rejection of a moral law that discriminates against women. If there is equal responsibility in sin, there ought to be an equal sanction.

This explains the challenge of Jesus to the scribes and Pharisees and to all present: "Let the one among you who is without sin be the first to throw a stone at her" (Jn 8:7). When Jesus is at last alone with the woman, he speaks to her in tender words: "Neither do I condemn you. Go, [and] from now on do not sin any more" (Jn 8:11). It is not difficult to imagine the impact of this incident and the hostility that Jesus the Nazarene awakened in those who saw this attack on the foundations of the social and religious order in which they lived and from which they benefited.

The freedom with which the Lord acts is likewise shown in the friendships that, as the gospel informs us, he has with some women. Both Luke and John tell us of his relationship with Lazarus and the latter's sisters, Martha and Mary, all of whom "Jesus loved" (Jn 11:5). In their house and company he found a welcome and repose. Luke reports a short but charming incident that has friendship for its central theme. This well-known passage comes immediately after the parable of the good Samaritan:

> As they continued their journey he entered a village where a woman whose name was Martha welcomed him. She had a sister Mary [who] sat beside the Lord at his feet listening to him speak. Martha, burdened with much serving, came to him and said, "Lord, do you not care that my sister has left me by myself to do the serving? Tell her to help me." The Lord said to her in reply, "Martha, Martha, you are anxious and worried about many things. There is need of only one thing. Mary has chosen the better part and it will not be taken from her." [Lk 10:38–42]

Jesus is welcomed into the home of Martha, who is probably the elder of the two sisters and whose name in Hebrew means "mistress; lady of the house." Martha thus treats Jesus as her neighbor and shows concern for him (in accordance with the teaching of the parable). Her sister, Mary, may have initially been helping with the household chores; at the moment, however, she is sitting and listening to the Lord's words. She is not practicing mere courtesy. Her attitude, of which Jesus approves, is highly meaningful. The learned men and doctors of the law were of the opinion that women were not capable of any deep understanding of the teachings contained in the law of God. Mary violates this standard. Seated there at the Lord's feet, she tries to gain a direct knowledge of the message; by so doing, she claims the right to enter into the enclosed preserve of male Jews.

Martha shows the familiarity of a friend when she reproaches Jesus for not telling Mary to be attentive to her sister. Martha has not seen that the Lord is in agreement with Mary's claim. His reply is an affectionate one, as the repetition of Martha's name shows, but it is also firm; he criticizes her for remaining prisoner of what she considers to be her proper role as a woman and mistress of the house. Martha should, like Mary, claim and fully occupy her place as a disciple of the Lord.

It needs to be said that, contrary to an interpretation often given, there is no opposition established here between Mary the contemplative and Martha the active woman. Contemplation and action are both essential dimensions of Christian life. Furthermore, the parable of the good Samaritan has just reminded us of the importance of actions done for the neighbor. Jesus does not reject the labors Martha undertakes in his service, but he lets her know that her condition as a woman does not limit her to those tasks; she has a right to other concerns. Domestic duties should not take up all her time, for in the final analysis not many things are necessary. It is not right that she should exert herself excessively in such duties while suppressing other dimensions of life to which she has a right.

Mary has chosen "the better part," which is to listen to the word of the Lord, to be a witness to it. This is the one thing necessary, because it gives meaning to everything else. Mary has dared to break out of what was regarded as the exclusive role of a woman. Jesus seeks by his actions and words to free Martha, too, from the conception of women that allows them only the secondary role of homemaker. In the Gospel of John the Lord tells his disciples that they are his friends and not his servants (see 15:14–15). He gives Martha the same message: "Be a friend, like Mary, and not a servant." Because friendship always supposes equality, the friendship of Jesus with the two sisters leads them to find themselves and thus sets them on the way to their full liberation.

Another important indicator: it is a woman (whose identity is not completely clear) who foretells the death of Jesus by her prophetic act of anointing his body. In response to the biased protest of those whose hearts are set on money, the Lord says that wherever the good news is proclaimed, her action will be told "in memory of her" (Mk 14:9; see also Mt 26:6–13 and Jn 12:1–8). The history of the church shows, however, that this command of the Lord has been forgotten. Only two other individuals who also play a prominent part in the passion story have been remembered: Judas, who betrayed Jesus, and Peter, who denied him.[9]

It is also women, as I mentioned earlier, who are the first witnesses to the resurrection of the Lord. John highlights the part played by Mary Magdalene (Jn 20:1, 18); Luke adds "Joanna, and Mary the mother of James" and "the others who accompanied them" (Lk 24:10). All these women must have held an important place among those who followed the teachings of Jesus; Luke in particular brings out their role at different points in his Gospel. The women tell the story to Peter and other disciples (see Jn 20:2,

18); according to Luke, the men are not convinced (Lk 24:11), but then find themselves obliged to reverse their opinion (24:12).

The high esteem that Jesus shows for women has made its way down the centuries despite entrenched resistances and despite having to evade clever strategems for maintaining traditional positions behind some changes in vocabulary. In any event, the behavior of Jesus must be the model and inspiration for those who make their own the message of the kingdom and regard Mary as "the perfect Christian."[10]

Blessed among Women

> During those days Mary set out and traveled to the hill country in haste to a town of Judah, where she entered the house of Zechariah and greeted Elizabeth. When Elizabeth heard Mary's greeting, the infant leaped in her womb, and Elizabeth, filled with the holy Spirit, cried out in a loud voice and said, "Most blessed are you among women, and blessed is the fruit of your womb. And how does this happen to me, that the mother of my Lord should come to me? For at the moment the sound of your greeting reached my ears, the infant in my womb leaped for joy." [Lk 1:39–44]

The Gospel episode we call the "visitation" tells of the meeting of two pregnant women. Mary, a Galilean, comes to Judah, the region where her son will one day be rejected and condemned to death. At her greeting, the child whom Elizabeth is carrying "leaps for joy" in her womb. A few moments later, the mother tells of what she has felt within her and describes the joy felt by the child who has until now been the focus of the events narrated in this first chapter of Luke.[11] Joy is the first response to the coming of the Messiah.

Elizabeth then utters a twofold blessing. As he always does in important statements, Luke here stresses the point that Elizabeth acts as one "filled with the holy Spirit" and that she cries out "in a loud voice." Mary is said to be "blessed among women." Her womanhood is singled out; it is as a woman that she is regarded as loved and given privileged status by God.[12] This interpretation is ratified in the second motif of Elizabeth's praise: "blessed is the fruit of your womb." The reference is, of course, to Jesus, but the emphasis is on the fact that he is now within the body of a woman, within her womb, fabric of her fabric. Mary's body thus becomes the sacred ark in which the Spirit lodges and makes known her greatness as a woman. Elizabeth then recognizes in her visitor "the mother of the Lord." Luke is undoubtedly placing on Elizabeth's lips an understanding that the Christian community achieved only after the resurrection. The important thing, however, is that this confession of faith emphasizes the motherhood of Mary. Her visit is an unexpected gift for Elizabeth.

Mention of Mary's motherhood is also found in other New Testament writings. Paul refers to the Son of God and adds the plainest possible description: "born of a woman" (Gal 4:4), which is true of every human being. John the Evangelist never mentions Mary by name but calls her simply "the mother of Jesus," and yet he has her playing an important role both at the beginning of Jesus' public life and at its end, beneath the cross (see Jn 2:1–12 and 19:25–27). Matthew has a description close to that of Paul, except that he gives the mother's name: "Mary of [whom] was born Jesus" (Mt 1:16). Immediately after the genealogy he has his own short "infancy Gospel."

Luke goes further. His emphasis on the womanhood of Mary shows that in his view this point is important if we are to understand what the Lord is trying to communicate to us. The birth of John the Baptist is announced to the father; that of Jesus, to the mother (see Lk 1:11–12 and 26–38). Furthermore, as I have already said, it is Elizabeth who acknowledges Mary as woman and mother.

In addition, we find another woman playing an important part toward the end of the Lukan infancy Gospel. The woman is Anna (the name means "grace, favor"), who is described as "a prophetess." When Jesus is presented in the temple, Anna praises God and speaks "about the child to all who were awaiting the redemption of Jerusalem." She prophesies about him in the temple, which "she never left." In this way she proclaims Mary's son as liberator of his people (Lk 2:36–38).

Several chapters later, in a passage found only in his Gospel, Luke once again puts on the lips of a woman a beatitude addressed to Mary: "While he was speaking, a woman from the crowd called out and said to him, 'Blessed is the womb that carried you and the breasts at which you nursed' " (Lk 11:27).

The context of this scene is important. Faced with people who refuse to recognize the meaning of the signs he performs, Jesus demands a stand for or against himself (see 11:23). When he had said this, a woman calls out, declaring that the mother of the Lord is blessed. John says that "the word became flesh" (Jn 1:14); Luke is more specific: he became flesh in the body of a woman. This is the point of the mention of Mary's womb and breasts. In his infancy Gospel Luke twice refers to Mary's womb (1:31 and 2:21, using different Greek words each time). The Lord's coming is a physical and not a "metaphysical" event, in the sense of something transcending the bodily sphere. We call his coming precisely his incarnation. The beatitude uttered by this unnamed woman (who uses words with an Old Testament flavor; see Gn 49:25) highlights a basic element of our faith: Jesus was born of a woman. That is how he introduced himself into human history.

The episode of the presentation recalls other aspects of Mary's womanhood:

When the days were completed for their purification according to the law of Moses, they took him up to Jerusalem to present him to the

Lord, just as it is written in the law of the Lord, "Every male that opens the womb shall be consecrated to the Lord," and to offer the sacrifice of "a pair of turtle doves or two young pigeons," in accordance with the dictate in the law of the Lord. [Lk 2:22–24]

Luke speaks rather vaguely of "their purification," when in fact there is question only of Mary's duty as a woman. According to Leviticus 12:2, a woman who gives birth to a boy "shall be unclean for seven days" (if the child is a girl, the uncleanness lasts for fourteen days). On the other hand, the actual presentation of the male child in the temple was not necessary. Its performance by Mary and Joseph may reflect their recognition that Jesus had a special mission. What is certain is that the mother was obliged to offer a sacrifice. According to the passage in Leviticus, which Luke cites, if she "cannot afford a lamb, she may take two turtledoves or two pigeons, the one for a holocaust and the other for a sin offering" (Lv 12:8; see also 5:7).

Mary's offering is thus what Vatican II rightly calls "the offering of the poor" (*LG* 57). Such were the circumstances of Mary, the virgin from the little town of Nazareth. She was a poor woman, and Luke points this out explicitly.

2. THE BELIEVER

Jesus, the Messiah, is the central figure of the gospels, and even of the sections dealing with his childhood. Mary plays an important role in the infancy narratives, but it is a subordinate role to that of her son. She is presented to us as a woman who believes in Jesus. Her attitude and her acceptance are related to the God who announces Christ. As we have just been seeing, Luke closely links the faith of Mary and her motherhood. She is the believer par excellence. However, the texts referring to her faith show it to be a process. She does not believe completely once and for all; rather there is a maturation and growth in her surrender to the Lord. Mary shows the way to all the disciples of her son.

Rejoice, Favored One!
The name of the child foretold to Zechariah is John, which means "Yahweh is favorable." And in fact the entire first two chapters of Luke's Gospel are concerned with the friendly, saving presence of God. Six months after the first divine communication, the same messenger of God announces to Mary the birth of Jesus the Savior. "In the sixth month, the angel Gabriel was sent from God to a town of Galilee called Nazareth, to a virgin betrothed to a man named Joseph, of the house of David, and the virgin's name was Mary. And coming to her, he said, 'Hail [or: Rejoice], favored one! The Lord is with you'" (Lk 1:26–28).

The angel's conversation with Mary begins with his urging her to be filled with joy. There are other ways of translating the angel's opening salutation, but "rejoice" is the one on which there is a growing consensus today. "Rejoice" puts us in a messianic setting, for joy is a characteristic accompaniment of the fulfillment of God's promises. Mary receives God's favor; "favored one" is a substitute for the name, Mary, in the angel's greeting. The Lord is with her: "you have found favor with God" (v. 30). Everything happens under the sign of God's free and unmerited love. Faith is the gift that sets the dialogue in motion; God relies on her, and this makes her in turn trust in him; it turns her into a person of faith. There is, therefore, no reason to be afraid; there is room only for self-surrender. Fear is the contrary of trust in God. The gaze that the Lord turns upon Mary solicits her faith; thanks to her response the young Jewish girl participates in God's work.

For in fact that which the angel announces will be the work of the Holy Spirit; the shadow of the Most High will cover Mary (see v. 35). We already know the role that Luke assigns to the Holy Spirit in the work of Jesus and his followers. There may be an allusion here to the dwelling of God in history; God is present now in the womb of Mary. Mary accepts this presence; this is the most important point made in the passage. Among her first recorded words are: "Behold, I am the handmaid of the Lord. May it be done to me according to your word" (v. 38). In the Magnificat Mary will again call herself God's "handmaid" (see 1:48). In both cases, this term (Greek: *doulos*) is more appropriate than "slave," a translation often used. Luke has in mind here the Hebrew word *'ebed* (servant), which signifies a belonging to God rather than a subordination or inferiority.[13] Those who proclaim the Lord's message are his servants, says Luke, citing Joel (in Acts 2:18), as are the preachers in Jerusalem (Acts 4:29), as well as Paul and Silas (Acts 16:17).

Attachment to God finds expression in being at God's service, in acceptance of God's will. This aspect of Mary's relationship with God emerges clearly in the second part of her answer to the angel. She does not ask for signs, as Zechariah had done (see Lk 1:18). She shows full confidence in God, whose word is always efficacious. She makes that word her own by her faith and in her body. This receptivity is the first requirement of servants; through it they bear witness to God's love. Jesus will say later on that the will of the one who sent him is his food (Jn 4:34), and in the depths of his agony he will pray that this will may be done beyond all else (Lk 22:42).

The word of God (*rhema*, which means both word and event, as I noted earlier) is a gift, but human beings must freely accept it. Mary's faith and humility do not prevent her from entering into a dialogue with the messenger of God. She does not simply listen to and accept his message; her faith is a free act, and therefore she inquires, she wants to know how that which has been made known to her will come about. The power of the Spirit stirs her to active participation; hers is the collaboration of one who knows that she is in the hands of God. Her assent to her motherhood brings us the Messiah; it speaks to us of God's will to life for every human being. In the Magnificat Mary says: "The Mighty One has done great things for me" (1:49). This fact is the source of the mission she accepts and takes up. We saw earlier that favor, or grace, and demand frame the experience of believers. Mary thus has her place in the history of salvation.

The miracle of the incarnation combines the power of the Spirit and the weakness of Mary. The son of this young Jewish woman has a role to play in history. "He will be great and will be called Son of the Most High, and the Lord God will give him the throne of David his father, and he will rule over the house of Jacob forever, and of his kingdom there will be no end" (1:32–33).

Such will be the responsibility of Jesus in his mission: his mission begins a new stage in the reign of God. Mary's motherhood, therefore, is more than a personal gift to her; it is a gift to the entire race. We see here a charism in the strict sense of this word — that is, a gift given to an individual for the good of the community. Mary is aware of all that her acceptance of God's will implies.

Elizabeth calls Mary blessed because she has trusted in God: "Blessed are you who believed that what was spoken to you by the Lord would be fulfilled" (1:45). She is blessed because she has accepted the gift of faith; she has believed in God. Thus the final verse of both the Annunciation and the Visitation stories emphasizes the point that Mary is a believer: she accepts God's will for her, and that is what motivates Elizabeth's statement.

This view of Mary is confirmed by Jesus himself. From a crowd that is listening to the Lord and following him, a woman cries out that his mother is blessed for having carried him in her womb. He replies: "Rather, blessed are they who hear the word of God and observe it" (Lk 11:28). The beatitude uttered by the woman should, in truth, apply to all who believe. Jesus is therefore not so much correcting her as making her statement more accurate, for his mother is, in fact, an object lesson in belief. In the passages I have been reviewing, Luke describes Mary as one who accepted God's plan from the very beginning. She is mother in her body and in her faith, or, more accurately, mother in her body because of her faith.[14] The son whom she carries in her womb is at the same time an expression of her faith. Motherhood and faith are inseparable in Mary.

The Synoptic Gospels contain a passage that is important in this context. I shall cite it from Mark:

His mother and his brothers arrived. Standing outside they sent word to him and called him. A crowd seated around him told him, "Your mother and your brothers [and your sisters] are outside asking for you." But he said to them in reply, "Who are my mother and [my] brothers?" And looking around at those seated in the circle he said, "Here are my mother and my brothers. [For] whoever does the will of God is my brother and sister and mother." [Mk 3:31–35; see Mt 12:46–50 and Lk 8:19–21]

The Gospels tell us on several occasions of the difficulty that the relatives of Jesus had in understanding his mission (see Jn 7:1–12). Mark makes this point, not without some harshness, in a passage that comes shortly before the one cited above. In the incident I am examining here, the relatives of Jesus (including his mother) are simply looking for him in order to see him (Lk 8:20) and speak with him (Mt 12:47). The Lord takes advantage of an opportunity to deepen the faith of his hearers: "My mother and my brothers are those who hear the word of God and act on it" (Lk 8:21). Matthew and Mark convey the same idea but speak rather of "doing the will" of God the Father. In addition, these two evangelists state expressly that before saying who his real family are, Jesus relates his words to those around him: "those seated in the circle," says Mark (3:34), while Matthew is even more specific: "stretching out his hand toward his disciples" (Mt 12:49). Once again, the point is made that Mary's motherhood acquires its full meaning thanks to her faith, to her discipleship.

The much-discussed episode of the wedding feast at Cana (reported by John) is an important one here. According to the story, Mary is among the first disciples of Jesus, all of them from Galilee, the region where John, like the Synoptic writers, locates the beginning of the Messiah's ministry. The mother of the Lord plays an important part in this first miracle of Jesus. Important, too, are the final remarks of the Evangelist: "Jesus did this as the beginning of his signs at Cana in Galilee and so revealed his glory, and his disciples began to believe in him. After this, he and his mother, [his] brothers, and his disciples went down to Capernaum and stayed there only a few days" (Jn 2:11–12). Mary accompanies her son and is among the disciples who "believed in him."

Mary is again shown as a follower of Jesus in a passage peculiar to John. She is said to stand by the cross, together with other women who had accompanied Jesus. Not only is she a disciple, but she is assigned a special dignity when Jesus makes of her a mother to his beloved disciple (Jn 19:25–27). Her presence in the midst of the Eleven, at the time when the church is about to be established (Acts 1:14), conveys the same meaning: she is a disciple of her son and is found in the midst of the community made up of his followers.

She Kept These Things in Her Heart

Faith always involves a journey. When Elizabeth says to Mary: "Blessed are you who believed," she is not making a timeless statement, as if Mary's faith had been full and complete from the beginning. Mary was a believer whose trust in the Lord grew amid uncertainties, anxieties, and joys. Luke makes this point in a passage to which I made passing reference earlier. He tells us that when the twelve-year-old Jesus went to Jerusalem for the

Passover, he remained there "but his parents did not know it." Then, "not finding him, they returned to Jerusalem to look for him" (Lk 2:43, 45). It was a painful search, but an instructive one:

> After three days they found him in the temple, sitting in the midst of the teachers, listening to them and asking them questions, and all who heard him were astounded at his understanding and his answers. When his parents saw him, they were astonished, and his mother said to him, "Son, why have you done this to us? Your father and I have been looking for you with great anxiety." And he said to them, "Why were you looking for me? Did you not know that I must be in my Father's house?" But they did not understand what he said to them. [Lk 2:46–50]

They did not understand, not yet. For Mary, too, things became only gradually clearer. Luke remarks: "His mother kept all these things in her heart" (2:51). Her meditation on them enabled her to gain a deeper understanding of Jesus' mission (see also 2:19). Her special closeness to the Lord did not exempt her from the difficult and endless process leading to an understanding of God's plans. She is the first disciple to be evangelized by Jesus.

Simeon, one of the individuals who appears in the infancy Gospel, has already given her a warning, in words whose meaning is debated. "Behold, this child is destined for the rise and fall of many in Israel, and to be a sign that will be contradicted (and you yourself a sword will pierce) so that the thoughts of many hearts may be revealed" (Lk 2:34–35).

This is a prophecy about the Messiah, but it has direct consequences for Mary. In earlier verses Simeon, inspired by the theme of the Servant of Yahweh (Is 40–55), had expressed his personal satisfaction at the coming of the Messiah, whom he recognizes in the little son of Joseph and Mary. He now speaks of the radical changes that Jesus will bring about as he carries out his messianic mission. He will overturn the present order: some will be lifted up, others will fall. The same idea had already found utterance in the Magnificat, in a passage to which I shall turn further on. The witness given by the Messiah will cause a division among his people, as he himself will later say: "Whoever does not gather with me scatters" (Lk 11:23). He will therefore be contradicted, resisted, and even rejected.

A short parenthesis in the text shows that Mary is not unaffected by the implications of Simeon's prophecy. She too—her soul—will be affected to the core by what happens to the Messiah. Mary is part of Israel. If we place ourselves in the context in which Luke is speaking, we must interpret the few words about Mary as an invitation to her to deepen her faith. Even she must recognize the signs of the Messiah (this is the meaning of the sword that will pierce her soul).[15] To accept Christ means to reject whatever is opposed to him or resists his message.

More than this, Mary has before her a costly journey. The suffering that the mother of the Lord will experience in her lifetime will be another way of sharing in the Messiah's work. This is not the primary meaning of Simeon's parenthesis, but it is an important consequence of what is said there. Christian devotion, set on this path by Augustine of Hippo, has been especially attentive to it. The devotion has given rise to the image of the Sorrowful Mother, though this is also inspired by John 19:25–27 (Mary beside the cross).

The poor, who are familiar with suffering, have always been very responsive to the suffering of Mary. This emerges beautifully from a text collected in the world of the Andes; despite its length, it is worth citing here in its entirety:

I am already deaf. My eyes are also worn out; I no longer have my teeth. All I have is this coca, which our Mother, Mary Most Holy, chewed. Therefore this coca is my food, my coffee, my everything; this coca alone is of use to me. In sorrows, in joys, it is only by eating this coca, sir, that I endure my life.
But did Mary Most Holy chew coca?
Yes, she chewed it.
Why did she chew it?
She was grieving for her son, for Jesus. Her son had been lost to her — that Jesus of Nazareth who had been born in the people of Jerusalem. Then, when her son grew up and disappeared, she went weeping after him, and in her endless grief she bit into some leaves of this bush. That is why it is now a comfort to all and to us to chew it when we are in distress.
And when she chewed the coca, what happened?
Then her endless grief and tears were allayed. And so, being now calm, she met her son. Then he said to her: "I am not lost; my father has commanded me, and what my father has commanded me I must do; now I shall go away." Saying this, he went away. So then, Mary Most Holy ate coca, and so we eat only coca in the cold of this high plateau. But the Virgin did not really *chew* it; she only bit into it. It is obvious that she simply bit into it; why should she chew it as I do?
Is coca pleasant?
Yes, sir, it is pleasant. It is as though it were meant for the cold of this high plateau. Here we are very high up; there is a great deal of wind and snow and hail; there are many hardships.
And so life is sometimes pleasant and sometimes bitter?
So it is, sir.[16]

The elderly peasant who speaks in this way understands Mary in terms of an ancestral custom of his people: the custom of chewing coca. He is able by way of it to be in communion with the suffering of the Mother of

God. By chewing coca he endures his life and faces up to the reality of his poverty. Suffering must also have caused Mary to chew coca. When the questioner expresses surprise at hearing this, the peasant reminds him that coca helps ease hardships. Then, concerned perhaps that he may have been "irreverent," he retreats a bit: the Virgin only bit into the coca and did not chew it as the American Indians do. The life of these people is both pleasant and bitter, like the coca. As a result, they see Mary as very close to them.

The messianic joy that Luke mentions several times in his first two chapters is not contradicted by the suffering that the mission of Jesus brings with it. On the contrary, the joy is heightened. For this is not an easy joy; it is paschal joy, it comes through suffering, just as definitive life comes through death.

3. DAUGHTER OF A PEOPLE

Mary is not an isolated individual, but a daughter of a people. Luke calls attention to this relationship and even goes so far as to identify Mary with Israel. His infancy Gospel is a tissue of biblical texts[17]; he uses them to announce the great themes of the kingdom, which is at the heart of Jesus' preaching.[18]

This approach achieves a sublime intensity in the song known as the Magnificat, which Luke places on the lips of the Mother of the Lord. Up to this point, Mary has said little; now Luke has her speak for ten verses.[19] Various attempts have been made to subdivide the text; no consensus has been reached. In my opinion, however, there is greater agreement on the deeper unity of the song and on seeing as its central point the assertion of the holiness of God: "Holy is his name" (1:49). This is the essential message conveyed by Mary's way of speaking about God.[20]

That is the viewpoint I shall adopt in this section. I shall not attempt a commentary on the Magnificat; many excellent ones already exist and will help in reflecting on what Mary says to us about God.

All Is Grace

It is often said that in the first verses (46–50) of the Magnificat—the verses some regard as forming the first part of the song—Mary speaks as an individual. That is why we find the expressions "my soul" and "my spirit," which are semitisms for the pronoun "I."

The fact of these expressions should not, however, make us forget that throughout the entire song (and not just in vv. 51–55, which some consider the second half of it) Mary expresses herself as a daughter of a people; in some sense, she represents this people, as I said earlier:

> And Mary said:
> "My soul proclaims the greatness of the Lord;

my spirit rejoices in God my savior.
For he has looked upon his handmaid's lowliness;
    behold, from now on will all ages call me blessed.
The Mighty One has done great things for me."
                    [Lk 1:46–49a]

Mary and, with her, her people sing of the greatness of God. God is the Lord, the Mighty One, who acts with power. The power of God is revealed in history through saving actions. There are many passages of the Old Testament that make this point (some of them have been cited in part one of this book). Yahweh, the God who is and is with us, will become the liberator of Israel. The Book of Exodus tells us that God said: "I have witnessed the affliction of my people in Egypt" (Ex 3:7). Deuteronomy is more specific: "He saw our affliction [in the Septuagint: *tapeinōsis*], our toil and our oppression" (Dt 26:7). This second passage is meaningful because it is part of the most important example of a "historical creed." Therefore, because he had witnessed this situation, Yahweh brought the people out of Egypt "with his strong hand and outstretched arm" (Dt 4:34) and established a covenant with it. From the standpoint of the faith of Israel, one must refer back to Israel's fontal experience if one is to understand an event of the magnitude of the Messiah's coming. This coming is also, and all the more, a manifestation of the power of God and of God's intervention in history.

Mary tells us that God saw "his handmaid's lowliness." "Lowliness" (or humility) translates the Greek word *tapeinōsis*, which has a definite connotation of affliction and oppression, as we saw a moment ago in the passage cited from Deuteronomy. The Greek *tapeinōsis* often translates the Hebrew word *'oni*, which signifies affliction caused by servitude and despoliation (or by sterility in the case of women; see Gn 16:11).[21] Mary, then, who is a servant and, in addition, a woman who has placed her life in the Lord's hands, is a "situation of humiliation."

God has "looked upon" the situation of Mary. The expression "look upon" is often used in the Bible with reference to the concern God has for those who suffer injustice and humiliation. It is a gaze of love that makes Mary happy. God will act in history in her behalf; God has the power to do so. Thus the covenant between God and the people is renewed.[22]

Contemplation of God's liberating power brings joy with it for those who benefit from God's action. At an earlier point we saw various expressions of this joy in the first chapters of Luke. Here, Mary exults (that is, leaps) for joy, in response to the exhortation of the angel Gabriel: "Rejoice!" (1:28). This is an attitude of great depth and fullness. "God my savior" is the source of her happiness; all will admit that she is happy, and will declare her blessed. In writing this, Luke may have had in mind the view that the first Christian communities had of Mary. The statement is a reminder, moreover, of what Isaiah says in 61:9–10: the nations will acknowledge those whom the Lord has liberated.

The joy is Mary's but it is also the joy of the entire people. At the birth of Jesus the shepherds are told: "Do not be afraid; for behold I proclaim to you good news [*euanggelizomai hymin*] of great joy that will be for all the people" (2:10). This joy is the subject of the angel's proclamation, for it is in fact a central element of the gospel. Joy enables Mary to proclaim the good news. The feeling of joy expands her heart and makes her even more disposed to receive the presence of God. In this way she becomes more a servant, more a person who places her entire trust in the Lord. It is out of a complete adherence to God, symbolized by her virginity, that Mary speaks of God and helps us to place ourselves in the presence of God's gratuitous love.

The second part of verse 49 contains the central statement of the Magnificat:

> . . . and holy is his name.
> His mercy is from age to age
> to those who fear him. [Lk 1:49b–50]

The Magnificat is a hymn of praise to the holy God. Psalm 111 praises God for the work of liberation and does so in words close to those of the Magnificat: "He has sent deliverance to his people; he has ratified his covenant forever; holy and awesome is his name" (v. 9). God's holiness gives meaning to the work of liberation. The mighty God is also merciful. Might and mercy are two aspects of God's greatness; God is a loving power, an efficacious love. God's mercy (Hebrew: *hesed*) makes God receptive and tender.

The exercise of God's power and mercy makes known to us God's greatness and holiness. "Holy is his name" is a statement that recurs throughout the Bible and one that Mary makes her own. Everything comes from God and from God's freely given, unmerited love. This idea is at the heart of biblical revelation and therefore also of the preaching of Jesus. At the Annunciation Mary was told: "the child to be born will be called holy, the son of God" (Lk 1:35). The literary form of the text makes us think that Luke's intention here is clearly to say that the holy one, the wholly other, is not a distant God. God becomes flesh, one of us, in the womb of Mary. The incarnation does not deprive God of transcendence but reveals to us what kind of holiness is God's.

God's holiness is that of one who fulfills promises (see Lk 1:55); who enters into our history in order to bring it into the sphere of the divine; who transforms the present world. God is the God who does justice, with all that the word "justice" implies in the Bible. To this end God makes an agreement with the people. It is as a member of this people that Mary speaks. Her contemplation of God's holiness is not an evasion of history;

her joy at the gratuitous love of the Lord does not make her forget the demands of justice. On the other hand, insertion into history and the building of a just world would lack real depth for Christians apart from the acceptance of God as the one absolute in our lives and as the ultimate foundation of our hope and our joy. Mary traces for us the path to this realization.

A Different History

The ways of God are not our ways (see Is 58). In God's plan, the least of history become the first. God's preference for the weak and oppressed runs throughout the Bible, as we saw from many passages cited earlier. The people of Israel have an obligation to bear witness to this predilection; the Messiah comes to proclaim it by his actions and words. Luke is, as we know, especially alert to this point. He therefore shows God's being revealed to the unimportant folk of history, to such 'anawim as Zechariah, Elizabeth, Simeon, Anna, and, above all, Mary. This revelation also speaks to us of the radical change of values and situations that is wrought by the coming of the Messiah. Mary's song expresses this in a forceful way:

> He has shown might with his arm,
>   dispersed the arrogant of mind and heart.
> He has thrown down the rulers from their thrones
>   but lifted up the lowly.
> The hungry he has filled with good things;
>   the rich he has sent away empty. [Lk 1:51–53]

These verses have been the object of indignant or fearful rejection and of fervent (if at times somewhat superficial) applause—when they are not causing headaches for the scholars. They are also, of course, an abiding challenge and reason for hope and joy among the Christian people. These three verses tell us how God (who is the subject of all six verbs) manifests power and mercy in history and makes the divine holiness present.[23]

First of all, God disperses the arrogant. "The might of his arm" is an expression that occurs frequently in the context of the exodus. It signifies the power by which Yahweh delivers the people. The verb used for "disperse" is a strong one; it means to put an enemy to flight. The thought is an echo (such as is found in, for example, Psalm 89:11, which may be one of the sources of the Magnificat) of what happened to the armies of the pharaoh. The power of God is exercised against the arrogant (the Greek word is *hyperēphanoi*), those who make a show of being more than they are, the proud and insolent.[24] These people are blusterers at heart. A literal translation of the text would be: "dispersed them in the thoughts of their heart." This is why some translate: "scattered the plans of the proud." Among these plans is the intention to humiliate the poor. These people feel that they were born to be in control and to be respected. Pride thus makes them enemies of God.

This verse does not say who they are who are contrasted with the proud; the next two verses will do this. But the preceding verse does speak of "those who fear him [God]" (v. 50). "Fear" of God is an important theme in the Bible, but the fear is not a fear of a powerful and even angry being. The idea here is different and reaches deeper: "fear" of God means respect for the plans, and trust in the person, of one who loves us faithfully. His servants (Mary, v. 48, and Israel, v. 54) are those who commit their lives to him. The proud are those who reject God's will, God's purpose, which is life, peace, and justice for all and especially for the poor and the unimportant people.

God's second action is described in the form of an antithesis in which rulers are contrasted with the lowly. By "rulers" is meant here those who use their power to dominate and oppress. Such rulers are brought low. The Bible is full of passages that say the same. One from Sirach that closely resembles the verse in the Magnificat sums up the thought very nicely: "The thrones of the arrogant God overturns and establishes the lowly in their stead" (Sir 10:14). God loathes those who take advantage of their power to mistreat and rob others. Jesus rejects this kind of power and offers himself as the model servant (see Lk 22:24–27).[25]

The lowly will be lifted up. I have already mentioned the meaning of the term "lowly" as represented by the Greek word *tapeinos*. The reference is to the humiliated, the poor, the oppressed. Mary has already spoken of her own "lowliness." Here she is speaking of the "lowliness" of the poor in Israel and indeed throughout all of human history. The parallelism is intentional and meaningful.

The holy God (who is powerful and merciful) is on the side of the weak and abused, not of their rulers. Paul says to the Christians of Corinth:

Consider your own calling, brothers. Not many of you were wise by human standards, not many were powerful, not many were of noble birth. Rather, God chose the foolish of the world to shame the wise, and God chose the weak of the world to shame the strong, and God chose the lowly and despised of the world, those who count for nothing, to reduce to nothing those who are something. [1 Cor 1:26–28]

A passage from Albert the Great, centuries ago, is clear on the social and historical implications of the verse on which I am commenting:

The rulers whom God throws down are those who glory in their power and misuse it by using it to oppress the poor. . . . They are the rulers we call "tyrants." Power worthy of the name is power exercised within the limits set by justice and equity. But the rulers of whom the Magnificat is speaking use their power tyrannically, that is, not according to reason but arbitrarily. It is these whom God throws down from their thrones.[26]

The common sense and evangelical inspiration of these words of the great Dominican make them fully applicable to our own day. If we attempt to strip the Virgin Mary's song of its historical sting, then we overlook the promises made in the Old Testament. More importantly, we take the wrong path to discovery of the spiritual meaning of a song that is so full of the presence of God that it requires no great efforts on our part to raise us up to contemplation and hope.

The third action of God displays the same inversion of situations. Here the hungry are contrasted with the rich. The latter are called in Greek *ploutountes* (rather than *plousioi*, as in other passages of Luke), a word that indicates that the ones who will go away empty are those who have "gotten rich": gotten rich, that is, at the expense of the poor and defenseless. I dealt with this aspect of riches in an earlier chapter when speaking of the idolatry of money (see chapter IV).

The poor are described in terms of a cruel and very basic deprivation— namely, hunger. The Greek word used for "hungry" here is *peinountes*, which is the word found in the beatitude of the hungry. As we saw in the latter connection (see above, chapter VI), the word is a forceful one and is to be more accurately translated as "the starving," those for whom hunger is like a sickness. The starving will be satisfied. Psalm 107 had said long ago: "He satisfied the longing soul and filled the hungry soul with good things" (Ps 107:9).[27] The contrast between rich and hungry is reinforced by the contrast between empty and full.

The reference to concrete or, as we sometimes say, material situations is clear. I regard therefore as very healthy the reaction of J. Dupont to those who in his judgment minimize the scope of what the Magnificat says about reversals of situations. He writes: "It is obvious that vv. 52–53 are not satisfied simply to relativize wealth and power."[28] For in fact they go further: they call us to commitments concerned with bringing into existence a history that differs from that of our experience.

It is important to point out, however, that we here in Latin America are not more alive to verses 51–53 than to the first part of Mary's song. We are indeed convinced that without commitment to the poor and those who count for nothing, there is no authentic Christian life. On the other hand, we are also convinced that without contemplation and acknowledgment of God's gratuitous love there is likewise no authentic Christian life. The spiritual meaning of the Magnificat is to be found precisely in this combination, which also finds expression in the structure of the song.

Paul VI sums this up accurately in his Apostolic Exhortation *Marialis Cultus* (37):

The figure of the Blessed Virgin does not disappoint modern men and women; rather she offers them the perfect model of the Lord's disciple: the disciple who builds up the earthly, temporal city while being a diligent pilgrim toward the heavenly, eternal city; who works for that justice which frees the oppressed and that charity which assists the needy; but above all, the disciple who is an active witness to that love which builds up Christ in people's hearts.[29]

Any exegesis, therefore, is fruitless that attempts to tone down what Mary's song tells us about the preferential love of God for the lowly and the abused, and about the transformation of history that God's loving will implies. Consequently, the text is not rendered more spiritual by emptying it of the God whom Jesus Christ came to reveal to us and making it insubstantial and inoffensive to those who enjoy unjust privileges in this world. The spiritual power of Mary's words consists in their ability to make us see that the quest of uprightness and justice must be located within the parameters of God's gratuitous love, or it loses its deeper meaning. At the same time, her words help us to understand that this free and unmerited love, which inspires our prayer and thanksgiving, requires of us a solidarity with those who live in circumstances contrary to the purpose of the God of Jesus Christ—namely, that all should have life.

The Magnificat anticipates the preaching of Jesus Christ on these themes (see Lk 4:16–18; 6:21–22). The meaning of her song has been powerfully summed up by John Paul II in his Encyclical *Redemptoris Mater* (37):

> Mary is deeply imbued with the spirit of "the poor of Yahweh". . . . Mary truly proclaims the coming of the "Messiah of the poor" (cf. Is 11:4; 61:1). Drawing from Mary's heart, from the depth of her faith expressed in the words of the *Magnificat*, the Church renews ever more effectively in herself the awareness that *the truth about God who saves*, the truth about God who is the source of every gift, *cannot be separated from the manifestation of His love of preference for the poor and humble*, that love which, celebrated in the *Magnificat*, is later expressed in the words and works of Jesus.[30]

Everything that has gone before is the work of God's mercy. Mary has experienced this truth and therefore she is thankful. The Jewish nation, too, has experienced it, and this is a new reason for gratitude on the part of the Mother of the Lord, who is a daughter of this people.

> He has helped Israel, his servant,
>   remembering his mercy,
> according to his promise to our fathers,
>   to Abraham and to his descendants forever.
>   [Lk 1:54–55]

In these verses "servant" represents the Greek word *pais*, which also means "child; son *or* daughter." Mary has called herself a servant; her life is in God's hands. God loves the people as a father loves his offspring. This theme occurs frequently in the Old Testament, for example:

> But you, Israel, my servant,
>   Jacob, whom I have chosen,
>   offspring of Abraham my friend—
> You whom I have taken from the ends of the earth
>   and summoned from its far-off places,
> You whom I have called my servant,
>   whom I have chosen and will not cast off—
> Fear not, I am with you;
>   be not dismayed; I am your God.
> I will strengthen you, and help you,
>   and uphold you with my right hand of justice.
>   [Is 41:8–10]

The mercy of God knows no limits; Abraham, the father of believers, trusted in it. The Lord's power to set free is at the service of a love that inspires complete confidence, confidence "forever," as Mary says at the end of the Magnificat. This love has been experienced by God's "servants," Mary and Israel. The Lord fulfills God's promises; holy is the Lord's name. This is the final word of Mary, "the perfect Christian," about God. It should also be ours.

CONCLUSION

As Jesus of Nazareth, the Galilean preacher, is leaving Jericho, a blind beggar (a man, therefore, who is doubly poor) acknowledges him as "Son of David," as Messiah (Mk 10:46-52). This incident takes place before the Lord is acclaimed Messiah in Jerusalem.

The blind man sees what others are unable to see. The Bible reveals to us the presence of a God who is linked to the "absent" folk of history: those whom others try to conceal from sight (see v. 48), but with whom the Lord wants to undertake a dialogue. Jesus, who already has a premonition of his death in Jerusalem, has time to spare for the suffering and hopes of this man. He says to him: "What do you want me to do for you?" (v. 51). He does not hastily impose his own will on the man, nor does he overwhelm him with help; rather he asks a question and wants to listen. He does not even ask the man the obvious question: "Do you want me to heal you?" He opens a space in which this marginalized and spurned individual can take the initiative. In Jesus' eyes, the poor are not mere objects of service or help; they are subjects of desires and rights, they are persons.

The beggar, who has "sprung up" and drawn near to Jesus (v. 50), addresses him fondly and confidently as "my teacher" (v. 51 NRSV: *Rabbuni*) and asks him for health and life. The Lord does not simply give him what he asks but also makes it clear that the blind man has played an active part in the giving of this gift: "Your faith has saved you" (v. 52). Bartimaeus (Mark has already, in v. 46, given us the name of this individual) then leaves the roadside, straightens up, and takes his place as a disciple. He follows the Lord on his way (see v. 52). The affectionate and respectful treatment given him by Jesus has caused him to be no longer a marginalized individual living on alms but a disciple who takes charge of his own life and commits it to the teacher.

That is why Jesus came: to bring life, and bring it in abundance (see Jn 10:10); life in all its dimensions, as we have just seen. This is the content of the kingdom; in it the God of life is revealed to us. I have tried to bring this out in these pages. Because God is life, God "makes all things new" (Rv 21:5). God is not reached by well-trodden paths nor on feet numb with fear. Faith is not compatible with an attitude of apprehensiveness; it can indeed live through periods of darkness and it can, according to classic teaching, live in a kind of half-light, but it cannot live in fear. John reminds Christians who suffer persecution and insults that "there is no fear in love . . . and so one who fears is not yet perfect in love" (1 Jn 4:18). Cowardice in the face of what is new is contrary to faith. This explains the exhortation of the psalmist: "Sing to the Lord a new song" (33:3).

This is something we must not forget on a continent where the majority live in an indescribable poverty resulting from radically inequitable and unjust social relationships, and where, consequently, we are daily faced with challenges that call for hitherto unknown responses. Recent years in Latin America have been filled with tension and intensity. The poor have struck out on numerous new paths; the price they have had to pay for recognition of their dignity as human beings has been, and still is, a heavy one. In this process—for it is in fact a process—the Christian faith is a source of inspiration for many. We are in the presence of experiences marked by great depth and richness. The Bartimaeuses of this continent, too, have ceased to stay at the roadside and have in recent years "sprung up" and drawn near to the Lord, the friend of life. Medellín and Puebla have been the expression of this new leap and at the same time have given the impulse for it. Their conferences have been stages on a journey that is difficult but also full of hope.

All this activity has arisen and continued in a context of death, as is evidenced by the quite recent events in El Salvador. There, two women of the people and six Jesuit priests were murdered because of their closeness to the poorest of the country and their commitment to the quest of peace for all.[1] The witness given by these dear friends, as by so many others, has made the master's teachings concrete for us. It inspires us in turn to make these teachings our own, freely and with a sense of responsibility; that is, it wants to say to us what the Lord said to Bartimaeus: "Your faith has saved you."

The love of God for all is the source of our joy and our commitment. God is close to us. God's presence, God's dwelling, among us enables us to say with Mary and the entire Bible that history is in the hands of the poor and that "holy is his name."

Faith welcomes this holiness; faith is a response to the gift that the Lord makes to us both of himself and of his preference for the poor. The result of this acceptance in faith is the establishment of an agreement, a covenant, with the God of life. The acceptance of God's kingdom is the expression of our faith in the God who is revealed in Jesus Christ, and it leads to solidarity with our brothers and sisters. Life is received and then given. "We know," says John, "that we have passed from death to life because we love our brothers" (1 Jn 3:14). This passage, this pasch, is celebrated in a church which, under the inspiration of the Spirit, "the father of the poor," seeks to prove its mission and its fidelity to the Lord by its solidarity with the least of history (see John Paul II, Encyclical *Laborem exercens*, 8).

Medellín was already asserting the need of a church that is "truly poor, missionary and paschal" (*Youth*, 15). It thus made its own the idea of a church of the poor, thereby applying to our situation what John XXIII had proposed to the universal church. The church in Latin America has walked this road, undertaking "a new evangelization," as Medellín had likewise suggested. The distance traveled in the last twenty years, while allowing us to see how far we still have to go, has provided the church with reserves of energy for the period ahead. In this setting, theological reflection nourished by the word of God must increasingly take the form of a hermeneutic of hope. This book, for its part, has been meant to help us give the reason for our hope (see 1 Pt 3:15) in the midst of so many problems and hardships, new forms of oppression, and struggles for justice.

On this continent hope is born in the midst of suffering; it takes the form of life that comes through death. Its ultimate motivation is found in the living God, the God of tender love, who stoops to us in our suffering, our faith, and our efforts to be in solidarity with the Latin American poor and to win their liberation. It is of this God and this reality that Vallejo was speaking when he said:

> God anxiously takes
> Our pulse, seriously and silent
> And like a father treating his child, gently,
> But gently, opens the blood-stained cotton-wool
> And with his fingers extracts HOPE.[2]

Thanks to this hope, which our people experience in the midst of suffering, we in Latin America can "walk before the Lord" like those who do so "in the land of the living" (Ps 116:9).

NOTES

INTRODUCTION

1. Ten years ago, in Peru, when the living conditions of the poor were worsening and leading to hunger, exploitation, and unemployment, over a thousand pastoral workers signed a statement saying: "God shows himself to be the God who gives life, preserves it, defends it, rescues it from oppression, and makes it permanent in the risen Christ. We believe in the Lord and therefore we believe in life" (*Danos hoy nuestro pan de cada día*, Lima, November 1979).

2. No. 68 (April 1985) of *Páginas* is dedicated to this meeting in Villa El Salvador.

3. See Gustavo Gutiérrez, *A Theology of Liberation. History, Politics, and Salvation*, trans. Sister Caridad Inda and John Eagleson (2d ed.; Maryknoll, N.Y.: Orbis Books, 1988). See also the Introduction to the second edition: "Expanding the View." [The second edition will be cited throughout. – Tr.]

4. See Gustavo Gutiérrez, *On Job. God-Talk and the Suffering of the Innocent*, trans. M. J. O'Connell (Maryknoll, N.Y.: Orbis Books, 1987).

5. For this reason, the Bible uses the same word (*yada* in Hebrew) in speaking both of the union of man and woman and of the knowledge of God.

6. On the relationship between the two testaments, see E. Beauchamp, *L'un et l'autre Testament. Essai de lecture* (Paris: Seuil, 1976), and H. Seebass, *Der Gott der ganzen Bibel* (Freiburg: Herder, 1982), esp. chap. 1.

7. See K. Kitamori, *Theology of the Pain of God* (Richmond: John Knox, 1965). The author adopts a perspective first suggested by Dietrich Bonhoeffer and cultivated by one sector of contemporary German theology.

8. Consuelo de Prado makes a very personal application of these words to the area of feminine spiritual experience in her article "Yo siento a Dios de otro modo," *Páginas*, no. 75 (February 1986). Eng. trans. in Elsa Tamez, ed., *Through Her Eyes: Women's Theology from Latin America* (Maryknoll, N.Y.: Orbis Books, 1989).

9. See the now classic debate over the Jesus of history and the Christ of faith. In a well-known lecture, and in his later work, Ernst Käsemann reminded us of the importance of the historical aspects of the witness of Jesus when it comes to recognizing in him the Christ of our faith. See his essay, "The Problem of the Historical Jesus," in his *Essays on New Testament Themes* (London: SCM, 1964), 15–47.

10. This point is well made, for the Gospels, in E. Arens, *Los evangelios ayer y hoy* (Lima: Ediciones Paulinas, 1989).

11. Homily in Salvador, Bahia, July 7, 1980, in *Pronunciamentos do Papa no Brasil* (São Paulo: Loyola, 1980), 192 (italics added).

12. I owe this idea to the stimulating article of A. Gesché, "Topiques de la question de Dieu," *Revue theologique de Louvain* (1974) 301–25.

13. In his excellent book *Dios de los cristianos* (Santiago: Ediciones Paulinas, 1988), Ronaldo Muñoz rightly says, in connection with reflections on God in the Latin American context: "In this perspective, it is understandable that the key theological question for us is not whether God exists but what the true God is like. Not simply *whether God* exists or not, but, above all, *what kind of God* it is that exists; how we can know and recognize him; how he is present in our lives and acts in our history; how we, individually and collectively, can respond to him in our basic outlook and concrete practice" (p. 28). Eng. trans., *The God of Christians* (Maryknoll, N.Y.: Orbis Books, and Tunbridge Wells: Burns and Oates, 1991). On this subject in the theology of liberation, see Victorio Araya, *God of the Poor* (Maryknoll, N.Y.: Orbis Books, 1987).

14. [Unless otherwise indicated, the citations of Scripture are from the *New American Bible* (1970), with Revised New Testament (1986). Any italics in the citations have been added by the author.—Tr.]

PART ONE. GOD IS LOVE

1. On this point see the reflections of John Paul II in his Encyclical *Rich in Mercy*, notes 52 and 61.

2. See Joachim Jeremias in, e.g., *The Lord's Prayer*, trans. J. Reumann (Philadelphia: Fortress, 1964). Jeremias's thesis has been much criticized but has successfully weathered the attack; see J. Schlosser, *Le Dieu de Jesus Christ* (Paris: Cerf, 1987), 179–209.

3. James Cone, *A Black Theology of Liberation* (New York: Lippincott, 1970; 2nd ed., Maryknoll, N.Y.: Orbis Books, 1986), 142.

4. Every kind of domination means death. Even in the controversial area of supposed masculine superiority, to call God "Father" is an expression of life. In this context, Elizabeth Schüssler Fiorenza reminds us of Jesus' command: "Call no one your father on earth, for you have one Father—the one in heaven" (Mt 23:9), and comments: "The monotheistic fatherhood of God, elaborated in the Jesus traditions as the gracious goodness usually associated with a mother, must engender liberation from all patriarchal structures and domination" (*In Memory of Her: A Feminist Theological Reconstruction of Christian Origins* [New York: Crossroad, 1983], 151).

CHAPTER I. GOD LIBERATES

1. As the reader may know, there are different interpretations of just how the Jewish people entered the land of Canaan. See the stimulating and well-documented work of Norman Gottwald, *The Tribes of Yahweh: A Sociology of the Religion of Liberated Israel, 1250–1050 B.C.E.* (Maryknoll, N.Y.: Orbis Books, 1979), who studies the historical and social context of the settlement. He maintains that there was a rebellion by oppressed Canaanite peasants in which slave workers belonging to Israelite tribes participated.

2. See N. Lohfink, *Option for the Poor. The Basic Principle of Liberation Theology in the Light of the Bible* (Berkeley: Bibal Press, 1987), 33: "The exodus or liberation of Israel from Egypt by Yahweh, its God, at the beginning of its history, is the central theme and even, in fact, the only theme of the confession of faith in the Old Testament."

3. Everyone knows of the detailed and extended treatment of this theme by G. von Rad in his classic *Old Testament Theology*, where he makes it the key element in an understanding of the Bible as a "history of salvation." Von Rad's thesis has prompted numerous other words and also evoked criticism. See N. Lohfink, *Le nostre grandi parole* (Brescia: Paideia, 1986), 87–104. Lohfink maintains that the important text, Dt 26:4–9, is to be interpreted rather in terms of a theology of history; he regards it "as a deliberately provided key for interpreting the Hextaeuch and the historical books connected with it, and even all the future events of Israelite history" (104).

4. See Gutiérrez, *A Theology of Liberation*, 89: "The Exodus is the long march towards the promised land in which Israel can establish a society free from misery and alienation. Throughout the whole process, the religious event is not set apart. It is placed in the context of the entire narrative, or more precisely, it is its deepest meaning. It is the root of the situation. In the last instance, it is in this event that the dislocation introduced by sin is resolved and justice and injustice, oppression and liberation, are determined. Yahweh liberates the Jewish people politically in order to make them a holy nation."

5. In connection with this passage (Dt 26:4–9) N. Lohfink points out the importance of the theme of poverty and says: "Taken by itself, this central passage of the Old Testament might hide from view all that makes it inconvenient for the Christian Churches to talk of an option for the poor and for a theology to call itself a theology of liberation" (*Option for the Poor*, 35).

6. On the importance of the image of the way in Christian life, see Gustavo Gutiérrez, *We Drink from Our Own Wells* (Maryknoll, N.Y.: Orbis Books, 1984), 72–89.

7. In his Encyclical *Rich in Mercy* (3), John Paul II speaks of Lk 4:16–20 as the "first messianic promise" (in *The Pope Speaks* 26 [1981] 24).

8. See Robert McAfee Brown, *Unexpected News* (Philadelphia: Westminster, 1984), 90: "If the exodus is the story that is paradigmatic for the Hebrew Scriptures, the incident in the synagogue at Nazareth is the historical paradigm for the Christian Scriptures."

9. See below, chapter VI.

10. [The author uses the Spanish *Biblia de Jerusalén* translation for this passage as being more literal than the *Nueva Biblia Española*, which he regularly uses, and enabling the reader to see more clearly the meaning of the passage and its connection with Luke. The only relevant change that might be made in the NAB text, which is cited here, would be to substitute "poor" for "oppressed" in v. 1. – Tr.]

11. Luke proceeds in a similar way in recording the sermon of Peter that marks the beginning of the church's preaching: in the citation from Joel 3 he omits the second part of v. 5, which adds: "on Mount Zion there shall be a remnant, as the Lord has said, and in Jerusalem survivors whom the Lord shall call." When this limitation is omitted, the passage of Joel takes on a more universal scope.

12. In connection with the passage in Matthew to which I have referred, Dupont writes: "The proclamation of good news *is identical with* the cures of the sick; 'proclamation of good news' is simply a formula that generalizes and makes explicit the significance of these cures. . . . In any case, one thing is certain: the good news proclaimed to the poor *can only be the news that they will cease to be poor* and to suffer from poverty. As the blind see and the deaf hear and the dead come to life, so the poor will not lack what they need; they will cease to be victims of an unjust

distribution of goods" ("Jésus annonce la bonne nouvelle aux pauvres," in *Evangelizare Pauperibus* [Atti della XXIV Settimana Biblica; Brescia, 1978], 183; italics added).

13. Synonymous parallelism, which is common in Hebrew poetry, means the repetition of the same idea in equivalent terms.

14. Roland de Vaux points out, however, in his *Ancient Israel: Its Life and Institutions*, trans. J. McHugh (New York: McGraw-Hill, 1961), that this precious command often remained a dead letter in the history of the Jewish people (175–76).

15. In his *Théologie de l'Ancien Testament* (Geneva: Labor et Fides, 1986), C. Westermann has rightly called attention to the theme of the blessing as being of great interest for reflection on Old Testament theology (see esp. 126–45). On the other hand, I am not convinced when the author thinks he sees a nuance of opposition between blessing and liberation. The subject calls for a closer and more profound analysis.

16. The tetragram consists of four consonants; the later addition of vowels makes possible its translation into modern languages as Yahve or Yahweh.

17. W. Eichrodt therefore says that this passage is concerned with the message of liberation; see his *Theology of the Old Testament*, I, trans. J. A. Baker (Philadelphia: Westminster, 1961).

18. See Gutiérrez, *A Theology of Liberation*, 95.

19. I am here following a suggestion of J. Linskens, professor of Sacred Scripture at the Mexican-American Cultural Center in San Antonio, Texas. W. Eichrodt had observed that "Yahweh" means " 'I am really and truly present, ready to help and act, as I have always been'. . . . The emphasis is not on passive, but on active existence" (*Theology of the Old Testament*, I, 190). Along the same line, G. von Rad says that "Yahweh" means "I will be there (for you)" (*Old Testament Theology*, I, trans. D. W. Stalker [New York: Harper & Row, 1962], 180). Following W. F. Albright, D. N. Freedman, in the *Journal of Biblical Literature* 79 (1960) 151–56, and F. L. Cross, "Jahweh and the God of the Patriarchs," *Harvard Theological Review* 55 (1962) 253, think that the form *yuhwi* is causative: "makes to be." Without accepting this view, R. de Vaux mentions it as possible in his *Early History of Israel*, trans. D. Smith (Philadelphia: Westminster, 1978), 349. See also J. Pixley, *Exodo* (Mexico City: Casa unida de publicaciones, 1983), 49; Eng. trans., *On Exodus* (Maryknoll, N.Y.: Orbis Books, 1987).

20. Many English versions correctly translate "Yahweh" as "Lord" (as the Septuagint did long ago), even though this entails some loss of the meaning peculiar to the name that God gives to himself. See the reflections of J. Severino Croatto, "Sabreis que yo soy Yave (Exodo 6)," *Revista Bíblica* (Buenos Aires) 45, new series, no. 10 (1983, no. 2) 77–94.

21. See H. Zorilla, *La Fiesta de Liberación de los Oprimidos* (San José, Costa Rica: Ediciones SEBILA, 1981).

22. See J. Dupont, *Etudes sur les Actes des Apôtres* (Paris: Cerf, 1967), 149 and 250.

23. Episcopal Conference of Chile, *Iglesia servidora de la Vida, Orientaciones pastorales 1986–1989* (Santiago, 1985), nos. 61 and 90.

CHAPTER II. GOD DOES JUSTICE

1. N. Lohfink points out that the theme of the Jewish nation as God's family is more frequently found, and more emphasized, in the Bible than the theme of

the people of God; see his *Le nostre grandi parole* (Brescia: Paideia, 1986), 127–44.

2. Karl Barth therefore says that the establishment of justice and right, which God calls for in the Bible, "necessarily takes the form of a restoration of the rights of threatened innocent persons, the oppressed poor, and widows, orphans, and foreigners" (*Church Dogmatics* 2/1 [New York: Scribner's, 1957], 386).

3. See the analyses of biblical texts on the theme of justice in José Miranda, *Marx and the Bible. A Critique of the Philosophy of Oppression*, trans. J. Eagleson (Maryknoll, N.Y.: Orbis Books, 1974).

4. See below, chapter VI.

5. James Cone, *A Black Theology of Liberation* (New York: Lippincott, 1970; 2nd ed., Maryknoll, N.Y.: Orbis Books, 1986), 143.

6. Paul is here quoting words that come from the world of Stoic philosophy, although it is not possible to determine a particular author for them.

7. John Paul II, Encyclical *Rich in Mercy*, no. 4: "The very word justice came to mean the salvation wrought by the merciful Lord" (*The Pope Speaks* 26 [1981] 30).

8. Pedro Casaldáliga, "Versión de Dios," in his *El tiempo y la espera* (Santander: Sal Terrae, 1986), 24.

CHAPTER III. GOD MAKES A COVENANT

1. See, for example, the classic work of W. Eichrodt, which I cited earlier.

2. Bartolomé de Las Casas, "Carta al Consejo de Indias," in his *Obras escogidas* (Madrid: BAC, 1958), 5:44.

3. See the outstanding analysis in J. Pons, *L'oppression dans l'Ancien Testament* (Paris: Letouzey et Ane, 1981); see also Elsa Tamez, *Bible of the Oppressed*, trans. M. J. O'Connell (Maryknoll, N.Y.: Orbis Books, 1982).

4. On the significance of the absence of the account of institution see my *A Theology of Liberation*, 149. John Paul II recalled the importance of this passage during his visit to Haiti, the poorest country in Latin America (Homily at Puerto Principe, March 9, 1983).

5. John Paul II writes as follows about the love of God in his Encyclical *Rich in Mercy*, note 52: "This love can be described as completely gratuitous and unmerited; as such its necessity springs from within: the heart demands it. It is, therefore, in a sense, a 'feminine' variation of the masculine fidelity to self that is conveyed by the word *hesed*. In keeping with this psychological origin, *rahamim* gives rise to a number of affections, among them kindness and tenderness, patience and indulgence (in the sense of a readiness to forgive)" (*The Pope Speaks* 26 [1981] 29).

6. Alejandro Romualdo, "Reza, cristiano, reza," in his *Poesia integra* (Lima: Viva Voz, 1986), 112.

7. On the relationship between gratuitousness and justice, see Gutiérrez, *On Job. God-Talk and the Suffering of the Innocent*, trans. M. J. O'Connell (Maryknoll, N.Y.: Orbis Books, 1987).

CHAPTER IV. IDOLATRY AND DEATH

1. On this subject see the important work of J. L. Sicre, *Los dioses olvidados. Poder y riqueza en los profetas pre-exílicos* (Madrid: Cristiandad, 1979).

2. Juan Luis Segundo made this very point a number of years ago in his book on God: "Our reflections begin by taking an interest in an antithesis that seems

quite out of fashion, the antithesis between faith and idolatry, rather than in the seemingly more topical antithesis between faith and atheism. What is more, we leave consistency and certainty behind right at the start in tackling the faith-idolatry antithesis that we regard as more deep-rooted; for the Christian as well as the professed atheist may stand on either side of this antithesis. We feel, in other words, that human beings are divided more profoundly by the image they fashion of God than by their subsequent decision as to whether something real corresponds to this image or not" (Juan Luis Segundo, *Our Idea of God* [= A Theology for Artisans of a New Humanity 2], trans. J. Drury [Maryknoll, N.Y.: Orbis Books, 1974], 12). See also Pablo Richard et al., *The Idols of Death and the God of Life* (Maryknoll, N.Y.: Orbis Books, 1983).

3. Franz Hinkelammert has an insightful development of this point in his *The Ideological Weapons of Death* (Maryknoll, N.Y.: Orbis Books, 1986).

4. It is not irrelevant to recall the importance of this passage from Sirach in the history of the church on this continent. Bartolomé de Las Casas attributes to it his prophetic vocation to defend the American Indians and, in general, the poor of the Indies. This is a commitment that continues to challenge us today. See my book, *Dios o el oro en las Indias (s. XVI)* (Lima: CEP, 1989).

5. See "mamōnas," in G. Kittel (ed.), *Theological Dictionary of the New Testament*, trans. by G. W. Bromiley (Grand Rapids: Eerdmans, 1985), 4:388–90.

6. The Greek word *plousios* is more often used when speaking of wealth.

7. Another passage that should be considered is the dialogue of Jesus with the rich young man (Mk 10:17–22 par.). It is the man's attachment to riches that prevents him from following Jesus. One must choose the one or the other if one is to enter the kingdom. The verses that follow the young man's departure (vv. 23ff.) speak of the obstacle that riches are to entrance into the kingdom.

8. In the passage just cited from Ezekiel, "going after wealth" translates the Hebrew *hlk'hry*, which is often used in the context of idolatry (see L. Sicre [note 1, above], 149).

9. The word used in Hebrew is *bs*, which means wealth (see Sicre, ibid.).

10. The *Testament of Judah*, which is one of the *Testaments of the Twelve Patriarchs* (among the Old Testament apocrypha), says: "My children, the love of money is a sure path to idolatry, because, when led astray by money, men call gods those that are no gods" (19, 1); trans. M. De Jonge, in H. F. D. Sparks (ed.), *The Apocryphal Old Testament* (Oxford: Clarendon Press, 1984), 547.

11. Bartolomé de Las Casas, *Entre los remedios* (1542), in *Obras escógidas* 5 (Madrid: Biblioteca de Autores Españoles, 1957–58).

12. Ibid.

13. This is the point Las Casas is making. He says it in so many words in his first book when speaking of those who cause "the deaths and carnage that bathe everything in human blood" and thus violate the commandment not to shed innocent blood but to seek justice, help the oppressed, grant judicial protection to orphans, defend widows, and feed the hungry. Those who act in this manner do not believe in the true God "but pour libations in honor of the Baals, that is, the idol that is proper to such evildoers and that controls them and keeps them subject and possesses them; in other words, the desire to have dominion, the boundless ambition for self-enrichment that is never satisfied and never finished and that is also a form of idolatry (Col 3). For, according to St. Jerome, 'Baalim' means 'my idol,' the one that controls me and possesses me. All this fits perfectly the ambitious

and the greedy or avaricious, and especially those preachers or, better, those wretched and unhappy tyrants" (*Del unico modo* 436).

14. Ibid.

15. *Memorial de Remedios* (1516), in *Obras Escógidas* 5:10b.

PART TWO. THE KINGDOM IS AMONG YOU

1. Sobrino adds: "In the image of 'father' Jesus sums up the truth that God is an absolute beginning and thereby the guarantor of meaning and that in this source there is love as the ultimate foundation of reality. But he qualifies this love" ("Dios," in C. Floristan and J. J. Tamayo [eds.], *Conceptos Fundamentales de Pastoral* [Madrid: Cristiandad, 1983], 252). This love also has a maternal face, according to Leonardo Boff, *The Maternal Face of God* (San Francisco: Harper and Row, 1987).

2. *El primer Nueva Coronica y Buen Gobierno* III (Mexico City: Siglo XXI, 1980), 1104.

CHAPTER V. THE GOD WHO COMES

1. On four occasions Matthew uses the word *anomia* to mean the rejection of God's will to life and justice. In 24:12, *anomia* is clearly opposed to *agape*: "Because of the increase of evildoing, the love of many will grow cold" (see also Mt 13:41 and 23:28). On the significance of these words, see J. Zumstein, *La condition du croyant dans l'évangile selon Mathieu* (Fribourg: Editions universitaires, 1977), 171–73; and D. Marguerat, *Le jugement dans l'évangile de Mathieu* (Geneva: Labor et Fides, 1981), 192–203.

2. *Shekinah* is a noun derived from the verb *shakhan*, which means to stay or dwell, and occurs frequently in the Old Testament. The word *shekinah* is not found as such in the Hebrew Bible but is used in the rabbinical writings (see the interesting article of J. Sievers, " 'Where Two or Three . . .': The Rabbinic Concept of *shekinah* and Matthew 18:10," in A. Finkel and L. Frizzed [eds.], *Standing Before God. In Honor of J. M. Osterreicher* [New York: Ktav Publishing House, 1981], 171–82).

3. Francis of Assisi, *The Canticle of Brother Sun*, in *St. Francis of Assisi. Writings and Early Biographies*, ed. M. A. Habig (Chicago: Franciscan Herald Press, 1973), 130. See the fine commentary of Noe Zevallos, *Comentario al Cántico del hermano sol* (Lima: CEP, 1987).

4. This "tiny whispering sound" recalls the metaphor of life-giving breath, which the Bible often uses to describe the unobtrusive action of the Spirit.

5. See below, section 4 of this chapter.

6. See my book, *On Job*, 67–81.

7. M. Díaz Mateos, *El Dios que libera* (Lima: CEP, 1985), 273.

8. On this important passage in the Gospel of John, see my book, *We Drink from Our Own Wells*, 38–42.

9. This lack of importance is a condition that children shared with women. When Matthew tells the stories of the multiplication of the loaves, he speaks of five thousand and four thousand men "not counting women and children" (14:21; 15:38). There is a similar expression in Ex 12:37.

10. The *Nueva Biblia Española* translates "Son of man."

11. Matthew is citing Mi 5:1. It is important to observe that the word used in

the ancient Greek translation of the Old Testament (the Septuagint) in this passage of Micah is different from that used in Matthew's Greek version of the passage. The Septuagint has *oligostos* ("smallest"), where Matthew has *elachistos*.

12. Who are "these least brothers of mine" (Mt 25:40)? Are they poor Christians or the poor generally? The point has always been the subject of debate. For myself, I stick to the choice I made in my *A Theology of Liberation*, 112–16: the text refers to the poor in general. Three detailed studies of Matthew adopt the same view: J. Zumstein (n. 1 of this chapter), 327–50; D. Marguerat (ibid.), 481–520, where the author discusses and refutes in meticulous detail the arguments for the restrictive interpretation; and a book devoted entirely to this passage of Matthew: X. Pikaza, *Hermanos de Jesús y servidores de los más pequeños (Mateo 25, 31–46)* (Salamanca: Sígueme, 1984). As L. Sabourin says in his *L'Evangile selon Saint Mathieu et ses principaux parallèles* (Rome: Biblical Institute Press, 1978), "even while acknowledging the value of arguments for the contrary view, the majority of modern exegetes prefer to see in 'these least brothers of mine' the poor in general" (331).

13. Homily at Edmonton airport (Canada), on September 17, 1984, nos. 3–4. The presence of God's kingdom implies that even now a profound change has taken place in history. "In the Bible the reign of God signifies that this world has been transformed, even in its economic dimension. Let us say immediately: this does not mean that there is no thought of the individual and the world to come; it means only that God, inspired by a truly divine passion, wants to impose his sovereign rule on this age and this society" (N. Lohfink, "Reino de Dios y economía en la Biblia," *Communio* [March–April 1986] 114).

14. J. Dupont, *El mensaje de las bienaventuranzas* (Estella: Verbo Divino, 1985), 6, cites Napoleon as saying in 1801: "A society cannot exist without an inequality of lots in life, and an inequality of lots in life cannot exist without religion. When a person dies of hunger alongside another who is swimming in abundance, it is impossible to accept such a difference unless there is an authority that can say: 'God wills it so; there must be poor and rich in this world, but in eternity there will be a different kind of distribution.' " All who think thus, even if they may express themselves in a less blatant way, consider the message that Jesus preaches, to be dangerous – namely, that the kingdom must transform history and that those who accept it must commit themselves to eliminating injustices and abuses, which are expressions of death.

15. As the reader may know, this passage in the Puebla Document owes much to the hand of Bishop Germán Schmitz.

16. For other aspects of the poem, see the excellent literary commentary of R. González Vigil, *Leamos juntos a Vallejo*, I. *Los Heraldos Negros y Otros Poemas Juveniles* (Lima: Banco Central de Reserva, 1988), 177–78.

CHAPTER VI. THE TIME CAME

1. See my *A Theology of Liberation*, 95–97.
2. [For this passage the author is using the translation of A. Levoratti and A. Trusso in *Biblia. El Libro del Pueblo de Dios* (Buenos Aires: Ediciones Paulinas, 1980). I continue to use the NAB. – Tr.]
3. On Zechariah, see G. Gorgulho, *Zacarías a vinda do Mesías Pobre* (Petrópolis: Vozes, 1985).
4. *Agape*, in *Los Heraldos Negros*, translated in R. Bly (ed.), *Neruda and Vallejo. Selected Poems* (Boston: Beacon, 1971), 195.

5. This is a central point made in God's discourses in the Book of Job; see my book, *On Job*, 79–80.

6. In the parallel passage Matthew, too, refers to this fact, but he seems to suggest that Jesus had a less direct knowledge of it: "When he *heard* that John had been arrested" (Mt 4:12).

7. The other Gospels also speak of the beginning of Jesus' preaching in Galilee; this is true even of John, who starts with the wedding at Cana (see 2:1–12).

8. Virgilio Elizondo has provided a stimulating presentation of this "Galilee theology" and its contemporary relevance in his book, *The Galilean Journey* (Maryknoll, N.Y.: Orbis Books, 1983). See also the recent painstaking study of S. Freyne, *Galilee, Jesus and the Gospels* (Philadelphia: Fortress, 1988).

9. The district of Galilee was not only looked down on but was suspected of being politically and religiously heterodox; see G. Vermés, *Jesus the Jew* (Philadelphia: Fortress Press, 1981).

10. It is in Galilee that the first groups of Jesus' followers come into being. Recent studies have alerted us to the sociohistorical conditions of the ministry of Jesus and the activity of his disciples. See, e.g., Gerd Theissen, *The Sociology of Early Palestinian Christianity* (Philadelphia: Fortress, 1978); Luise Schottroff and Wolfgang Stegemann, *Jesus and the Hope of the Poor*, trans. M. J. O'Connell (Maryknoll, N.Y.: Orbis Books, 1986); G. Lohfink, *Jesus and Community* (Philadelphia: Fortress, 1982); R. Aguirre, *Del movimiento de Jesús a la Iglesia cristiana* (Bilbao: Desclée, 1987). This is a very profitable lode for the understanding of the Gospels.

11. Our word "Amen" comes from the same root as the Hebrew *'emet*, which means truth, fidelity, firmness, trust.

12. Following the *Biblia de Jerusalen*, I adopt here the so-called more difficult reading of these verses. There are manuscripts that read "the kingdom of God and its justice." [The NAB and other modern versions such as the REB and the NRSV all have "his justice." – Tr.]

13. See section 4 of this chapter, below.

14. On Paul's complex ideas of flesh and body see my book, *We Drink from Our Own Wells*, 54–71.

15. This parable is, in fact, framed by two similar sentences. Just before this passage, at the end of the previous chapter, Matthew reports a saying of Jesus to his disciples: "Many who are first will be last, and the last will be first" (Mt 19:30). On the basic unity of Mt 20:1–16, see Luise Schottroff, "Human Solidarity and the Goodness of God. The Parable of the Workers in the Vineyard," in Luise Schottroff and Wolfgang Stegemann, *The God of the Lowly. Socio-Historical Interpretations of the Bible*, trans. M. J. O'Connell (Maryknoll, N.Y.: Orbis Books, 1984), 129–47.

16. As we shall see further on (chapter VII), the fourth beatitude (Lk 6:22–23) has its own field of meaning and represents a different perspective.

17. J. Dupont thinks that Luke's version of the beatitudes is closer to what Jesus actually said; see his meticulous and discerning analysis in *Les Béatitudes* I and II (Paris: Gabalda, 1958, 1960).

18. Luke's predilection for these themes has always inspired studies of the social context he has in view; see the works listed above in note 10 of this chapter.

19. *Ptochos* appears 34 times in the New Testament; 24 of the occurrences are in the Gospels. Another Greek term also found in the New Testament is *penes*; this, however, refers rather to those with few resources.

20. The word *plousioi* (the wealthy) occurs 11 times in Luke (3 in Matthew, 2 in

Mark). The reader will profit from the article of G. Soares-Prabhu, "Clase en la Biblia: los pobres biblicos ¿una clase social?" *Revista Latinoamericana de Teología* 12 (Sept.-Dec. 1987) 217–39.

21. The Letter of James clearly echoes this contrast between rich and poor, and forcefully indicts the exploitation of the poor by the rich and powerful (see Jas 2:1–9; 4:13–17).

22. See J. Dupont, *Les Béatitudes* II, 143–218; S. Legasse, *Jésus et l'enfant* (Paris: Gabalda, 1969); H. R. Weber, *Jesús y los niños* (Lima: CELADEC, 1980).

23. On this passage see my book, *On Job*, xi–xiii.

24. On the meaning of this parable J. Dupont writes: "The replacement of the guests involves a shift from one social group to another." Further on, he says: "From whichever side we approach the subject, namely, the identification of the addressees of the parable of the wedding guests, we reach the same result: the story is addressed to the representatives of Israel's religious elite, that is, first and foremost to the Pharisees. Moreover, it challenges them in their consciousness of what separates them from and opposes them to 'sinners,' namely, that they regard the latter as the scum of the chosen people" ("La parabole des invités au festin dans le ministère de Jésus," in his *Etudes sur les évangiles synoptiques* [Louvain: University Press, 1985], 689 and 690).

25. J. Jonson thinks that the irony comes from the polemical context; Jesus is answering the criticism that he seeks the company of drunkards and gluttons. See his *Humour and Irony in the New Testament* (Leiden: Brill, 1985), 156–57.

26. See Albert Nolan, *Jesus before Christianity* (Maryknoll, N.Y.: Orbis Books, 1976), 23: "Sinners made up a clearly defined class of society, the same class to which the poor, in the broadest sense of this word, belonged."

27. "Here we are confronted with a paradox. If we 'spiritualize' this gospel message about the poor too soon, as it were—that is, out of proper order and sequence—and maintain that the 'poor' in the gospel are *first and primarily* the 'spiritually' poor rather than plainly and simply the materially poor (if we may so call them, in contradistinction to the classic concept of the 'spiritually poor'), then we have an easy time with God. We 'humanize' God. We make him more accessible to human understanding. Now God will love, first and foremost, the good, the 'meritorious'—just as do ourselves. But if, instead, we unflinchingly and courageously take the gospel statements at their face value, then what we have is God's love for the poor first and foremost simply because they are poor, simply because they are literally and materially poor. Now we have no easy God at all. Now we are faced with the mystery of God's revelation, and the gift of his kingdom of love and justice" (G. Gutiérrez, *The Power of the Poor in History*, trans. R. R. Barr [Maryknoll, N.Y.: Orbis Books, 1983], 95).

28. J. Dupont has made a key contribution to the understanding of this point (see *Les Béatitudes* II, 13–90, and many other passages of this work) by showing that the correct perspective for understanding the beatitudes is theocentric: the beatitudes are a revelation about God. The starting point is the literal interpretation of the poor, the hungry, and those who mourn. This is a central thesis in his study of the beatitudes. Nor is his an isolated, even if very authoritative, voice; rather, as J. Schlosser says, this interpretation "is on the way to becoming the prevailing one in contemporary exegesis" (*Le règne de Dieu dans les dits de Jésus* [Paris: Gabalda, 1980], 449, note 91).

29. L. Alonso Schökel, *¿Donde está tu hermano?* (Valencia: Institución San Jerón-

imo, 1985), 29 and 31. For the reasons given, the author proposes the following translation of Gn 4:4–5: "The Lord looked with favor on Abel and his sacrifice and looked with less favor on Cain and his sacrifice."

30. H. De Witt is of the opinion that the Hebrew text (the Masoretic text) deliberately omits whatever Cain may have said to Abel (4:8; the translations make up for the omission, inserting: "Let us go out in the field") and that the writer's intention is to indicate a breakdown of communication between the brothers. See *He visto la humillación de mi pueblo. Relectura del Génesis desde América Latina* (Santiago, Chile: Editorial Amerinda, 1988), 145.

31. Karl Barth, *Church Dogmatics* 2/1 (New York: Scribner's, 1957), 386.

32. As the reader will know, this conception, which is solidly anchored in the Bible, is formulated in the light of, and owes its prevalence to, the experience of the church in Latin America. It is to be found in Latin American theological work, in Medellín, and, above all, in Puebla, as well as in the practice and thinking of many today in the universal church. The expression "preferential option" is found over and over again in the teaching of John Paul II, from his visit to Mexico in 1979 down to his Encyclical *Sollicitudo rei socialis* (1988). It is also found in the Instruction *Libertatis conscientiae* of the Congregation for the Doctrine of the Faith (68).

CHAPTER VII. THE ETHICS OF THE KINGDOM

1. See Hugo Echegaray, *Anunciar el Reino* (Lima: CEP, 1981), 261.

2. Francisco Moreno cites this text and correctly notes that the question reveals an ethical uneasiness that "will recur over and over again throughout the entire Christian community as it reflects critically on its faith in the light of the word of God." See his *Salvar la vida de los pobres* (Lima: CEP, 1986), 92.

3. This picture is carefully painted in the excellent study of J. Zumstein, *La condition du croyant dans l'évangile de Matthieu* (Fribourg: Editions universitaires, 1977).

4. C. Duquoc, "Une parabole de l'agir de Dieu," *Lumiere et Vie*, no. 183 (September 1987) 95. The entire number is devoted to the Sermon on the Mount.

5. Of the seven occurrences of the word "justice" (*dikaiosynē*) in Matthew (as opposed to one in Luke and none in Mark), five are in the Sermon on the Mount: 5:6; 5:10; 5:20; 6:1; 6:33). The other two are connected with the person of John the Baptist: 3:15 (the first words that Matthew attributes to Jesus) and 21:32.

6. "Long of spirit" (Eccl 7:8) signifies a patient person; "low of spirit" (Prov 16:19) signifies a humble person (according to the NRSV and REB). The Qumran documents contain such expressions as these: "By means of the poor [or humble] of spirit (*'anwey ruah*) God brings down those whose hearts are closed and obdurate" (1 QM 14, 7).

7. See my book, *A Theology of Liberation*, chapter 13.

8. See the detailed study of F. Camacho, *La proclama del Reino* (Madrid: Cristiandad, 1987), who is following the lead given by J. Mateos in his translation of the beatitudes in the *Nueva Biblia Española*.

9. This point is well brought out in Camacho, 115.

10. These two passages are peculiar to Matthew; there are no parallels in Mark and Luke.

11. See J. Dupont, *Les Béatitudes* III (Paris: Gabalda, 1973), 473–543. His anal-

yses are an important source of what I say in these pages on the beatitudes.

12. Romano Guardini, *The Lord*, trans. E. C. Briefs (Chicago: Regnery, 1954), 70.

13. See Walter Brueggemann, *The Land: Place as Gift, Promise, and Challenge in Biblical Faith* (Philadelphia: Fortress, 1977).

14. This cruel experience finds expression in the words of an Andean peasant: "Our forebears told us that our lands were very extensive. There was land for all. But now almost nothing is left to us. They have driven us into the uplands as if we were just cattle. For us there is no prairie, no hillside, no watered valley." The words are cited in the pastoral statement *La tierra, don de Dios, derecho du un pueblo* (March 30, 1986), signed by Bishop J. Calderon and prelates A. Quinn, F. d'Alteroche, and M. Briggs, and made available in *Pàginas*, no. 77 (May 1986).

15. Aware of the situation of the Peruvian peasantry, the bishops of Sur Andino write (in the statement mentioned in note 14): "The peasants have a lively memory of their history, which provides the ground for their hope. They know of their successes and their failures, and this historical experience helps them seek ways of surviving in face of the aggression they experience and the threats they receive, as they try to safeguard the values passed down to them. This causes them to celebrate before the Lord their present condition, their labors, their struggles and hopes. In summary, our Andean people have a profound experience and understanding of God, who created the earth for all and is defender of the poor. The Andean family and community possesses standards of harmony, justice, and reciprocity that are connected with the kind of thinking about the land which Israel developed and with the ethics of the kingdom as proclaimed by Jesus to the poor who will inherit the land."

16. H. Hendricks makes an interesting point when he reminds us of the rich meaning of the biblical word "merciful." The Hebrew word *hesed*, which underlies the Greek adjective used by Matthew (*eleēmōn*), means more than pity or compassion for those in trouble; it means an ability to enter into the sufferings of others so as to feel and see things as they do (see Mt 9:13; 23:23). The merciful, therefore, are those who identify with others; the contrary attitude is that of persons who insist on their own needs and rights. See H. Hendricks, *Sermon on the Mount* (Manila: East Asian Pastoral Institute, 1979), 30. The mercy of which I am speaking contains an important element of sympathy; it implies that one opens one's heart to the poverty and suffering of others.

17. The word *dipsychos* is peculiar to James and not found in any other New Testament book.

18. The *New Jerusalem Bible* translates "inconsistent" in Jas 1:7–8 and "you waverers" in 4:8.

19. P. David, *Commentary on James* (Grand Rapids: Eerdmans, 1982), 74, shows the Old Testament roots of James's word "double-minded"; this information is not irrelevant to a letter so full of Semitisms. See also J. Adamson, *James. The Man and His Message* (Grand Rapids: Eerdmans, 1989), 133.

20. The *Biblia de Jerusalén* translates Mt 5:9 as "those who seek peace." "Making" or "building" is more literal; the adjective *eirēnopoioi*, which is not found elsewhere in the Bible, means "makers or builders of peace." But the choice of this translation does not mean forgetting that peace is a gift as well as a task.

21. The Septuagint reveals this rich complexity by using, without distinction, 25 words (one of them being *eirēnē*) to translate *shalom*. On the wealth of meaning

that the word has in the Bible as a whole, see Walter Brueggemann, *Living Toward a Vision* (New York: United Church Press, 1976).

22. See L. Wisser, *Jérémie, critique de la vie sociale* (Geneva: Labor et Fides, 1982), 38. The author shows that in Jeremiah "the practice of social justice is a constitutive element of the knowledge of Yahweh" (249).

23. There is agreement among those well informed about this theme. See the reasons given by J. Dupont for rejecting "peaceful" and "pacifist" as translations: *Les Béatitudes* III, 635–44.

24. J. Dupont says of the Lucan beatitudes: "Jesus was speaking of the poor as such, the afflicted and the hungry without any reservation. Their suffering was enough to make them privileged before God. Luke applies these promises to his Christian readers, evidently out of a desire to inspire them in the difficult situations of their lives" (*Les Béatitudes* III, 28).

25. We find something similar in Peter's exhortations to Christians: "Even if you should suffer because of *righteousness* [or justice], blessed are you" (1 Pt 3:14), and "if you are insulted for the name of *Christ*, blessed are you" (1 Pt 4:14).

26. Samuel Rayan, *The Holy Spirit* (Maryknoll, N.Y.: Orbis Books, 1978).

27. [The author once again takes his translation of this and the ensuing passage of Zechariah from *Biblia. El Libro del Pueblo de Dios*. I continue to use the NAB. — Tr.]

28. In this passage, "kindness" translates *hesed*, while "compassion" translates a word we met earlier: *rahamim*, which signifies compassion that springs from a mother's heart.

29. Elsa Tamez, *Bible of the Oppressed* (Maryknoll, N.Y.: Orbis Books, 1982), 22–24.

30. On the contrast between rich and poor in this letter, see Pedrito V. Maynard-Reid, *Poverty and Wealth in James* (Maryknoll, N.Y.: Orbis Books, 1987). The author sketches the historical and social setting of the letter.

31. The verb *moranthē*, here translated "loses its savor," means literally "is made foolish" and suggests a link with Mt 7:26 where the person who listens to the words of Jesus "but does not act on them" is called a *moros*, "fool." The connection between the two passages is significant.

32. It is a mistake to regard this letter as something like a short treatise on slavery. Slavery is not Paul's concern in the letter, although what he says about it would later have an important influence in this area. On the debated subject of slavery in Paul, see the study of R. Lehmann, *Epître à Philémon. Le christianisme primitif et l'esclavage* (Geneva: Labor et Fides, 1978). See also José Comblin, *Epistola aos Colosenses e Epistola a Filemón* (Petropólis: Vozes, 1986), 85–107. Both authors give us the historical and social context of this short letter of Paul.

33. See, e.g., the opening of the Letter to the Colossians; here, in a passage that has a purpose similar to that of the verse on which I am commenting, Paul writes: "We have heard of your faith in Christ Jesus and the love that you have for all the holy ones" (Col 1:4).

34. *Splangchna* is the word Luke uses, but in a verb form, when he says that the Samaritan "was moved with compassion" (*esplangchnisthē*) toward the wounded man (Lk 10:33). See my commentary on this text in my book, *A Theology of Liberation*, 113.

35. As a fugitive slave, Onesimus was at the mercy of slave-hunters and could fall under the law, since his situation in the society of the day was now an irregular

one. Given this situation, Paul was protecting him when he returned him to Philemon and commended him as a brother.

36. In the final four verses of the letter, Paul says goodbye to his friend and calls down the grace of Jesus Christ on him and his community.

37. In his article, "Reino de Dios y economía en la Biblia," *Communio*, March-April 1961, N. Lohfink offers a different and stimulating interpretation of the text from Leviticus and therefore of Jesus' answer. According to him, one's "self" means one's "family." Therefore, to love another as oneself means "to treat him as though he were a member of one's family" (119). The idea is, therefore, to extend to those outside the household and one's own people—that is, foreigners—the attitude cultivated toward those who belong to the family. It means making neighbors of those far off, as we are taught also in the parable of the good Samaritan (see Lk 10).

Part Three. Under the Inspiration of the Spirit

1. See H. Mottu's provocative analysis of this famous passage in his book *Les confessions de Jérémie. Une protestation contre la souffrance* (Geneva: Labor et Fides, 1985), 30–36.

2. On Micah see Juan Alfaro, *Micah. Justice and Loyalty* (Grand Rapids: Eerdmans, 1989).

Chapter VIII. My Eyes Have Seen You

1. This chapter, originally written as a preliminary sketch of my book *On Job. God-Talk and the Suffering of the Innocent* (Maryknoll, N.Y.: Orbis Books, 1987), can now serve as a summary of the conclusions reached there.

2. [The author uses the Spanish translation of Job by L. Alonso Schökel and J. L. Sicre in their *Job. Comentario teológico y literario* (Madrid: Cristiandad, 1983), which is based in turn on the version of Mexican writer José Luz Ojeda. Unless otherwise indicated, I use the *New Jerusalem Bible* translation of the Book of Job.—Tr.]

3. In his earlier translation of the Book of Job (1976), L. Alonso Schökel says that "the Book of Job is a play with very little action and a great deal of passion" and that passion characterizes "its search and its language" ("Introducción" to the Book of Job in the *Nueva Biblia Española*, 1288). This point is developed in the extensive commentary of Alonso Schökel and Sicre cited in note 2, above. W. Vogels has very perceptively shown the importance of language as a theme in the Book of Job; see his "Job a parlé correctement. Une approche structurale du livre de Job," *Nouvelle revue théologique* 102 (1980) 835–52. My own thoughts on Job are indebted to both of these excellent studies.

4. [This verse is translated from the author's Spanish text.—Tr.]

5. R. H. Tawney has observed that "like the friends of Job," people of this mentality "saw in misfortune, not the chastisement of love but the punishment for sin" (*Religion and the Rise of Capitalism* [New York: Mentor Books, 1963], 219).

6. Further on, Job repeats his position: "I am innocent [Hebrew: *tam*]; life matters not to me, I despise my existence" (9:21 [translated from the author's Spanish text]). This assertion of innocence will become the surest conviction of his destitute life: "Far from admitting you to be in the right, I shall maintain my integrity to my dying day. I take my stand on my uprightness, I shall not stir: in my heart I need not be ashamed of my days" (27:5–6).

7. Psalm 73 is on the same theme.

8. L. Alonso Schökel describes the passage as follows: "This is a pessimistic triptych on a society divided into oppressors and oppressed. As found in the text, the pictures or scenes form a series of violent contrasts which underscore the injustice of the oppressors and the misfortune of the oppressed" (in Alonso Schökel and Sicre [note 2, above], 357).

9. [These verses are translated from the author's Spanish text.—Tr.]

10. [Verse 21 is translated from the author's Spanish text.—Tr.]

11. [Verses 20–21 are here translated from the author's Spanish text.—Tr.]

12. [This entire passage is translated from the author's Spanish text.—Tr.]

13. See above, chapter II.

14. César Vallejo, *Obra poética completa* (Lima: Mosca Azul, 1974), 423.

15. [This passage is translated from the author's Spanish text.—Tr.] In v. 6 I have adopted the translation proposed by D. Patrick, "The Translation of Job XLII, 6," *Vetus Testamentum* 26 (1976) 369–71. See my *On Job*, 126–27; to the bibliographical references given there I can now add J. Hartley, *The Book of Job* (Grand Rapids: Eerdmans, 1988). Although Hartley does not reach the same conclusions as D. Patrick (whom he does not cite), he acknowledges that the key verb, *nhm* (usually translated as "regret" or "repent"), does not imply "grieving over a wrong done" or "an attitude of remorse" (535, note 5, and 537).

16. The real intention of the author of the Book of Job is to destroy a false image of God and to look for an ultimate solution to the problem of suffering (on this point, see G. Ravasi, *Giobbe* [2nd ed.; Rome: Borla, 1984], 813).

CHAPTER IX. HOLY IS GOD'S NAME

1. On Marian devotion in Latin America, see A. González Dorado, *De María conquistadora a María liberadora. Mariología popular latinoamericana* (Santander: Sal Terrae, 1988). It is worth noting that the first Marian devotion to arise from our own midst—namely, devotion to the Virgin of Guadalupe—gives simple and beautiful expression to the Virgin's predilection for the poor and unimportant folk of history as represented by Diego, an Indian. See Virgil Elizondo, "Our Lady of Guadalupe as a Cultural Symbol: 'The Power of the Powerless,' " in *Liturgy and Cultural Religious Traditions* (*Concilium* 102; New York: Seabury, 1977), 25–33.

2. In his attractive treatise on Mariology, *María evangelizada y evangelizadora* (Bogotá: CELAM, 1988), Carlos J. González gives some guidelines "for avoiding excesses" (25–27).

3. Karl Rahner, *Mary, Mother of the Lord*, trans. W. J. O'Hara (Freiburg: Herder, 1962), 36.

4. I. Gomá Civit, *El Magnificat. Cántico de salvación* (Madrid: BAC, 1982), 10.

5. In both cases, the JB [like the NAB and other versions—Tr.] gives "things" as the translation of the Greek noun *rhema*, which also means "word." This Greek word is often used in the Bible to translate the Hebrew *dabar*, which likewise has the two meanings of word and thing (or event). In Hebrew, the prophetic word is always *dabar*.

6. As the reader may know, the document approved at Puebla had this description of the poor in the body of the text; the final version placed it in a footnote. See also my book, *The Power of the Poor in History*, 161, note 17.

7. This is not the place for a detailed exegesis of these passages. I cannot,

however, refrain from pointing out that the second account has frequently been interpreted in a way that justifies an unacceptable inferiority of women.

8. The fact that there are two stories has given rise to some odd interpretations in the course of church history. There is, for example, an interpretation that maintains that the first account has to do with the creation of souls, and says that at this level man and woman are equals; the second account has to do with the creation of the body, an area in which woman is inferior to man.

9. Elisabeth Schüssler Fiorenza makes this point in her forceful book *In Memory of Her* (p. xiii); the title of her book is, of course, derived from this passage of the gospel.

10. A detailed study of the role of women in the Gospels may be found in Ben Witherington III, *Women in the Ministry of Jesus* (Cambridge: Cambridge University Press, 1984).

11. As everyone knows, there is a deliberate parallelism in the stories having to do with John the Baptist and Jesus. Lukes uses this device as a way of showing the difference between the two men; everything is oriented toward the second. It is likely that the reason for this approach (the same holds for the Gospel of John) is the presence of disciples of the Baptist, for whose sake it was important to bring out the uniqueness of Jesus.

12. Elizabeth's words remind us of those which Uzziah spoke to Judith: "Blessed are you, daughter, by the Most High God, above all the women on earth" (Jdt 13:18). Nor may we forget that Judith is a feminine personification of the Jewish people and, as such, also a prefiguration of Mary.

13. See C. J. González (note 2, above), 87–88.

14. The Greek word *menoun*, which is translated as "rather" in Lk 11:28, would perhaps be better translated as "yes indeed, but" or "yes, but rather"; see J. A. Fitzmyer, *The Gospel according to Luke* II (= chapters X-XXIV) (Garden City, N.Y.: Doubleday, 1985), 928.

15. See Raymond Brown, *The Birth of the Messiah* (Garden City, N.Y.: Doubleday, 1977), 460–66, who also gives a rundown of the different interpretations of this text; see also Fitzmyer (note 14, above), 429–30.

16. "María Santíssima había mascado coca," in *Pastoral Andino*, no. 4 (October 1974), 4. The interview, in Quechuan, is with an 86-year-old peasant.

17. I. Gomá Civit (note 4, above) says that the infancy Gospel is "saturated with Hebraic turns of language translated into Greek" (5). José I. González Faus is correct when he describes Mary as "memory" of her son and her people (see his *Memoria de Jesús. Memoria de un pueblo* [Santander: Sal Terrac, 1984], 15–32). On the idea of Mary as "Daughter of Zion," see Rene Laurentin, *Structure et Théologie de Luc I-II* (Paris: Gabalda, 1964).

18. Ivonne Gebara and Maria Clara Bingemer aptly note that Mariology must be linked to the theme of the kingdom; see their *Mary: Mother of God, Mother of the Poor* (Maryknoll, N.Y.: Orbis Books, 1989).

19. There is considerable discussion of the source of this song, one of the most obvious ones being the song of Hannah in 1 Sm 2:1–10. It is not for me to go into the details of this discussion here. The reader can find further information in the works cited in this chapter.

20. There are even those who think that the entire song takes the form of a chiasmus (a symmetrical arrangement of a text, with the ideas being repeated in inverse order starting from a central point: a, b, c—c¹, b¹, a¹). The center here would

be the words "Holy is his name." On the literary form of the Magnificat, see the state of the question in J. Delorme, "Le Magnificat: la forme et le sens," in *Vie de la Parole. Etudes d'exégèse et d'herméneutique biblique offerts à P. Grelot* (Paris: Desclée, 1987), 175–94.

21. The corresponding verb, *tapeinoō*, means "to oppress, to abuse." The Hebrew word *'oni* has the same root as *'ani* and *'anaw*, two of the words most commonly used to signify the poor, the helpless, those who live bowed down. As often happens, the same words can acquire a meaning that refers to interior dispositions, to an interior attitude. Zephaniah 2:3 describes as spiritually poor (*'anawim*; NAB: "all you humble of the earth") those who possess these qualities. See the still instructive book of a teacher whose thought affected me deeply: A. Gelin, *The Poor of Yahweh*, trans. Mother Kathryn Sullivan (Collegeville: Liturgical Press [1964]).

22. W. Vogels observes, rightly and accurately: "A reading of the Magnificat in the light of salvation history ... shows us that it is a song soaked in the theology of the covenant and of poverty" ("Le Magnificat, Marie et Israel," *Eglise et théologie* 6 [1975] 295).

23. The verbs in Greek are in the aorist tense. There is a great deal of disagreement regarding the most suitable tense to be used in translating them (the *Biblia de Jerusalén* [and the NJB and NAB — Tr.] uses the past tense; the *Nueva Biblia Española* uses the present). In any case, it is clear that they describe an ongoing action of God. J. Dupont, however, thinks that the verbs refer to the annunciation to Mary, and that they illustrate a "use of the aorist for a future action, but one looked upon as already virtually completed" ("Le Magnificat comme Discours sur Dieu," *Nouvelle revue théologique* 102 [1980] 334).

24. In Ps 89:11 the Greek word *hyperēphanous* translates the Hebrew *rahab,* a pejorative name for Egypt, the oppressor of Israel (see Is 30:7; Ps 87:4). See the survey of this word in the Bible in I. Gomá Civit (note 4, above), 109–17.

25. J. Dupont (note 23, above) sees in the use of the word *dynastai* (rulers) instead of *dynatoi* (powerful) a sign of the pejorative tone taken in the song when speaking of such persons (337).

26. Albert the Great, *In Lucam*, in his *Opera Omnia* (Paris, 1904) 22:138 (cited in E. Hamel, "Le Magnificat et le Renversement des Situations," *Gregorianum* 60 [1979] 56).

27. The Septuagint uses the same Greek word (*peinountes*) for "hungry" in Ps 107:9.

28. J. Dupont (note 23, above) 335–36, note 28. He takes into consideration what is said in E. Hamel (note 26, above) 72 and R. Brown (note 15, above) 362.

29. Translated in *The Pope Speaks* 19 (1974–75) 75.

30. Translated in *The Pope Speaks* 32 (1987) 185.

CONCLUSION

1. The women were Mrs. Julia Elba and her daughter Celina; the Jesuit priests were Joaquin López y López, Ignacio Ellacuría, Segundo Montes, Juan Ramón Moreno, Amando López, and Ignacio Martín-Baró.

2. *Trilce XXXI*, translated in Jean Franco, *César Vallejo. The Dialectics of Poetry and Silence* (New York: Cambridge University Press, 1976), 38. It is the author of the present book who has capitalized the word "hope" in the citation.

General Index

INDEX OF BIBLICAL CITATIONS

211